Labour Statistics for a Market Economy

Challenges and Solutions in the Transition Countries of Central and Eastern Europe and the Former Soviet Union

EDITED BY IGOR CHERNYSHEV

Prepared for the International Labour Office

CENTRAL EUROPEAN UNIVERSITY PRESS
BUDAPEST · LONDON · NEW YORK

First published 1994 by
Central European University Press
H - 1021 Budapest,
Hűvösvölgyi út 54, Hungary

Distributed by
Oxford University Press, Walton Street, Oxford OX2 6DP
Oxford New York Athens Auckland Bangkok Bombay
Calcutta Cape Town Dar es Salaam Delhi Florence Hong Kong
Istanbul Karachi Kuala Lumpur Madras Madrid Melbourne
Mexico City Nairobi Paris Singapore Taipei Tokyo Toronto
and associated companies in Berlin Ibadan
Distributed in the United States
by Oxford University Press Inc., New York

The designations employed in ILO publications, which are in conformity with United Nations practice, and presentation of material therein do not imply the expression of any opinion whatsoever on the part of the International Labour Office concerning the legal status of any country, area or territory or of its authorities, or concerning the delimitation of its frontiers.

The responsibility for opinions expressed in studies and other contributions rests solely with their authors, and publication does not constitute an endorsement by the International Labour Office of the opinions expressed in them.

Reference to names of firms and commercial products and processes does not imply their endorsement by the International Labour Office, and any failure to mention a particular firm, commercial product or process is not a sign of disapproval.

For the provenance in their original form of the papers appearing here, please see the opening page of each chapter.

British Library Cataloguing in Publication Data
A CIP catalogue record for this book is available from the British Library.

ISBN 1 85866 008 4

Library of Congress Cataloging in Publication Data
A CIP catalog record for this book is available from the Library of Congress.

Produced and designed by John Saunders
Printed and bound in Great Britain by Biddles of Guildford

Contents

Preface

The national use of probability sampling techniques, the introduction of high-speed computing machines, the development of systems of economic accounting and, recently, the widespread availability of electronic means of data collection and dissemination could be named as some of the instruments that have marked turning points in the development of official statistics in the last half century.

Along with the changes that have come about in the political and economic systems of Central and Eastern European countries and the former Soviet Union, modern official statistics in those countries are now witnessing another major revolution in the course of their history: the transition from one statistical system to another within a short period of time.

This transition comprises a number of elements. One concerns data requirements which have radically changed in scope. For example, in the field of labour statistics, unemployment and labour cost did not form part of the statistical agenda in the past, but have emerged virtually overnight as essential information.

In parallel, the means of data collection have metamorphosed. The statistical infrastructure, previously based on a vast network of reporting units (enterprises), is now turning into a modern scientific system based on sample surveys, addressed directly to the economic or social agents, who are individuals, households or production units. In the field of labour, unemployment is being measured on the basis of labour force surveys using a representative sample of households, while labour cost is to be measured on the basis of a sample of enterprises.

This change in the means of data collection has serious implications for the statistical infrastructure, not only with regard to new statistical tools, such as sampling frames and business registers, or survey methods and interviewing techniques, but also with regard to the mental attitude needed to face the statistical challenge and to design solutions.

What makes the transformation particularly difficult is that it is taking place in an adverse environment, with reduced levels of resources and a public often reluctant to provide the required information. None the less, the requirements of a market economy and a democratic society imply a mega-fold increase in the demand for statistical information, from a host of impatient and data-hungry policy-makers, analysts and the press.

This volume, ably put together and edited by Mr Igor Chernyshev, describes some of the major issues of statistical transition in the field of labour. Under each broad topic, the ILO statistical standards or the ILO points of view are first presented. Then, through of series of articles prepared by national experts for various symposia, specific issues of application are described. The twenty-six articles that make up this book form a timely and authoritative pool of information which can be shared by all statisticians, whether themselves directly involved in the transition problems, or simply interested in understanding the various aspects of the statistical revolution that is taking place today in Central and Eastern European countries and the former Soviet Union.

Farhad Mehran,
Chief Statistician,
International Labour
Office, Geneva

Notes on contributors

Farhad Mehran Chief Statistician of the ILO. Holds a Harvard PhD degree. Taught at Rutgers University, United States, and the College of Statistics, Teheran, and was Deputy Director of the Iranian Statistical Office before joining the ILO in 1979. Co-author of the ILO publication *Surveys of economically active population, employment, unemployment and underemployment: A manual on concepts and methods,* he has published many papers on labour force surveys and related topics and on income distribution.

Ralf Hussmanns Joined the ILO Bureau of Statistics in 1987, where he is in the Employment and Unemployment Statistics Section. Co-author of the ILO publication *Surveys of economically active population, employment, unemployment and underemployment: A manual on concepts and methods.* He has developed the ILO international guidelines on the measurement of employment in the informal sector which were adopted at the 15th International Conference of Labour Statisticians in January 1993. Previously worked as a researcher with the Federal Institute for Population Research in Wiesbaden, Germany, and then with the Federal Statistical Office.

Eivind Hoffmann Chief of the Employment and Unemployment Statistics Section, Bureau of Statistics, ILO. Holds a graduate degree in economics from the University of Oslo, Norway. Worked in the Department of Research at the Norwegian Central Bureau of Statistics and headed the Division of Labour Market Statistics. Before joining the ILO in 1984, headed the group for research on spatial data at the Norwegian Computer Centre. He is the major architect of the revised International Standard Classification of Occupations (ISCO-88) and was responsible for the revision of the International Classification of Status in

Employment which was revised at the 15th International Conference of Labour Statisticians in January 1993.

Marie-Thérèse Dupré Member of the Conditions of Work and Life Statistics Section, Bureau of Statistics, ILO. Works in the field of statistics of wages, hours of work and labour cost. She is engaged in developmental work on the revision of existing international guidelines on wage statistics and on the measurement of income from paid and self-employment.

Igor Chernyshev Member of the ILO Bureau of Statistics since 1986, he previously worked with the Central Statistical Office of Ukraine. Holds a Master's degree in Economics and Statistics from the Kiev State University. His responsibility has been the ILO-comparable employment and unemployment estimates project, which has resulted in the regular publication of comparable data since 1990. He is currently organizing and coordinating the ILO technical support in the field of labour statistics to the countries of Central and Eastern Europe and the former Soviet Union.

Regis Rassou Chief of the Conditions of Work and Life Statistics Section, Bureau of Statistics, ILO. He is a chartered statistician who graduated from the Institute of Statisticians in the United Kingdom. After a period of service with the Central Statistical Office in Mauritius, he joined the ILO Bureau of Statistics in 1969, where he has been responsible for various statistical topics related to conditions of work and life.

François Eyraud After his Doctorat d'Etat in Economics at the Faculty of Economy of Aix-en-Provence (France), he worked for ten years as a researcher with the National Centre of Scientific Research and as a Professor of Economics at Aix-en-Provence. Both his work and publications are related to the problems of labour economics and occupational relations. Member of the ILO Labour Law and Labour Relations Branch since 1989, where he has been responsible for issues dealing with remuneration and collective bargaining.

Mirjana Scott Former member of the Employment and Unemployment Statistics Section, Bureau of Statistics, ILO. Graduated in economics and statistics from the University of Belgrade. Worked on the revision of the International Standard Classification of Occupations (ISCO-88).

Vladimir Gouriev Formerly Director of the Social Statistics Department of the Statistical Committee of the Commonwealth of Independent States and former Deputy Chairman of the State Committee on Statistics of the USSR. Holds a Master's degree in Statistics from the Moscow Institute of the National Economy. He is the author of several books on labour and social statistics.

Iraida Manykina Deputy Director of the Population and Labour Statistics Department of the Statistical Committee of the Commonwealth of Independent States. Formerly Director of the Labour Statistics Department of the State Committee on Statistics of the USSR. Holds a Moscow Institute of the National Economy PhD degree. She has contributed to the development of the System of Balances of Labour Resources, which has been considered a major instrument of labour statistics analysis in the former centrally planned economies.

Tatiana Gorbacheva Director, Labour Statistics Department of the State Committee on Statistics of the Russian Federation. Graduated from the Moscow State University, she holds a Master's degree in Economics and Statistics. She has been developing new concepts and definitions of labour statistics in the Russian Federation based on international recommendations and national practices of countries with a market economy. She was responsible for the preparation and conduct of the first Russian Household Labour Force Survey.

Klaudia Kiseleva Senior Economist of the Labour Statistics Department of the State Committee on Statistics and Analysis of the Republic of Belarus. She is in charge of a group of specialists responsible for the preparation for the first Labour Force Survey in Belarus.

Valery Ouvarov Deputy Director, Department of Migrant Workers, Ministry of Labour of the Russian Federation. Holds a Master's degree from the Moscow Institute of Economics and Statistics. He participated in a number of ILO Workshops and Seminars on the development and use of national occupational classifications. Author of a number of publications on labour migration, employment, classification and description of occupations.

Staliy Makovlev Formerly First Deputy Director of the Department of Labour Organization, Wages and Economic Mechanism at the State Committee for Labour and Social Affairs of the USSR. He was responsible for the development of a new national classification of occupations.

Bohuslav Mejstřík Senior Statistician of the Labour Force Section of the Czech Statistical Office. Graduate of the Prague School of Economics, he has been responsible for the conduct of Labour Force Surveys in the Czech Republic.

Jaroslav Kux Formerly Director of the Social Consumption and Services Statistics Division, Federal Statistics Office of Czechoslovakia. Graduate of the Prague School of Economics, author of numerous technical papers and publications on methodological and practical issues of labour statistics, he initiated the conduct of Labour Force Surveys both in the Czech and the Slovak Republics.

Janusz Witkowski Director of the Labour and Population Income Statistics Department of the Central Statistical Office of Poland, Professor of Demography at the Institute of Statistics and Demography of the Warsaw School of Economics. His main field of expertise being social aspects of population development and labour statistics and labour market policy, he has been responsible for the improvement of a labour market information system in Poland as well as the development of concepts, methodology and conduct of Polish Labour Force Surveys. Author of several books and more than sixty papers, articles and reports on population development, migration, social and labour mobility, unemployment and the labour market situation.

Irina Vantu Economist of the Social Statistics Department, National Commission of Statistics of Romania. She works in a group of specialists which is responsible for the preparation of the first Labour Force Survey in Romania.

Andras Keleti Formerly Deputy Director of the Department of Labour Statistics of the Hungarian Central Statistical Office and Head of Household Survey Section. Holds a Budapest University PhD degree. He was responsible for the preparation and conduct of the first Labour Force Survey in Hungary.

György Lázár Head of the Labour Market Information and Analysis Department of the National Labour Centre of Hungary. Graduate of the Budapest Technical University. He participated in the ILO Meeting of Experts on the revision of the International Standard Classification of Occupations, 1968 (ISCO-68) in 1984 and was Chairman of the Committee which revised the International Classification of Status in Employment at the 15th International Conference of Labour Statisticians in 1993. He contributed significantly to the development of a new Hungarian Standard Classification of Occupations.

János Fóti Deputy Director of the Department of Population Census of the Hungarian Central Statistical Office. Holds a PhD degree from the Budapest Institute of Economics. He actively participated in the preparation and conduct of the last three Population Censuses in Hungary. He is the leader of the team which developed a new Hungarian Standard Classification of Occupations based on the International Standard Classification of Occupations (ISCO-88).

Introduction

I. CHERNYSHEV

Official statistics provide an essential element in the formation of a democratic society with a free-market economy, serving the government, the economic actors, social partners and the public with data about the economic, demographic, labour and social situation.[1] The market system functions at its best when all the economic partners have the maximum information at their disposal. This information must be timely, reliable and comprehensive.

In the former traditional centrally planned economies, the basic purpose of economic statistics was to generate data so that the authorities could elaborate national plans, transpose them into directives to enterprises, and monitor the implementation of plans at all levels.

The introduction of market-oriented reforms in the countries of Central and Eastern Europe (CEECs) and the former Soviet Union (FSU) made obsolete many of the purposes and uses of the data generated by a plan-oriented system as well as the systems and mechanisms used to collect the basic information needed. At the same time, the reform gave rise to new requirements for information at the macro and micro levels.

It was soon realized that the revolutionary changes in Central and Eastern Europe represented both a challenge and an opportunity for official statistics, in the supply of relevant and reliable data: a challenge because the institutional framework and reporting system which provided the basis for statistics was rapidly disappearing or undermined; an opportunity because this had made it necessary to re-examine

[1] 'Fundamental Principles of Official Statistics in the Region of the Economic Commission for Europe': adopted during the session of the United Nations Economic Commission for Europe, at the Palais des Nations, Geneva, on 15 April 1992.

the old data collection procedures and instruments (i.e., variables, definitions and classifications) for relevance and reliability, and in many cases to replace or supplement them by new instruments which could be used to monitor the transition process and ensure reliable statistics in the future.

This is universally applicable to any field of economic and social statistics and is also true for labour statistics. The systems of labour statistics were to some extent inadequate even before the radical changes in the countries of Central and Eastern Europe and the former Soviet Union because they were based on erroneous idealistic assumptions about how their economic system functioned in practice.

Some major challenges that Central and Eastern European countries and countries of the FSU will have to meet in the field of labour statistics are: (i) measurement of employment (both in state and private sectors) and unemployment, (ii) collection of reliable wage statistics, and (iii) development of new national economic classifications compatible with those internationally recognized and adopted.

UNEMPLOYMENT

In 1930, the Soviet Union proclaimed the total abolition of unemployment.[2] Consequently, unemployment, which had been measured in millions at that time, officially disappeared. The justification was that, since the State guaranteed its citizens the right to a job, unemployment would cease to exist by definition. After the installation of the central command system in CEECs, Soviet statistical practices were adopted in full. As a result, unemployment statistics became non-existent, while the phenomenon of unemployment, as it is generally understood in market economies, continued to exist both in the region and the former Soviet Union.

With the collapse of the administrative command system in CEECs and the FSU, the restructuring processes of transition to a market economy reopened the issue of unemployment with new force. Open unemployment has become an increasingly serious problem in the region. Under these circumstances, the national statistical institutions and governments suddenly realized that they did not have at their disposal adequate statistical instruments to measure the number of unemployed and provide information on the real situation in their labour markets. The message from the international statistical community was short and clear: these countries must carefully and urgently

---

[2] *Narodnoye Hoziaystvo SSSR v 1987 g.* (National Economy of the USSR in 1987), Statistical Year Book. *Finansy i Statistika*, Moscow, 1988, p. 664.

examine the possibilities of establishing new statistical infrastructures in the vital areas of employment and unemployment. The main instrument for providing such statistics on a comprehensive and consistent basis in market economy countries is a Labour Force Survey based on a probability sample survey. This work has begun.

WAGES

As mentioned above, so-called 'labour markets' in the former centrally planned economies of Central and Eastern Europe and the FSU were severely regulated and distorted, and a central wage-fixing system was an integral part of them. Average monthly wages and salaries were calculated as a ratio of the total amount of wage funds available to (in practice distributed to) a given enterprise and the average number of employees. Only those wage earners and salaried employees who worked for a complete month were counted, i.e. persons who because of illness, unpaid leave or other specific reasons were absent from work and did not receive their full compensation in terms of wage or salary were excluded.

The introduction of new wage legislation and principles of remuneration adopted in market economies created a different income and psychological situation in CEECs and the FSU. Wages became the subject of negotiations between workers' and employers' organizations and the government. The principles of tripartism have begun to be laid down in these countries. As a result, central wage fixing has begun to lose ground and the collection of reliable wage statistics in public, private and co-operative sectors of the national economy has become a real challenge for labour statisticians.

NEW NATIONAL CLASSIFICATIONS

A comprehensive classification has much in common with a set of geographical maps of a country. In the same way as maps, it can be described in terms of coverage, scale, types and depth of information provided about enterprises, population groups, wages, education and other economic and social phenomena. Having embarked upon the road of radical reforms leading to a market oriented economy, the countries of Central and Eastern Europe and the FSU discovered that without such 'maps' it would be extremely difficult, if not impossible, to develop a new statistical infrastructure and to build a new system of labour statistics.

The national economic and occupational classifications which existed and partly continue to exist in CEECs and the FSU have reflected the central command system and differ both conceptually and structurally from similar classifications used in market economies. These divergencies originated partly from the differences between the System of National Accounts (SNA) and the System of Balances of the National Economy or the Material Product System (MPS) and partly from differences in the detailed breakdown and conceptual treatment of industries and sectors of economic activity. Moreover, certain classifications used outside the region were not in existence at all. A good example of this is the classification of status in employment.

Hence a rapid development of national classifications which could be used for both internal and international analysis and comparisons became a priority area of national programmes to revise official statistics for the period of transition from a planned to a market economy. These have already been adopted or are being developed in CEECs and the FSU.

THE INVOLVEMENT OF THE ILO

Since 1989 the ILO has been actively involved in assisting Central and Eastern European countries and the former Soviet Union to revise and restructure their labour statistics systems in order to meet the above-mentioned challenging requirements resulting from their transition to a market economy. This assistance was provided by means of technical missions of the ILO Bureau of Statistics' staff members to CEECs and FSU countries, international expertise in terms of comments on various technical documents and survey questionnaires and expert consultancies as well as the organization of regional workshops and seminars covering the most topical issues which these countries have been struggling to handle.

This book covers a wide range of issues and gives insight into the difficulties and challenges of daily work in the national statistical institutions of Central and Eastern European countries and the former Soviet Union. It provides a better understanding of the transition processes, both in the national economies and in the labour statistics that are currently operating in this part of the world.

The book is a collection of articles and papers either published in the ILO *Bulletin of Labour Statistics* or presented at one of the many international workshops and seminars organized by or jointly with the ILO specifically for CEECs and the FSU. These articles and papers were written by ILO staff members and leading national labour statisticians who have been directly involved in the difficult but exciting process of the revision and rebuilding of national labour statistics systems. The articles and papers are grouped together by specific topics in four parts and reflect different ways of attaining one common goal – the development of new statistical tools to gauge new phenomena and patterns of population behaviour resulting from the transition to a market economy.

The book is addressed to a wide audience of readers who want to know more about particular aspects of the subject, those who are directly involved in the process of transition, users of statistics, researchers, planners, journalists, politicians, trade unionists and others who may be interested in knowing about the fascinating challenges faced by CEECs and the FSU while they are on the move to a market economy.

Part I

Major challenges in labour statistics

1

Labour force, employment and unemployment*

III. PAST EXPERIENCE AND NATIONAL PRACTICES IN MEASURING THE ECONOMICALLY ACTIVE POPULATION AND IN USING ECONOMIC CLASSIFI-CATIONS

3.2. The Workshop noted that in a number of Central and Eastern European countries the economically active population included the employed only. It was generally reported that the concept of unemployment was rather new to those countries and, as a result, unemployment statistics were rarely available. At the same time it was widely recognized that unemployment statistics would increasingly become important in the context of the transition that is under way in the countries of Central and Eastern Europe.

3.3. Therefore, it was suggested that consideration be given to the development of a system of unemployment indicators distinguishing between different types of unemployment, i.e., structural, frictional, seasonal and general unemployment . . . Workshop showed strong interest in learning more about international standards and practices adopted by market economy countries to collect statistics of unemployment, particularly the instrument of Labour Force Surveys . . .

3.10. The Workshop was informed by participants that the Central and Eastern European countries lacked current labour force statistics as well

* Extract from the Report of the UN/ILO Workshop on Economic Statistics in Population and Housing Censuses and Surveys (Moscow, 21–29 December 1990).

as the technical capability and resources to develop them. The present situation relied chiefly on the system of labour or manpower balances and on enterprise or establishment statistics. Enterprise statistics were reported to be very reliable and the response rate was quite high because of state ownership. This situation could change as a result of labour migration from state-owned enterprises to co-operatives as well as other changes which were occurring or may occur.

3.11. However, the Workshop was informed by participants that the countries had no current labour force statistics based on Labour Force Surveys as carried out periodically in the Western countries.

3.12. In this context, participants raised many issues and discussion focused on various aspects of Labour Force Surveys, e.g. sample design, periodicity, interview methods, cost of the survey, etc. Some participants informed the Workshop about their present efforts to carry out a household survey including testing the survey questionnaires and training in progress. Notwithstanding, it was stressed that survey capability development was one area where countries would require much technical support and assistance in the future . . .

IV. MEASURING THE NUMBER OF ECONOMICALLY ACTIVE, EMPLOYED AND
    UNEMPLOYED PERSONS AND HOURS OF WORK

4.4. This agenda item was introduced by a representative of the ILO Bureau of Statistics on the basis of his paper entitled 'International standards on the measurement of economic activity, employment, unemployment and underemployment' (INT/90/R94/40). The paper describes the basic concepts and definitions laid down in the international standards presently in force concerning statistics of the economically active population, employment, unemployment and underemployment, as adopted by the Thirteenth International Conference of Labour Statisticians (ICLS) in 1982. The paper discusses also particular issues that may arise in survey applications of the International Standards concerning the measurement problems and the appropriate statistical treatment of particular categories of workers . . .

4.6. Topics covered in the presentation included: the concept of economic activity as used in delimiting the SNA production boundary; the minimum age limit to measure the economically active population; the conceptual framework for measuring (i) the currently active population (labour force) and (ii) the usually active population; the international definition of employment distinguishing between persons in paid employment and persons in self-employment and, in both cases, between persons at work and persons with a job/enterprise but temporarily not at work during the reference period; the one hour criterion embodied in the international definition of employment; the 'important contribution' provision for persons engaged in the production of goods and services for own and household consumption: the notion of formal job attachment in the definition of temporary absence from paid employment; the international definition of unemployment and its three criteria (without work, actively seeking work, and current availability for work); and the concept of visible underemployment and its measurement in terms of (i) the number of persons visibly underemployed (i.e., persons involuntarily working less than normal duration and seeking, or available for additional work) and (ii) the quantum of visible underemployment (i.e., the time available for additional employment aggregated over all persons visibly underemployed) . . .

XI. RECOMMENDATIONS

The participants at the UN/ILO Workshop on Economic Statistics in Population and Housing Censuses and Surveys:

- having been informed that several of the countries represented at the Workshop have already taken concrete steps to modify and strengthen their statistics on employment and unemployment through the preparation for regular Labour Force Surveys and the adaptation of the ISCO-88 and ISIC, Rev. 3;
- recognizing the importance of accurate and timely statistics on the economically active population, employment and, in particular, unemployment, as stressed by several high-level meetings on statistics in countries under transition in Central and Eastern Europe and elsewhere;
- recognizing the need for labour statistics of a country to be based on a combination of reports of enterprises and organizations, enterprise surveys and censuses, household surveys and censuses, and administrative records;
- recognizing the need for countries to strengthen the basis for their establishment statistics, in particular through improved registers of establishments;
- recognizing the needs for countries to adopt and adapt international

statistical classifications, definitions and standards to the greatest extent possible, consistent with national experiences, circumstances and resources;

will recommend that

- the national statistical agencies and interested and responsible ministries take concrete steps to identify the best means to strengthen statistics on employment, unemployment and underemployment, wages, hours of work, labour productivity, strikes, prices, etc., and to allocate the necessary resources to this important task);
- the competent international and regional organizations be prepared to assist national governments, individually or on a regional basis, to adapt international standards and recommendations to national circumstances and to make adequate preparations to carry out censuses and new forms of surveys. Such assistance should take the form of:
  - advice on the formulation of project preparation and plans;
  - identification of qualified experts to provide advice;
  - advice on the proper understanding and procedures for developing national standards and classifications taking into account the international ones, in particular, ISIC, Rev. 3 and ISCO-88;
  - organization of training seminars, at the national or regional level as appropriate, in such cases as application of international recommendations and standards in censuses and Labour Force Surveys, the design of questionnaires, sampling and field work, as well as proper coding of industry and occupation. . . .
  - organization of a special workshop on wage statistics.

2

Wage and labour cost*

3. REVIEW OF EXISTING WAGES STATISTICS IN TRANSITION ECONOMIES

3.2. The economic and social restructuring taking place in Central and Eastern European Countries (CEECs) is triggering changes in their statistical systems, including their wage statistics system. The main use of these systems in the past was in the administration of wage funds, within the framework of setting and monitoring production plans. They produced data on wages and certain forms of non-wage payments made by enterprises to their workers.

3.3. The system was characterized by exhaustive and compulsory reporting of enterprises to statistical offices through their relevant ministries. Data reporting usually covered the State and Cooperative sectors, and at least all large enterprises and budgetary institutions in selected industries. Data were collected on employment, total payments and in some cases working time.

3.4. While that system is still operating in some CEECs, it was evident to the meeting that some changes were already occurring in others. These changes, however, were not significant enough to meet the demand for the type of statistics required in market economies.

3.5. But shifting from one system to another is not an easy process. A number of technical problems have got to be resolved. For instance, the

* Extract from the Report of the ILO Workshop on Wage Statistics (Prague, 25–29 November 1991).

change of statistical unit from the enterprise to the establishment implies the building-up of a register of establishments, in order to provide more precise and consistent data on the geographical and industrial distribution of employment and wages.

3.6. The register should also be extended to cover more appropriately the private sector (especially the smaller enterprises). Such an extension raises further problems such as non-response or low quality responses, and an agreed definition of what constitutes the private sector comparable to the concept of the private sector in market economy countries. On the question of non-response or more reliable information, the issue of the choice between compulsory and voluntary statistical reporting was raised. It was suggested that neither approach taken independently was desirable, but that perhaps some type of combination of both should be envisaged.

3.7. The meeting also suggested that use of administrative sources (such as social security or tax records) should be examined as a complementary source of wage statistics. The inclusion of income or earnings questions in Labour Force Surveys, and of expenditure and income questions in household surveys, should also be considered.

3.8. There was a feeling in the meeting that occupational data were important and could provide more comparable wage data across industries and regions.

3.9. The meeting also considered the possibility of using carefully designed sampling methods in lieu of the present exhaustive enumeration. It expressed interest in data on pay systems, wage structure and distribution; in the use of international classifications of economic activities and occupations; and in the measurement of labour cost. It noted that there were some difficulties of terminology, and that the concept of labour cost in particular would need to be more explicitly defined in the context of CEECs, both for national and internationally comparative purposes.

4. MAIN USES OF WAGES STATISTICS IN MARKET ECONOMY COUNTRIES

4.1. . . . wage fixing in market economies, whether by governments, unions or employers, has three basic objectives:

(i) Wage *levels* have an impact on *macro-economic stability* and economic growth (although there is no real level);

(ii) Wage *structure* has an impact on the *allocation* and mobility of labour (through the 'compensatory' role of wage differentials), and also on *equity* (which raises issues of 'equal pay' and 'minimum wages');

(iii) Wage *systems* have an impact on the *efficiency* of production (through 'payment by results' and other flexible systems, and also through supplementary payments and benefits).

4.2. These uses of wage statistics have clear implications for the programme of statistics which should be undertaken:

(i) Data on the general level of wages and non-wage labour costs, on an internationally comparable basis;

(ii) Disaggregation by geographical region, industrial sector and occupation (for questions of allocation); and also by age/seniority and firm size, and covering atypical employment (for issues of equity);

(iii) Information on types of payment by results and supplementary benefits (with provision to cover systems which do not yet exist in the countries concerned).

4.3. . . . wage determination through 'collective bargaining', in various forms, has several advantages: in creating a balance of forces, in ensuring mutual commitment, and also in providing flexibility to adapt to new situations. Collective bargaining created its own needs for statistics – both in ensuring that the parties have access to reliable and up-to-date data and, where appropriate, in gathering information on the bargaining process itself. . .

5. INTERNATIONAL RECOMMENDATIONS AND NATIONAL PRACTICES IN SELECTED MARKET ECONOMY COUNTRIES

5.1. . . . there are four main agreed concepts in wage statistics, which are progressively broader:

WAGE RATE   Price of labour
(for normal hours of work)

EARNINGS   Receipts of employees
(for hours actually worked or paid for)

| COMPENSATION OF EMPLOYEES (SNA) | Cost to employer of employee remuneration |
| LABOUR COST | Cost to employer of employment of labour |

In addition, there is a provisional definition, more related to the purchasing power of the worker:

| EMPLOYEE INCOME | Receipts by virtue of current status as employee |

3

Classification of occupations*

4. The objective of the Workshop was that participants both from Central and Eastern European countries (CEECs) and market-economy countries should be in a position to appreciate the problems and possibilities involved in developing useful tools for the restructured economies of the CEECs and thereby to be able to advise their superiors accordingly and prepare necessary plans for the development of such tools and their supporting institutions . . .

6. The discussion on specific areas of use of occupational classifiers, i.e. job classification and job evaluation, in the pay administration, and effective management of individual enterprises in market economy countries, established that:

(a) there is normally no direct link between the national standard occupational classification and the job and pay classification systems used by private or public employers;
(b) the job classification systems used by an enterprise or a branch of the economy for pay administration and the management of human resources and production must, as much as possible, be tailored to the specific organizational and technological circumstances of the enterprise or industry in consultation and negotiation with organizations representing the workers. Such systems also need to

---

* Extract from the ILO Workshop on the Role of National Occupational Classifiers of the Central and Eastern European Countries in the Economic Restructuring (Geneva, 3–6 December 1990).

develop as the technological and organizational circumstances change;

(c) In order to adequately monitor changes in the absolute and relative pay of different groups of workers, all social partners are concerned that statistics on wages, etc. should be collected according to a standard national occupational classification at an appropriate level of detail.

7. The discussion on the use and organization of information about the tasks performed in jobs as a basis for planning curriculum and development of vocational training programmes established that:

(a) the task information needed to develop specific vocational training programmes is normally much too detailed to be included in a standard national occupational classification system (NOC). The NOC therefore is of limited usefulness in the development of specific training modules and curricula;

(b) in order to be able to identify broader areas of priority for vocational training and in order to organize such training, it is an advantage to use the classification structure of a NOC, particularly if this structure can reflect similarities in skill level and skill specialization.

8. The discussion on the use of standard occupational classifications by services charged with job placements and the redeployment of labour established that:

(a) an occupational classification providing a common 'language' for job contents (tasks) and job titles to be used by employers, jobseekers and employment-service officers is only one of the instruments which are needed for successful placement or redeployment of workers. However, it represents an important tool for recruitment and the redeployment process, in that it provides a consistent framework for the collection and dissemination of such information;

(b) the more aggregate levels of the NOC will normally be adequate for the basic sorting of vacant jobs and workers into main areas of skill requirements and competence;

(c) to serve as a useful tool in the redeployment of workers, the basic task descriptions at the detailed level of the NOC must be supplemented with descriptions on skills and training needed to achieve the transition from one occupation to another. Information both on tasks and on the additional training requirements for occupational mobility must be kept up to date.

9. The discussion on the development and use of a NOC for the collection and presentation of occupational statistics established that:

(a) any occupational classification to be used for the collection and presentation of statistics must correspond to the needs of the users of these statistics and consequently be developed in dialogue with them. Some of these users are concerned with the areas discussed above;

(b) there are significant advantages to have as a basis for producing occupational statistics a NOC which serves as a common starting point for the various users of occupational classifications. The implementation of the NOC in data collections to be used to produce occupational statistics should be carried out in a way which will ensure the high quality of the statistics which are consistent with the principles of the NOC. This can be achieved only by adequate maintenance and updating of the statistical instruments, such as coding indices used to implement the NOC so the statistics can reflect the changing occupational structure of the economy, and by close communication with the other users of the NOC;

(c) there are significant advantages to developing (or revising, as the need may be) a NOC on the basis of the international model (ISCO-88) because it represents a well-defined conceptual structure and because this makes it easier to draw upon the experience of other countries, as well as facilitating comparisons with them. However, the detailed structure of the international model needs to be evaluated carefully and, if necessary, modified in the light of national circumstances and based on a sound body of information about the actual tasks of jobs found in the national economy. . .

10. The participants at the Workshop expressed their great appreciation of ISCO-88 and gave their full support to its use as a starting point for the revision of their national occupational classifiers.

RECOMMENDATIONS

The participants at the Workshop would like to make the following recommendations about the future work on job and occupational classifications in Central and Eastern European countries:

(1) In market-oriented economies, individual branches of the economy or even individual enterprises will tend to develop job classifications

and pay administration systems suited to their particular circumstances. Such systems should, as far as possible, be developed in consultation and negotiation with workers' organizations . . .

(2) A basic standard national occupational classification system (NOC) will be needed to serve as a tool to be used in areas such as the monitoring of the development of wages, incomes, employment and unemployment, labour market analysis and education planning for the implementation of vocational training programmes, vocational guidance, job placements and immigration administration. The NOC can either be used directly or as a basis for developing more tailor-made tools for particular areas of application;

(3) Responsibility for the basic NOC should be given to a national organization which has an operational need to ensure the complete and consistent coverage of all occupations existing in the economy and to ensure proper maintenance and updating of the classification . . . It should also be given the necessary resources to carry out these tasks;

(4) Basing the development of new or revised national occupational classifications on an international model such as the *International Standard Classification of Occupations, 1988* (ISCO-88) will have advantages – such as a reasonably well-defined conceptual basis, possibly to benefit from the experience of other countries and a basis for making comparisons with them. However, when using ISCO-88 as a model, it is important to base the national occupational classification on thorough investigations into the tasks, organization and skill requirements of actual jobs in the country to the largest extent possible . . .

(5) There is a need for the countries of Central and Eastern Europe to consult and co-operate among themselves to learn from each other's experience, as well as that of other countries, in the process of modifying and revising their respective classification systems to be used for the new approaches to pay administration, vocational training, employment services and occupational statistics. Furthermore, the international institutions, in particular the ILO and European Community, should provide assistance to CEECs in their attempts to modify and improve their national classification system and the supporting institutions . . .

4

Measuring employment trends, labour shortages and skill gaps in transition countries

E. HOFFMANN and I.CHERNYSHEV*

This chapter will use the term 'transition countries' to designate those countries in Central and Eastern Europe which have embarked on a transition from centrally controlled to more open and market-oriented economic, social and political systems. For this reason the first part of this chapter (and Annex 1) will give a brief review of the information available in the ILO Bureau of Statistics on statistics which can be used to describe employment trends in Bulgaria, the former Czech and Slovak Federal Republic (CSFR), Hungary, Poland, Romania and the former USSR. However, all countries which are open to outside influences through foreign trade and whose policy makers or managers initiate change can in some sense be said to be in 'transition'. Therefore the discussion in the second part may have some relevance beyond these countries.

It was almost immediately perceived that the revolutionary changes in Central and Eastern Europe represented both a challenge and an opportunity for official statistics, as regards the supply of relevant and reliable data: a challenge because the institutional framework and reporting system which provided the basis for statistics was rapidly disappearing or undermined; an opportunity because this has made it necessary to re-examine the old data collection procedures and instruments (i.e. variables, definitions and classifications) for relevance and reliability, and in many cases replace or supplement them by new

* This chapter was originally written for the joint EUROSTAT/ISTAT/OECD International Conference, Rome, July 1991, entitled 'Labour Market Indicators for Transition: Monitoring Labour Market Developments in Central and Eastern European Countries'.

instruments that can be used to monitor the transition process and ensure reliable statistics in the future. In the second part of this chapter the implications of this 'statistical revolution' with respect to methods for measuring employment trends, labour shortages and skill gaps will be reviewed, with a view to reaching some practical conclusions as to the type of statistics which should be collected and how, when employment trends are being monitored, the measurement of labour shortages and skill gaps is a priority.

Though they might have been included, the words 'policy indicators' have been omitted from the title of this chapter deliberately, because 'policy indicators' are often seen as magic numbers, which, if they move in specified directions or pass certain thresholds, will trigger specific government actions or, at least, a review of relevant, current policies with a view to changing them. They also are perceived as summarizing complex situations or developments in a manner which is intuitively easy to understand. Preferably they should also be relevant for explicitly stated policy concerns and/or able to indicate the type of policies needed. The problem is, however, that very few such 'policy indicators' can be found in modern democratic market economy countries. The unemployment rate, the consumer price index, the surplus or deficit of the balance of payments, the growth in GNP are examples of indicators which are keenly followed by policy makers in government and economic organizations as well as by the press and which may lead to re-evaluations of current policies, but no policies are determined by specific movements of a single or a small set of indicators, although the actual amount of money given from the central budget to regions may in some countries (and the European Community) be determined by e.g. their observed unemployment rates. (One possible exception: some economy-wide collective pay agreements include clauses that trigger new negotiations or automatic wage adjustments once the consumer price index has passed a predetermined value. Policies designed to limit the effects of such clauses may therefore be considered as 'triggered' by the movement of the CPI.)

Another interpretation of 'policy indicators' is that they are statistical numbers which can be used to judge and plan the (required) scope of policies once these have been decided: 'How many persons will be affected?' 'How much money will be required?' With this perspective it is more relevant to talk about 'policy relevant statistics' than 'policy indicators', and to define the task of the statistician as that of developing statistics which will be relevant both for the description of developments of concern to the political and economic decision-makers and for the formulation and dosage of policies related to those concerns. Generally speaking 'policy relevant statistics' will describe distribution and levels, direction and speed of change as well as 'gainers' and 'losers' in current or recent developments. This type of statistics on 'employment trends', 'labour shortages and 'skill gaps', and how to collect them, will be the focus of the rest of this chapter, rather than the definition of specific 'policy indicators'.

THE STARTING POINT FOR EMPLOYMENT AND RELATED STATISTICS

Established practices

All the transition countries have one state institution, the State Committee for Statistics or the Central Statistical Office, which is responsible for the collection, processing and publication of employment statistics covering the whole national economy.

As there was practically no private economic activity, checking and fulfilment of state plans and ensuring information requirements for the Communist Party were the main tasks of the statistical services in the centrally controlled economy. Therefore, almost to the very end of 1990, both the reporting system and the system of statistical indicators reflected the perceived needs of a centrally controlled economy, and the overwhelming majority of *employment statistics* (among others) were collected from compulsory *continuous full-scale statistical reportings* which covered all *state* enterprises, institutions and organizations as well as state and collective farms. This means that from about 85 per cent (Poland) to 95 per cent (former USSR) of those employed were covered by these compulsory reports.

In practice the statistical reporting procedures were executed in the following manner: once or twice a year the Central Statistical Office forwarded to the regional statistical offices several sets of questionnaires to be sent to *all* enterprises, organizations, institutions and agricultural units of that region. It was compulsory for these units to fill out and return these questionnaires to district statistical offices. The returns were processed regionally and sent to the Central Statistical Office in the form of aggregate totals. This system made it possible to have up-to-date information on employment by sex, occupation and sector within two weeks of the reference date at national level and within 5–10 days at regional level.

Data on self-employment in private agricultural and non-agricultural activities, unpaid family workers and temporary and seasonal workers have been taken from special annual or half yearly 'sample surveys' and from micro-censuses of agricultural activities (usually every 3–5 years).

Some data on employment were also available from social security registers and other types of social records, e.g. on the number of free-lance
intellectual workers (Hungary). Information on employment in the
armed forces was provided by the Ministry of Defence, but not
published.

In general the employment data for this group of countries can be
considered to have been satisfactory, even if their quality and coverage
would differ from country to country. Thus, the Bulgarian publications
did not reveal employment by sex and age groups. Age group distribution seems to have posed a problem for the USSR as well. These data are
only available from special employment surveys and censuses which
were carried out infrequently.

According to the official sources of the transition countries, there was
no unemployment until 1990. Consequently no data on unemployment
were collected and, as a rule, the transition countries would not use the
term 'labour force' or 'economically active population' in their official
publications. However, official statistics referred to the 'labour
resources' which consist of 'economically active population' (in the ILO
understanding) plus 'full-time students of working age' plus 'persons
engaged in housework' less 'non-working invalids' less 'persons on
early retirement and receiving beneficiary pensions' (miners, workers
and employees of the chemical industry, etc.).

The ILO Bureau of Statistics has studied the concepts and definitions
used in the transition countries to count their labour force. Annex 1 gives
a brief review of these concepts and definitions and the adjustments
needed in order to arrive at the estimates which are comparable in terms
of coverage. Such estimates (up to 1989) are shown in Table 1 in the
Annex. (For further information see Chernyshev & Lawrence, 1990 and
1992.) We consider that, up to that year, the statistical accuracy of the
coverage of the relevant labour force variables is not disputed.

Current developments

The economic and political reforms in the transition countries have
made it urgently necessary also to introduce reforms in their statistical
practices with respect to their measurement of the labour force and its
components:

(a) On the employment measurement side the transition to market
    economies has raised or will raise a number of challenges. We have
    already recognized those related to the closing of inefficient enter-
    prises and, in particular, the creation (and demise) of tens of
    thousands of co-operative and private firms and organizations.

(b) All transition countries became aware of unemployment and most of them started to collect corresponding data at the beginning of 1990 (except Bulgaria and the former USSR). As a rule these statistics are derived from employment offices where people register for unemployment compensation. The employment offices which existed in the past are currently being totally restructured, their roles redefined and the number of offices dramatically increased. However, in many cases these offices are not yet equipped to analyse the structure of available jobs and the skills of job-seekers or to communicate available information to potential employers or to a national information bank. No (outside) statistical expert has evaluated reports that in early 1991 there were, for example, 240,000 unemployed in the former CSFR (2.8 per cent of the labour force) or 2 million in the former USSR, or statements about unemployment growth. In particular estimates of changes in unemployment should be treated with care until the scope and administrative procedures of these offices are well established.

From the information available in the ILO, it is quite evident that all transition countries have decided to introduce Labour Force Surveys as a major source of statistics on employment and unemployment. Existing national experience with surveys on social and demographic issues and on time-use, combined with available international guidelines on concepts and definitions and experience with effective questionnaire design, make it likely that relevant national competence is available to design the questionnaires, process the returns, and analyse and present the results. However, relevant experience of the practical and management problems (such as establishment of field organization, etc.) for in-the-field sampling and data collection for surveys of the scale necessary for an LFS, are not readily available, in particular given the tight time schedules needed to get up-to-date statistics.

All transition countries have approached the ILO, EUROSTAT and national statistical organizations in Western Europe and North America for technical assistance in preparing and managing the LFS type of surveys.

Concerning the major classifications to describe the labour force, the situation seems to be as follows:

(a) The classification of education is generally considered to be satisfactory.
(b) The existing industrial classifications were based on the division of the economy into a 'productive' and a 'non-productive' economic

sphere. This distinction is no longer considered to be relevant or useful. As all transition countries are introducing the SNA system of national accounts and have been able to provide employment data according to ISIC, rev.2 (1968), at least at an aggregate level, it should not represent a major difficulty to introduce revised industrial classifications based on ISIC, rev.3 (1990) or NACE, rev.1 also for employment statistics.

(c) The occupational classifications used were also based on a distinction between 'productive' and 'non-productive' jobs (or 'manual' and 'non-manual' labour), for pay administrative purposes. The countries did not provide employment data according to any level in the ISCO-68 classification. The development of new occupational classifications based on ISCO-88 has been identified as an important challenge which many of the countries seem prepared to undertake. Work has started in Bulgaria, the Czech Republic, Hungary, Poland , Romania, Slovenia and the former USSR.

It should be noted that most of the transition countries will carry on with the current reporting systems for state and certain types of co-operative enterprises and farms. With modifications this instrument, which is already in place, is expected to permit the collection of reliable statistics on average employment and earnings from the establishments covered - to supplement the LFS results and provide the core of the establishment based employment statistics which may emerge as part of the statistical programmes to be built on the new business registers now under development. This will, however, take time. It has been mentioned, for example that in the former CSFR hundreds of new co-operatives and private businesses were registered daily, but that only 30 per cent of these became operational.

FUTURE STATISTICS ON EMPLOYMENT TRENDS AND SKILL SHORTAGES

Monitoring employment trends

As we have seen, the measurement of employment trends in transition countries was based on regular reporting by a limited and very stable set of establishments and organizations. That certain components of total employment were not covered or only covered in a rudimentary fashion did not matter very much as long as they could be assumed to constitute small and stable proportions of the total. These assumptions could be made with some confidence about most of the groups. (In some countries data for the 'armed forces' were included, and hidden, in the totals and in others they were excluded and only available to the proper authorities.) The transition processes have undermined the basis for these statistics in two ways: (i) an increasing part of economic activity is carried out outside the establishments subject to the established reporting systems; and (ii) the authority of the government, i.e. the statistical authorities, to demand (correct and) detailed statistical reports on employment and other aspects of operations are eroded as and when the establishments have to operate independently of government control and support. Neither during the transition process nor afterwards is it realistic to assume that the measurement of employment trends can be reliably based on establishment surveys, given the expected increasing importance of small and medium-sized establishments and their expected chaotic 'demography'. Since transition countries by definition and in practice do not have a *stable* administrative basis for employment statistics, the only stable basis for monitoring employment, and unemployment, will be household-based labour force sample surveys (LFSs), and concrete steps to start such surveys in 1991 or 1992 were taken in most of the transition countries.

The strength and weaknesses of LFS data (relative to establishment and administratively based employment statistics, where they are realistic alternatives) are well known. One important advantage of LFSs for the transition countries is that the conceptual and method-ological problems in using them for measuring employment and unemployment levels and changes are well understood and that many different countries have relevant experience from which transition countries can learn, cf. Hussmanns *et al.*, 1990 and ILO, 1990. An LFS is in many ways as close to an 'off-the-shelf' survey instrument as you can find in official statistics, and preparations can concentrate on the organizational and financial problems involved in launching the surveys. One important consideration is the frequency of observation and release of results. Given the expected limited capacity to carry out interviews, the advantages of continuous operations, the need to break down some data at regional levels, and for current data, interviewing representive samples every month for publication of quarterly averages (as in Norway) seems to be a sensible solution, which will make it possible to develop certain aggregate indicators on a monthly basis as the time-series become longer and their behaviour better understood.

To get estimates of the number of employed persons will not be suffi-cient. There will be demand for information about the type of activities people are employed in and the type of persons who are employed and unemployed. This means that classifications of industry, occupation and education/training will be needed as well as coding indexes and guidelines on how to use these classifications effectively in household surveys. The work to modify existing classification systems, whether national ones or international models such as ISIC, rev.3, ISCO-88 and ISCED, and to develop the tools needed to use them effectively, is probably as difficult and demanding of resource as the preparations for the LFS itself, but also as necessary. Such tools are not documented in detail in sources which are easily accessible, but see Chapter 9 in Hussmanns *et al.*, 1990.

What about the existing infrastructure and procedures for measuring employment? Should they be abandoned because they will cover a decreasing proportion of total employment, at least until adequate business registers have been established? Probably not, unless there is a straight trade-off in terms of resources for labour force statistics. There will still be great interest in data on the development of employment in the former centrally controlled enterprises, whether they remain in the state sector or are taken over by national or foreign private owners. The development of new instruments for collecting establishment-based employment and wage statistics, which can also provide a basis for analysing *ex post* the impact of the transition process, will also be one of the many challenges faced by the national statistical authorities. Not only the content and scope of the enterprise-based labour statistics may change as a consequence, but also the quality of the reported data. The direction of this quality-change is difficult to predict, as the presumed negative impact on 'willingness' to report resulting from greater operational freedom may be off-set by less need to appear to satisfy centrally formulated plans and regulations.

Measuring labour shortages and skill gaps

Current and future 'skill shortages' are frequently expressed concerns of employers and educational planners in many countries and have, at least according to the anecdotal evidence which has found its way into Western news media, been identified as one of the major bottlenecks to the transition process. Therefore it is certainly legitimate to request that statistics on such shortages should be developed and published regularly. 'Shortage of skill X' is commonly understood to mean that there is unsatisfied demand at prevailing wages and working conditions for workers who have the capacity to carry out the tasks and duties of type X or of occupation X, or who have received training of type X. Thus one needs to be able to define and measure both 'unsatisfied demand' and a relevant concept of a 'type X worker'.

In Hoffmann, 1991, it is suggested that

'Shortage of skill X' in a particular geographically defined labour market can be defined to exist when 'vacancies' above a predetermined threshold have been observed for workers of type X for more than N reference periods,

where this 'predetermined threshold' has been set for the particular labour market by analysing the 'normal' or 'balanced' situation, given the data collection instruments used and the particular features of that labour market. Obviously, such thresholds would have to be re-established from time to time as the functioning of the markets or the measurement instruments change.

If this definition is acceptable one crucial element in any effort to measure current labour shortages will be the definition and measurement of 'vacancies'. From the discussion in Hoffman, 1991, it seems clear that to obtain measurements of 'vacancies' which conceptually and methodologically are parallel to 'unemployment' as measured in LFSs will be complicated because of the need to cover the whole universe of possible demand for labour services. Particularly relevant to the situation in the transition countries is the need to have good business registers as part of the total sampling frame, given that these registers are very much under development at the moment.

A further complication is the need to find relevant typologies for 'type X worker'. The common variables used to indicate workers' skills are 'occupation' and 'education/training/qualifications' (different terms are used in different countries), and for both we have both national classifications and international models which can be used as bases for revision of the existing ones if necessary. However, the anecdotal evidence on the concerns expressed concerning 'skill shortages' in transition countries indicates that neither variable will adequately reflect these concerns. Two problems are involved, namely (a) that the classifications will reflect those types of skills which are (or have been) present in the country, while the shortages mainly are related to skills for which there has been very little or no demand in the past ('professional accountants' are frequently mentioned as an example); and (b) that while the type of skill may be represented in the classifications, the shortage is related to particular types of experience, for example related to the functioning of enterprises in a market economy, for which no appropriate typology has been developed and tested − neither in the transition countries nor elsewhere.

What are the options if 'something', however flawed relative to the ideal in terms of coverage, group identification and conceptual adequacy, is better than 'nothing'? Looking at the demand side it is convenient to distinguish between (i) direct observation of (outcomes of) search activities; and (ii) inquiries to (potential) 'employers' about search activities and their outcomes. Features of both approaches will be outlined after a brief discussion of *relative wages* as an indicator of the presence of 'labour shortages'.

Development of relative wages. According to standard economic theory, one of the expected outcomes of persistent excess demand for (shortage of) a particular type of labour would be that the relative price of this type would increase. In principle we should therefore be able to draw conclusions about the existence of excess demand for particular groups of workers by observing changes in relative remuneration between groups of workers with different skills or qualifications, as indicated by the following statement about the situation in Britain (from *The Economist*, 13 April 1991, p. 36): 'Skill shortages are easing too, so that companies do not need to pay more to recruit and retain staff'. However, (i) at least during the transition period the market economy is not yet in place; (ii) in practice relative wages have proved to be quite 'sticky' and actual wage rates are determined by a range of different factors and can vary quite significantly between individuals even when they belong to the same narrowly defined 'skill' or occupational group and have the same formal qualifications; (iii) wages only represent a proportion, which varies over time and between groups, of total compensation received (i.e. of the total 'price' for labour). To some extent problems (ii) and (iii) may be less important if one can focus on the relative wage rates of newly hired persons. However, we do not know of any examples of official statistics which use this approach to indicate short- or medium-run labour shortages. On the other hand, changes in the balance between supply and demand of different types of labour market groups have been used to explain longer-term shifts in the relative incomes of these groups.

Observing search activities

Vacancies reported to public employment agencies give the most common basis for vacancy statistics in the countries which have developed systems of public employment services. Statistics on such 'vacancies' are often used to monitor the state and development of the labour market, alone or in conjunction with data based on the registration of job seekers, in particular unemployed persons, at the same offices. Most of the coverage problems discussed in Hoffmann, 1991, will be even more important in transition countries where the employment services are only now being developed. In addition, this development process does in itself represent a problem for the validity of statistical time-series, as they can be expected to reflect the development of the services as much as the underlying labour market developments.

Vacancies advertised in newspapers and journals are also used as a basis for monitoring labour market developments and business cycles in some countries. The methods used vary from very simple measurement of column lengths in one or a few papers and journals at weekly or monthly intervals, with no or very limited classification by type of work or employer, to highly developed 'clipping operations' where industry, occupation and qualification required are coded for all job advertisements appearing during a reference period and efforts are made to eliminate duplicates. This source can only give statistics relating to new or re-advertised vacancies, but the fact that most examples of this type of statistics have been developed by private organizations for sale to customers may indicate that they have been found useful. Again these statistics, even from the most sophisticated operation, will only cover the type of vacancies for which newspaper or journal advertising is an important channel for recruitment, and in the transition countries we may expect that measured changes will tend to reflect changes in the means used by employers to find workers, and in the services offered by newspapers etc., as much as real changes in the demand for labour.

A possible third source of indicative statistics on certain types of 'skill shortages' can be found in the *work permits given to foreigners*, if these are allocated on the basis of applications submitted by, or with the support of, employers. If the relevant authorities can be persuaded to formulate questions about type of work to be performed and the type of qualifications which the permit seeker has in a way which will give adequate information for coding, then this may provide interesting statistics on the need to supplement the national pool of labour. However, it is an unfortunate paradox with this source that honest answers can only be expected if they do not influence whether or not a work permit will be granted – in which case the immigration authorities will have no interest in whether or not this part of the application form has been completed adequately.

Statistical surveys of employers

The only approach that can lead to measurement of vacancies or skill shortages and that will not be 'contaminated' by the institutional changes of the transition process is to survey units which may be looking for labour services, asking about possible search activities. This represents the parallel to the measurement of unemployment through household labour force surveys. As observed above the scope of the vacancy definition is such that the sampling frame for this type of survey in principle should include all economic units, i.e. households as well as all public and private establishments. In practice such surveys have only covered sub-sets of public and private establishments, although it would be interesting to carry out experiments asking about labour demand in household surveys. Questions to households could cover both the household's own demand for labour services and what household members know about demand at their place of work, i.e. by their employers or themselves as self-employed persons. In fact, household surveys may be the only way of covering the vacancies in small and informal sector establishments, which may represent a higher proportion of total vacancies than they do of total employment, not only for specific worker categories but also overall, as the rate of turnover of employment in such establishments may be significantly higher than in larger ones.

A possible design of a full-scale 'vacancy survey' is outlined in Hoffman, 1991. However, a simpler approach may be more realistic in the context of transition countries – namely a variant of the approach used in the Swedish Labour Market Tendency Surveys, cf. Statistics Sweden, 1990. As in the Swedish approach, the selected employers would be asked (1) whether they had been looking for new workers during a recent period ('Yes/No' and how many); (2) whether they had actually hired new workers during the period ('Yes/No' and how many); (3) whether those hired had the qualifications most wanted ('Yes/No'); (4) would have to be given extra training by the employer ('Yes/No'); (5) how the employer saw the supply of workers with and without relevant experience ('Good/Balanced/Poor'); (6) whether recruitment had been easier or more difficult than previously; (7) whether additional recruitment is expected in the forthcoming period ('Yes/No') and (8) by how many? The Swedes can draw probability samples of employers of workers who have particular types of education or training (by linking their person and business registers) and can therefore formulate the questions as pertaining to particular qualifications. Transition countries do not have this possibility, but must select employers in general from whatever registers they have. The questions outlined above therefore have to be about workers in general, but should be supplemented with questions designed to ascertain (a) the types of jobs or tasks for which the employer has been recruiting, and (b) the type of qualifications he/she would like the new workers to have. These questions should be asked before question (3) and would have to be open for later coding of occupation, experience and qualification.

CONCLUDING REMARKS

The focus of this chapter has been on instruments for describing the current situation with respect to employment trends, labour shortages and skill gaps. It can be argued that government policies which can lead to improvements in these areas must be based on information referring to longer-term prospects, as these policies can only be expected to have significant effects over the long term – in particular if one is talking about policies for the training and re-training of a significant number of persons in the labour force, and that the proper focus of the chapter therefore should have been on indicators which have such longer-term perspectives. This view may have some merit, but the following observations seem relevant:

(a) Relevant medium- and longer-term time-series which in the future can be used as a basis for constructing medium- to longer-term indicators and projections will have to be built from observations of current situations;

(b) Questions such as 'Will this country have enough engineers to ensure economic growth after year 2000, or enough nurses to meet the demand for health services resulting from the increase in the number of old age persons?' are being addressed by the use of quite sophisticated demographic and economic projection models which try to link demographic, economic and educational developments. Not only do such models have to be based on data about current and past developments, these data also have to reflect structural features of the society which are common to both the observation and projection period. In transition countries such structural features are likely to be limited to the demographic aspects of the models, almost by definition.

Political concerns and priorities change over time because the circumstances and institutions as well as the external environments of a country are changing. (Some of the changes in policies or priorities are temporary, and may even seem misguided with hindsight, while others are lasting and reflect new perspectives on the society or new insights into the way in which it functions.) As a consequence it is not possible to identify stable sets of statistical 'policy indicators' related to employment trends, labour shortage and skill gaps. However, the experiences of other countries demonstrate that, although no single statistical instrument will satisfy all requirements, the existence of a (quarterly) labour force survey supplemented with establishment based employment information in selected areas will provide a very good basis for the formulation and implementation of policies requiring employment trends data. For the formulation and implementation of policies for which one would like to have statistics on 'labour shortages and skill gaps' it is much less easy to be confident that the instruments outlined in this chapter will be appropriate and adequate, because the phenomenon itself is more complex, and because there is less international experience in developing, testing and using the concepts and tools.

REFERENCES

Chernyshev, I. & Lawrence, S. (1990): 'ILO-comparable annual employment and unemployment estimates: Results and short methodological presentation.' *Bulletin of Labour Statistics*, 1990-4.

Chernyshev, I. & Lawrence, S. (1992): 'ILO-comparable annual employment and unemployment estimates: Updated results and methodology (no.3).' ILO *Bulletin of Labour Statistics*, 1992-4.

Hoffmann, E. (1991): *Measuring vacancies and excess labour*. Mimeographed paper. Bureau of Statistics, International Labour Office. Geneva, May 1991.

Hussmanns, R., Mehran, F. & Verma, V. (1990): *Surveys of economically active population, employment, unemployment and underemployment: An ILO manual on concepts and methods*. International Labour Office, Geneva, 1990.

ILO, 1990: *Statistical sources and methods. Volume 3. Economically active population, employment, unemployment and hours of work (Household surveys)*. Second edition. International Labour Office, Geneva, 1990.

Statistics Sweden, 1990: *Arbetskraftsbarometer 1990* (Labour market tendency survey 1990). Statistics Sweden, Stockholm, 1990.

Annex 1 (ILO-comparable annual employment and unemployment estimates: updated results and methodology) and relevant tables are to be found at the end of this volume.

5

Revision of labour statistics systems in the countries of the Commonwealth of Independent States in the light of the ILO international recommendations

I. CHERNYSHEV, V. GOURIEV and I. MANYKINA*

In May 1990 the then USSR ratified the Labour Statistics Convention, No. 160, adopted on 25 June 1985 by the International Labour Conference of the International Labour Organization at its Seventy-first Session. The principal significance of this ratification (the earlier 1938 Convention, No. 63, had not been ratified by the USSR) was the USSR's recognition of how important international contacts were at that time and how important it was to ensure comparability of statistics on the utilization of available labour resources and on the relationship between earnings and other economic variables.

One may say that statistical practice in the republics of the former Soviet Union (FSU) was broadly in line with the ILO international recommendations, i.e. labour statistics were collected regularly, covered the whole territory and provided data for all the working and non-working population, etc. Nevertheless, there existed a number of divergences in concepts, definitions and systems of indicators used, classifications applied and methods of data collection employed. Furthermore, a number of concepts (e.g. 'unemployment' and 'labour cost') were not subject to statistical analysis since they were not considered to be a feature of Soviet society.

However, the processes in progress in the economy and labour organization have made it more than ever necessary to bring national statistics closer into line with international standards. This is particularly true as

---

* This chapter is a slightly modified version of an article first published in the *Bulletin of Labour Statistics*, 1992, No. 4, and is exclusively concerned with the experience of the countries of the CIS: Armenia, Azerbaijan, Belarus, Georgia, Kazakhstan, Kyrgyzstan, Moldova, the Russian Federation, Tajikistan, Turkmenistan, Ukraine and Uzbekistan.

regards indicators of the economically active population, employment, unemployment and hours of work. After 1990, new labour statistics were sent to the ILO (such as strikes, occupational injuries and consumer price indices). In the case of 'labour cost', it was decided to initiate the development of appropriate methods for its measurement during 1992.

Despite some improvement in the exchange of information at the international level, much work remained to be done to modify statistical structures, systems of indicators and programmes for *ad hoc* surveys and other statistical observations to bring them closer to the ILO international recommendations and allow more detailed analysis of the new processes taking place in the labour markets of the countries of the Commonwealth of Independent States.

The main areas of this activity are described below.

STATISTICS OF EMPLOYMENT AND UNEMPLOYMENT

General situation

Since more and more jobs would become redundant as the intensification of labour proceeded and the State discontinued subsidizing inefficient and unprofitable enterprises, it was expected that the number of unemployed in the CIS countries could increase dramatically by the end of 1992 and in the first half of 1993, particularly in big cities. Any attempt to slow down this process artificially (for instance, by issuing a special decree to halt the release of redundant workers from state enterprises) would inevitably have increased invisible unemployment and labour hoarding.

A legal guarantee that the labour problems arising from the new economic conditions would not be neglected by the State was provided by the *Basic Principles of Labour Legislation* adopted in the CIS countries during 1992. Within the framework of the Basic Principles, national and regional programmes of employment were drawn up to make provision for all the available means of activating the labour market: creation of new jobs, introduction of effective vocational guidance for the unemployed and marginal groups, their training and retraining. Privatization and conversion, as well as the encouragement of new flexible forms of employment (incentives for small enterprises, favourable conditions for self-employment, attractive remuneration schemes for homeworkers and out-workers, etc.), were to be used extensively in order to reduce the pressure of redundant labour on the labour market.

Administrative data

An essential part of implementing the revised employment policies was the ensuring of a timely supply of policy-makers, at all levels, and providing the public with reliable and comprehensive statistical information on labour supply and demand. In order to cope with this task, a statistical reporting system by the state employment offices was introduced. The indicators collected in these reports were determined jointly by the statistical institutions and labour administration in accordance with the international recommendations adopted by the 13th International Conference of Labour Statisticians in 1982. They enable data to be provided on persons registered at state employment offices for job placement in sufficient detail to classify them as placed in employment or unemployed. Quarterly reports supply data on the number and movement of unemployed persons, classified by sex and place of residence. Annual reports gave further information on the structure of the unemployed by age, level of education, cause of leaving the job and other factors.

However, the instability and uncertainty of the processes which occurred in the labour markets of the CIS countries also created a need for operational reporting. Thus in June 1991, in addition to quarterly and annual reports, approval was given for a monthly report providing a limited range of statistics on job placement and employment as shown in Figure 5.1.

By the second day of the month following the reference period, lower-level (district and urban) offices of the employment service were required to submit data in this form to their supervisory bodies and to the statistical authorities in their area. In the CIS countries in general, processing of the results was completed by the 15th of the month following the reference period.

Combined efforts on employment and social protection against unemployment also need operational data from enterprises on the number of workers who have lost or are expected to lose their jobs as a result of redundancy. The reporting of such data was introduced into statistical practice in January 1992. These reports were used for short-term projections of changes in the labour market, determination of the resources required by the State Employment Funds and for preparing additional social security measures in the CIS countries.

Labour Force Surveys

When the revision of labour force statistics began in the CIS countries, it was proposed, *inter alia*, to restrict the collection of unemployment data

Code	Category	No. of persons
01	Not gainfully employed at the beginning of the reference period	
02	Registered during the reference period	
03	Placed in a job during the reference period	
04	*Of Code 03*, the number who lost their previous job because of redundancy	
05	Not gainfully employed by the end of the reference period	
06	*Of Code 05*, those who are recognized as unemployed	
07	*Of Code 06*, the number who lost their previous job because of redundancy	
08	*Of Code 06*, those undergoing vocational training as arranged by the employment office	
09	*Of Code 06*, those engaged in community and social work	
10	*Of Code 06*, those receiving unemployment allowance	
11	Demand of enterprises for wage-earners and salaried employees at the end of the reference period	
12	*Code 11* including wage-earners	

Fig. 5.1 Report on job placement and employment of persons registered at the employment office

to compulsory reports provided by state employment offices. However, from the experience of countries with a developed market economy and from the first practical steps taken by the national statistical institutions in that field, it became evident that a large number of the unemployed did not register with employment offices. This was a crucial point which stimulated an active discussion between labour statisticians and labour administrators and which finally tipped the balance in favour of the introduction into statistical practice of regular household Labour Force Surveys (LFSs). Another no less important argument was that unlike employment offices, household surveys would also look into employment issues that would permit more detailed analysis and forecast of unemployment changes in time and the collection of information to supplement the data being reported by enterprises and organizations. Furthermore, by conducting LFSs to study employment and unemployment, the national statistical institutions would be making a definite contribution to international comparability of labour statistics in accordance with the requirements set out in the ILO Labour Statistics Convention, No. 160.

In November 1991 the GOSKOMSTAT USSR organized a Seminar on Labour Statistics for the newly independent states which led to a set of recommendations urging them to conduct LFSs to measure employment and unemployment on a regular basis, using the relevant ILO international recommendation. The ILO Bureau of Statistics was invited to the Seminar and its representatives actively participated in the discussions.

In July 1992, the Statistical Committee of the CIS (STATCOM CIS) organized a follow-up International Seminar on Labour Statistics, which gathered together senior labour statisticians from seven of the CIS member countries (Armenia, Belarus, Kazakhstan, Kyrgyzstan, Moldova, the Russian Federation and Turkmenistan) as well as from Estonia, Latvia, Lithuania and Georgia. The ILO Bureau of Statistics was again invited to this Seminar and was represented, as before, by the ILO Chief Statistician and another member of the Bureau. At the end of the Seminar a new set of revised recommendations was adopted by the participants. One of the major conclusions was that all countries represented at the seminar showed a great interest in measuring their labour force through the LFS techniques. Also, the participants reiterated their request that the ILO should assume its role as an international coordinator of the efforts of the FSU countries to launch a comprehensive and harmonized Labour Force Survey.

In conducting the surveys, it was recommended that a single methodology should be used, based on an agreed minimum number of statistical items, which would permit comparison between countries within the territory of the FSU and with foreign countries.

Based on the decisions of the seminars and with the ILO's technical assistance, STATCOM CIS prepared a master LFS questionnaire and a set of recommendations on how to organize and monitor an LFS. The Russian Federation was the first CIS country to conduct a full-scale LFS (early November 1992), preceded by a pilot survey in the Orlov Region in June 1992. The official title of the survey is 'Population Sample Survey of Employment' (PSSE). In November 1993, the second round of PSSE was carried out. The ILO Bureau of Statistics provided substantial assistance to the Russian Federation's GOSKOMSTAT both in their preparations for a pilot and a full-scale PSSE. With the kind permission of GOSKOMSTAT a methodological description of this survey and its questionnaire are presented in Annexes 2 and 3 respectively. Ukraine is the second country of the CIS to launch a regular LFS, beginning in October 1995. A pilot survey was conducted in the Chernigov Region in November 1992 in which two ILO experts participated. A trial LFS took place in October 1993.

In both cases, the sample frames were built up on the basis of the decennial population censuses (conducted in January 1989) and compiled from the lists of census enumeration districts. The use of data from the 1989 population censuses presented a number of advantages: the very costly process of establishing a sample was avoided, the sample was established by computer, a number of intermediate selection steps involving determination of actual place of residence of families and direct selection of actual families and individuals in the age groups observed were avoided, and a single data base was employed containing demographic, social and economic information on the population (both actual families and individuals). The principal drawback of using the census address lists was the administrative, territorial and other changes of the past two years which had occurred in the FSU countries. However, allowance for such changes was made when drawing up the sample (by means of current statistics and projections) and preparing instructions for the interviewers and Regional Statistical Offices, etc.

OBSERVING THE DEVELOPMENT OF A MIXED ECONOMY

As has already been stated, labour statistics must be reviewed, not only to bring them closer to international standards but also to meet domestic needs in view of the growing range of statistical indicators requiring measurement and analysis as the CIS countries move from a command economy to a mixed (state, private, individual, etc.) mode of production during their transition to a market economy.

Despite the fact that in the CIS countries state ownership was still predominant, other forms of ownership and methods of management such as private farms, leasing relationships and banking structures became increasingly common. Trading and commodity exchanges had been set up. Privatization was in progress. State enterprises were being taken over by collective and private ownership in manufacturing, construction, agriculture and other sectors. In order to account appropriately for such processes, employment statistics for these new forms of economic activity started to be collected regularly and published by industry.

REVISION OF NATIONAL ECONOMIC CLASSIFICATIONS ON THE BASIS OF INTERNATIONAL STANDARDS

As has already been mentioned above, in addition to changes in items of observation, there were changes in the concepts used in statistics and new statistical categories were being brought into practice.

A very important part of bringing statistical practice in the CIS countries closer to international practice is the review of the existing national economic classifications. This began through the combined efforts of the statistical bodies and other economic departments and research institutes and in close collaboration with the ILO Bureau of Statistics and the UN Statistical Office.

In order to convert statistical data for international comparison, conversion tables were prepared between the then current edition of the former *All-Union Classification of Economic Sectors* (OKONH) and the third edition of the *United Nations International Standard Industrial Classification of All Economic Activities* (ISIC), which served to convert OKONH into ISIC categories and vice versa. Later, another statistical classification in wide use was reviewed: *The All-Union Classifier of Wage-Earner Occupations and Salaried-Employee Posts and Tariff Rates* (AUOC). It is intended to convert the former AUOC and the grading and rating handbooks in the Single Classification of Occupations, on the basis of the underlying principles of the *International Standard Classification of Occupations 1988* (ISCO-88), in order to standardize the nomenclature of occupations and make it possible for the CIS workers and employees to move out into the international labour market. It is envisaged to begin introducing new National Classifications of Occupations in the CIS countries in 1994-95.

When these tasks have been completed, statistical bodies will be able to conduct subsequent surveys of occupations on the basis of the new National Classifications of Occupations. That will undoubtedly improve analysis and ensure comparability.

The Russian Federation and Ukraine were the first two CIS countries to set up teams in charge of the development of new occupational classifications. This work is carried out jointly by their respective statistical institutions and Ministries of Labour, and international expertise is provided by the ILO. Recently, the ILO Bureau of Statistics organized training for two Ukrainian project managers in Geneva.

The changes taking place in the economy and in the labour market made it necessary to develop and introduce *National Classifications of Status in Employment* (NCSE). Since no such national classification existed in the CIS countries before, the only classification able to serve as a basis is the *ILO International Classification of Status in Employment* (ICSE), which currently suggests the following basic groups: employees, employers, own-account workers, unpaid family workers, members of producers' cooperatives, persons not classified by status. ICSE was revised by the 15th International Conference of Labour Statisticians held in January 1993 and its new version has been carefully studied by the CIS countries. Obviously, the CIS countries will come up against various problems in developing their NCSE but that should not be seen as a reason to discourage them from this work. Difficulties will be overcome progressively as both national and international classifications are further developed and improved. Use of this classification will undoubtedly assist in the analysis of changes in the current social structures in the labour force, which already fall outside the framework of the traditional Marxist subdivisions of labour into manual, non-manual, collective farm, etc.

NEW PROCESSES AS REFLECTED IN THE LABOUR MARKET

During the period of transition a certain deterioration in labour discipline and time-keeping became noticeable. Rejection of former methods of management did not always or not immediately lead to their replacement by new economic methods. As a result labour discipline has been weakened and the length of time enterprises stand idle for lack of raw materials or disruption of supplies from cooperatives has increased.

Reduced output, lower imports and the continuing breakdown of existing economic relationships, both inside the individual CIS countries and between them, caused the closure of many enterprises and works as a result of disruption of material and technical supplies.

In the USSR, *statistics on working time lost* used to be compiled on the basis of compulsory reports from enterprises and organizations. STATCOM CIS proposed retaining this source of information in the future for the CIS, since it considers that it was not really advisable to study the use of working time by means of household surveys.

The new processes appearing in the labour market include strikes, which are now unfortunately firmly ensconced in economic life. Hence *strike statistics* are a very new field. In setting up a reporting system for strikes, use was made of the experiences of countries with a market economy and methodological recommendations from the ILO Bureau of Statistics.

Data on strikes are currently collected by statistical bodies either from managements or directly from strike committees. It is expected that in the future the trade unions will also be involved in this work.

LABOUR FORCE FLOWS

The processes of transition in all CIS member countries led to a marked increase in labour force migration of all kinds: between enterprises under different forms of ownership, between different sections of industry, between different parts of a country, and between different CIS countries.

Labour force flows

In forecasting the direction and scale of *labour force flows*, the intersectoral analysis of the redistribution of the labour force and of structural changes in occupations is of paramount importance. Unlike countries with a market economy, where such processes are observed through household surveys, the CIS countries used to study this subject on the basis of information collected from enterprises and organizations. Although, as mentioned earlier, it involves a considerable workload, STATCOM CIS continues to believe that this source of information offers the considerable advantage of greater reliability and greater detail in the nomenclature of economic sectors, branches of industry and occupations.

Analysis of the structure of employment by sector shows that, against a background of declining employment in the productive sector, the number of those employed in the non-productive sector is increasing.

The scale and direction of labour force flows between various branches of industry may be studied through analysis of current structural changes in jobs and occupations. Since 1980 there has been a steady decline in the number of assistant workers, freight handlers, navvies, road workers and some other occupations of unskilled and low-status labour. As modern, more productive machinery has been brought into manufacturing, the number of machine operators has declined. Among salaried employees there has been a fall in the number of accountants, statisticians, draughtsmen and copyists. As a result of increasing demand for high quality engineering and removal of the need to perform functions outside the field (for example, organizing socialist emulation, clerical tasks, etc.), the number of engineers will also go down. With time, as conversion proceeds, labour force flows between the different branches of industry will be affected by reduction in the armed forces, cuts in workers in the military and industrial complex, and the like. There will be a steadily increasing demand for labour in the service sector.

Labour turnover

An item of continuing statistical observation is *labour turnover*. Various definitions of labour turnover exist; however, frequently, it is used to mean labour-force flow for any reason. Statistical observation in the field would be facilitated if the ILO proposed a standard definition of that category. In the CIS countries, labour turnover refers only to leaving the job at an individual's own request or for a breach of labour discipline. Therefore, this aspect of analysing labour-force flows differs from the earlier topic by restricting attention to the narrower contingent of workers who leave an occupation or a job for the reasons given above.

Level of labour turnover is generally measured by the *rate of labour turnover*, which is the ratio between the number leaving for the given reasons and the total of those employed. This indicator is used to analyse sectoral and territorial differences in turnover levels and the way they change in time.

Statistical analysis of labour turnover used generally to be based on data collected through annual statistical reports and *ad hoc* sample surveys. Such reports would usually include *labour force flow statistics* relating to changes in the labour force during the reference period such as flows of wage-earners, or both wage-earners and salaried employees, into and out of employment. Here, those taken on by an enterprise or organization were classified by the form of recruitment, and persons leaving by the reason for doing so. There existed the following forms of recruitment: organized recruitment; recruitment under directives from corresponding ministries or departments of persons graduating from full-time higher and secondary-specialized education, including vocational and technical schools; persons transferred from other enterprises, institutions and organizations; persons recruited by the enterprise and organization itself.

Statistical reports used to include the following reasons for leaving employment: transfer to other enterprises, institutions and organizations; as a result of the ending of a contract or completion of work; in order to follow a course of study; call-up for the army, retirement or other reasons governed by the law; at the individual's own request; dismissal for absenteeism or other breaches of labour discipline.

Sample surveys of causes of labour force flows, which were conducted on a regular basis before 1989 in manufacturing and construction, represented another important source of information for statistical analysis.

In the 1980s labour turnover in many sectors of the economy of the Soviet Union took a clear downward trend. For example, in 1986 labour turnover in manufacturing had declined from 16 to 12 per cent in comparison with 1980 and in construction from 23 to 17 per cent. To some extent that was the result of a series of measures to strengthen labour discipline adopted by the Soviet Government in the 1980s, which included both penalties and incentives. That decline in labour turnover unjustifiably weakened interest in statistical study of the problem.

The Russian Labour Flexibility Survey

In 1988-9, however, labour turnover began to increase again (e.g. labour turnover in manufacturing had already reached 14 per cent by 1989).

That was to some extent due to the appearance of new forms of independent activity and new forms of management. Labour turnover has also been increased by inter-ethnic conflicts and the resultant forced migration of population.

Although there was a return to existing forms and means of analysing labour turnover, it should be said that since such methods make insufficient allowance for economic variables it was difficult for them to determine the full range of causative and consequential relationships in the field. Hence, when the need arose for new labour policies and labour incentives in the transition to a market economy, it was decided to make a major change in the statistical procedures for studying such problems.

Plans were being made for a new survey to be conducted in the second half of 1991, when a proposal was received from the ILO for a very similar statistical study. The joint (GOSKOMSTAT of Russia and the ILO) survey, entitled 'Russian Labour Flexibility Survey' was conducted in late 1991, with the second round (which included an update of a fractional sample) in early 1992, in Moscow, the Moscow Region and St Petersburg and covered 501 industrial enterprises, giving a useful opportunity to compare the Russian methods with those from outside and add new techniques of data collection and processing to its procedures.

The survey questionnaire allowed, *inter alia*, data to be collected on indicators characterizing labour force flows into and out of employment, occupational structure, labour turnover, its causes and the measures being taken to reduce it, etc. Also, the questionnaire contained a special set of questions destined for interviewing managements and provided statistics on output and financial activity of surveyed enterprises, which allowed the determination of the relationship between the way the work of the staff was organized and the results of economic activity.

The survey findings were used as a basis for recommendations on effective labour policy which were presented by the ILO and actively discussed by the participants at the *Conference on Employment Restructuring in Russian Industry*, which was held under the ILO auspices in close collaboration with GOSKOMSTAT of the Russian Federation in Moscow and St Petersburg in October 1992. Finally, a set of recommendations on how to develop an effective labour policy was sent to all enterprises taking part in the survey to assist them in applying more acceptable methods of dealing with their staff.

CONCLUSIONS

It is quite evident that the CIS countries have embarked on the road to a radical revision and restructuring of their national statistical systems. The Republic of Belarus, the Russian Federation and Ukraine have each developed their own *State Programme for the Transition to the System of Accounting and Statistics Adopted in International Practice*. These State Programmes were endorsed by the governments and have become legal documents at the national level. Each State Programme contains a special chapter on labour statistics. Other CIS countries are in the process of developing similar programmes.

The ILO, the UN Statistical Office, the International Monetary Fund, the World Bank, the Organization for Economic Co-operation and Development (OECD) and the Statistical Office of the European Communities (EUROSTAT) are providing extensive technical assistance to these countries in their effort to implement the above programmes.

The ILO Labour Statistics Convention, No. 160, has been ratified by Belarus, the Russian Federation and the Ukraine, thereby committing the three countries to compile labour statistics in conformity with relevant international standards and practices.

The CIS countries are conscious that the road both in economic and statistical transition to a market economy will not be a short and easy one and that it will require both strength and patience. However, they are very determined to reach the end and emerge with new statistical systems which will permit complete integration into the international statistical community and greatly facilitate comparability across countries.

Annexes 2 (Methodological description of the Labour Force Survey in the Russian Federation) and **3 (Questionnaire used in the Russian Federation)** are to be found at the end of this volume.

6

Some aspects of labour analysis in the CIS countries

I. MANYKINA*

The general labour market situation in countries of the Commonwealth of Independent States (CIS) is extremely complex. In a society where the command-administrative way of linking manpower with the means of production was in force until very recently, the development of market relations is painful both for the economically active population (employed or seeking work) and for employers.

The economic situation, which in all the CIS countries is characterized by a dramatic decline in production, decreasing investment and falling living standards, is having a profound impact on the labour market. The national economy of the CIS countries has been set back several years on many fronts. Thus, in the Russian Federation, the net national income (net product) was at the level of 1976 in 1992, the public labour productivity at the level of 1977.

The number of people employed in the state sector (excluding joint stock companies) fell by more than 10 per cent over 1992 in the CIS as a whole, due to the decrease in production volume and the redistribution of the labour force among various sectors of the economy.

The development of other forms of property and methods of economic management is becoming more and more evident. The number of peasant individual farms is increasing. On 1 July 1991 peasant farms in the Russian Federation numbered 25,000, on 1 January 1992 they numbered 50,000 and on 1 July 1992, 127,000. In the CIS as a whole, 387,000 farms were registered in total on 1 July 1992.

* This chapter was originally written as a paper for the Joint ECE/ILO/OECD Work Session on Labour Statistics and Issues of Concern for Transition Countries, Paris, December 1992.

The process of state property privatization is increasing (albeit more slowly than expected): on 1 April 1992, private enterprises numbered around 80,000 and on 1 August they numbered 160,000. At the end of 1992, nearly 3 million citizens were employed in joint stock companies and economic associations. Forms of business activity are becoming more and more varied – such business associations of citizens and legal persons as partnerships, companies, inter-industrial, regional and other associations have been spreading out in the CIS countries.

EMPLOYMENT AND UNEMPLOYMENT

In 1991 the total number of those employed in the CIS countries amounted to 131 million. This number covers employees of the state and private enterprises (including those working in cooperatives, collective farms, joint stock companies and societies, etc.) as well as farms, family enterprises, private production and persons engaged in individual labour. More than half of those employed in the CIS countries are concentrated in the Russian Federation (74 million people); Ukraine has 25 million employed, Kazakhstan and Uzbekistan have 8 million each, Belarus 5 million, and in the other states there are 3 million or fewer employed in each.

The transition of the CIS countries' economies to multi-structural development is accompanied by a growth in labour force and job turnover (see Table 6.1). This turnover is characterized by a considerable excess in the number of those made redundant over the number of those hired and by the creation of new jobs. The hiring of new workers balances the number of those made redundant by only 70–80 per cent in a number of the CIS countries (the Russian Federation, Belarus, Moldova).

The share of those who left their jobs due to redundancy, among the total value of turnover of those who left their jobs, amounted to 12.5 per cent in Kyrgyzstan, 10 per cent in the Russian Federation and Belarus, 8.5 per cent in Moldova and 7 per cent in Kazakhstan in 1992. The highest share of the redundant employees (due to staff reduction) relates to science facilities (32 per cent in Belarus, 24 per cent in Moldova, 18 per cent in Kyrgyzstan); the lowest relates to health care (1-2 per cent in Kazakhstan and Moldova, 3 per cent).

The newly formed organizational structures do not fully absorb the surplus manpower forced out of the state sector, so there is a reduction in the number of jobs available. In particular, the organizations' and enterprises' demand for labour, reported to the employment services, amounted in January 1992 to 16,000 in Azerbaijan (as opposed to 13,000

Table 6.1 Labour force and working places, turnover in the first half of 1992.

	Turnover of labour force in January–June (in thousands)			Number of employees planned for redundancy in July–September (thousands)	Number of vacant working places at the end of June (thousands)	Number of working places planned to open in July–September (thousands)
	Employed	Number who left employment	Number of those who left who were redundant			
Belarus	269	417	41	30	36	1.7
Kazakhstan	123	128	9	19	34	4.9
Kyrgyzstan	127	179	22	5	5	0.7
Moldova	103	143	12	12	10	0.5
Russia	6,772	8,110	802	402	625	11.7

in August), 50,000 and 24,000 respectively in Belarus, 58,000 and 51,000 in Kazakhstan, 570,000 and 364,000 in the Russian Federation, 33,000 and 29,000 in Uzbekistan (data on Uzbekistan is given for July 1992). This trend is a cause for concern, bearing in mind that in the near future it could lead to an imbalance of demand and supply in the labour market.

The activity of the employment services could promote the decrease of tension in the labour market. However, less than half of the unemployed seek help from these services (and in some regions less than a third). Since the beginning of July 1992 the number of placements with the assistance of an employment service has been declining in many CIS countries, as shown in Table 6.2.

The existing system of professional and vocational training and re-training does not create favourable conditions for the promotion of employment. The extent of professional education is decreasing annually. Educational facilities within enterprises are being dismantled. The number of employees dealing with the organization of training are being reduced, as well as the funds allocated for professional education. The real demand of enterprises for personnel of certain professions is underestimated.

The system of training for the unemployed population, entrusted to employment services, is being developed extremely slowly. The number of people undergoing training at the instigation of employment services in August 1992 was 6,900 in the Russian Federation, 1,100 in Azerbaijan,

Table 6.2   Placement in employment of unemployed population

	May ('000)	June ('000)	July ('000)	August ('000)
Azerbaijan	2.1	2.2	2.6	2.4
Armenia	0.4	0.4	0.4	0.4
Belarus	5.7	6.9	6.2	7.0
Kazakhstan	7.8	7.9	8.0	8.0
Kyrgyzstan	0.9	1.1	1.0	0.8
Moldova	1.4	1.6	1.2	1.0
Russian Federation	53.4	60.4	54.7	53.4
Tajikistan	0.9	1.4	1.1	1.1
Turkmenistan				
Uzbekistan	11.0	13.0	8.3	9.3
Ukraine				

600 in Belarus, 100 in Kyrgyzstan, 300 in Tajikistan and 300 in Uzbekistan.

Over the year of 1992, unemployment has grown each month in the majority of the CIS countries (Table 6.3). In the Commonwealth as a whole (on 1 October 1992), 1.5 million people were registered as seeking employment and 525,000 people as unemployed. More than half of the unemployed were women. More than 70 per cent of the unemployed were in the most active age group (from 23 to 54 for women and from 23 to 59 for men).

In 1991, when the process of registration at employment services had just begun, the share of office employees (white-collar workers) among the unemployed amounted to nearly two-thirds. This high proportion was caused by a sharp reduction of administration bodies in early 1991. In 1992, however, the balance between blue- and white-collar workers among the unemployed had shifted towards blue-collar workers. By the middle of 1992 they accounted for 60 per cent of the unemployed while office employees only accounted for 33 per cent. The proportion of those with no profession (seeking a job for the first time) was 7 per cent.

The fact that graduates of the higher and specialized secondary educational institutions have difficulty finding employment is another cause for concern. Their number in the Russian Federation amounted to nearly 2,000 or 3 per cent of those unemployed, 8 per cent in Belarus and 9 per cent in Kazakhstan.

The majority of those unemployed are blue- and white-collar workers made redundant from enterprises and organizations. At the end of August 1992 they reached 40 per cent in the Russian Federation and over 50 per cent in Belarus of the total number of those recognized as unemployed.

Intensifying migratory pressures are aggravating the unemployment problem. Approximately 10 million migrants were registered in the CIS countries at the end of 1992. About a quarter of the total number of migrations was traditionally inter-republican. However, recently this index has become considerably higher in republics with an unstable internal situation caused by racial tensions. Thus in 1992 the proportion of citizens who departed from their town settlements among the total number of migrants was 42 per cent in Moldova, 45 per cent in Turkmenistan, 50 per cent in Kyrgyzstan, 56 per cent in Uzbekistan, 71 per cent in Tajikistan, 73 per cent in Georgia and 87 per cent in Azerbaijan.

A special variety of migrants, forced migrants or so-called refugees, appeared in the territory of the former USSR as a result of internal national conflicts. The problems of refugees affected almost all republics

Table 6.3   Number of unemployed registered at the employment services (at the end of month under review)

	Jan. (1000)	Feb. (1000)	March (1000)	April (1000)	May (1000)	June (1000)	July (1000)	Aug. (1000)	Sept. (1000)
Azerbaijan	4.9	5.5	7.0	7.9	7.2	7.2	6.8	6.6	6.2
Armenia	-	-	-	6.1	8.9	14.5	20.8	29.3	35.6
Belarus	2.6	3.4	4.2	5.1	5.8	7.1	9.7	12.2	14.9
Kazakhstan	4.5	6.7	9.2	11.8	13.6	15.6	19.6	22.4	25.0
Kyrgyzstan	0.2	0.3	0.5	0.7	0.8	0.8	1.1	1.2	1.4
Moldova	-	0.2	0.3	0.4	0.4	0.6	0.9	1.2	1.6
Russian Federation	69.2	93.1	118.4	151.0	176.5	202.9	248.0	294.2	367.0
Tajikistan	-	-	-	0.5	1.3	3.5	3.6	5.5	5.5
Uzbekistan	-	-	-	-	-	-	1.4	2.1	3.6
Ukraine	-	-	-	-	-	-	-	-	63.9

of the former USSR. Over 700,000 citizens who were forced to leave their places of permanent residence had registered by the beginning of 1992. Armenians, Azerbaijanis, Turks-meshetins and Ossetians were the largest groups. It is possible that the flow of Russian-tongue refugees will increase considerably due to the growth of national conflicts in the Caucasus and in the region of Central Asia.

The Russian Federation remains the major recipient of refugees both of native and other nationalities. On 15 February 1992 the number of refugees from other CIS states in the Russian Federation rose to 223,000, of whom 49,000 were Turks-meshetins, 48,000 Armenians, 43,000 Russian-speaking citizens and 7,000 Azerbaijanis.

In 1991 and especially in 1992 another new problem – forced underemployment – emerged in the majority of the CIS countries. In the USSR, underemployment had existed only in the form of voluntary transition to a shorter working day or week (it was mostly connected with women having small children). However, in 1992 the reduction of operations or temporary halting of production took place due to breaching of inter-industrial links, or the irregularity in supply of raw materials and accessory parts. In order to keep skilled workers, the management of such enterprises transferred them to a shorter working day or offered them unpaid leave or leave with reduced pay rather than cancelling their contracts. For example, 25 per cent of industrial enterprises (mainly in military and light industries) were working according to such a schedule in August 1992. The number of these non-working employees was near 2 million. They were not included in the number of unemployed, although their situation was sometimes even worse than that of the unemployed registered at employment services.

REMUNERATION OF LABOUR

Wages policy has changed in accordance with the transition to a market economy. In particular, the role of the state has changed, many of its functions having been transferred directly to enterprises. Now enterprises independently establish the forms of labour remuneration and material incentives. Many wage restrictions have been removed. The practice of various social payments (public transport expenses, public catering etc.) is widely applied.

The lack of a universal system of social security and of equal opportunities in procuring funds for wages indexation has led to an increasing gap in the level of earnings (see Table 6.4).

In all the CIS countries, the growth of average wages continued throughout 1992. However, almost all the growth was caused by the

Table 6.4   Average monthly wages during the first half of 1992 in CIS
countries

	Average monthly cash wages		Average monthly cash wages as % of cash wage in same period of 1991		Average real wage as % of wage in same period in 1991	
	January–June (Roubles)	July (Roubles)	January–June (%)	July (%)	January–June (%)	July (%)
Azerbaijan	1,055	2,510	443	763	-	-
Armenia	853	1,382	300	349	45	40
Belarus	2,778	4,733	741	847	93	91
Kazakhstan	2,156	3,794	644	1,031	75	120
Kyrgyzstan	1,099	1,822	398	528	46	56
Moldova	1,842	2,680	606	747	68	86
Russian Fed.	3,215	5,793	814	1,042	98	111
Tajikistan	1,116	1,873	455	669	-	73
Turkmenistan	1,569	-	535	-	-	-
Uzbekistan	1,121	2,013	433	621	73	111
Ukraine	3,142	-	1,012	-	-	-

necessity for compensation for the rise in prices. Thus, for example, the average monthly cash wages' growth in the Russian Federation was 814 per cent from January to June 1992. Taking into consideration the decrease in the rouble's purchasing power, the real value of wages in the second half of 1992 could be assessed at only 98 per cent of wages in January 1992

In the majority of CIS countries, real wages have been decreasing along with the high growth of cash wages. Changes in the labour remuneration rates are characterized by higher growth in areas such as industry, construction, transport and forestry while in areas such as science, health care, culture, art and some other non-productive branches the wages' growth rate was lower than in the national economy as a whole. For example, in Belarus in June 1992, wages in the industrial sector multiplied by ten, and in the field of health care by eight; in the

Russian Federation they multiplied by twelve and eight respectively.

The wages of workers in low-paid jobs have grown more slowly than the wages of those in better-paid categories. As a result, pay differentials have greatly increased: the decile ratio (the ratio of the labour remuneration rate of 10 per cent of the workers with the highest wages and that of 10 per cent of the workers with the lowest wages) changed only slightly in the 1970s and 1980s, but in 1991 it went up to 6.

LABOUR CONDITIONS

The development of market relations has been accompanied by decreasing attention to conditions of work. According to the registration data on unhealthy industrial conditions (dustiness, gas-pollution, noise, vibration, radiation and other factors, exceeding minimum allowable concentration) in the Commonwealth as a whole on 1 January 1992, about 8 million people were employed there of whom 1.3 million were engaged in hard manual labour and about 1 million were working on equipment not meeting the requirements of industrial safety.

In 1992, as compared to 1991, the proportion of employees working under conditions hazardous to health among the total number of employees rose in industry from 17 per cent to 21 per cent (by 795,000 employees), in construction from 6 to 8 per cent (by 61,000), and in transport from 7 to 9 per cent (by 114,000). This trend is observed in all the CIS countries. As to women, 2.1 million (34 per cent) work under harmful labour conditions (the total percentage of women's employment in the inspected branches was 41 per cent). The majority of women working under such conditions are concentrated in the industrial sector.

The existing system of privileges and compensation for unhealthy and other unfavourable working conditions stipulates the award of: additional annual paid leave, a shorter working day, higher wages or extra payments, free medicinal-preventive meals, free milk or other equivalent food, the right to a privileged pension according to age and years of service. An employee can be granted one or more privileges.

The number of employees enjoying at least one of the above privileges represents 16.2 million (43 per cent of the total number of employees) in industry, construction, transport and communications, which is considerably higher than the number of employees working under unhealthy or other unfavourable working conditions.

The considerable excess of the number of employees enjoying the above privileges over the number of employees actually working under harmful and other unfavourable labour conditions depends, on the one hand, on the disparity of the compensatory mechanism and the actual labour conditions and, on the other hand, on defects in the definition of the level and concentration of conditions hazardous to health in the work place.

One of the most common privileges is additional leave. In 1991 this was granted to 13.6 million employees in the inspected branches. Nine million received free milk and other equivalent food, 8.1 million had been given higher tariff rates or extra payments, 5.7 million received a privileged pension, 1.1 million had been granted shorter working hours and 1 million received free medicinal-preventive meals.

There has been no progress in the field of safety measures. The level of industrial injuries has been slightly reduced (5.4 victims among every 1,000 employees against 5.7 in 1990), but the level of fatal injuries remains high: approximately 2 out of 100 victims were killed. The indicators of industrial disease rate are also growing (for example, in the Russian Federation in 1991 there were 2.08 employees registered sick in every 10,000 against 1.96 in 1990). The majority of industrial diseases are in the chronic group, caused by dust and gas-pollution, which accounts for more than one-third of cases, or by noise and vibration, which accounts for about a quarter of cases.

BRIEF CONCLUSIONS

This analysis of the labour market situation in the CIS countries has shown that over the last two years the following trends have stood out: a sharp decline in production; acceleration of redundancy; increased labour force turnover among branches of the economy, regions and various sectors of the economy,

It should be pointed out that in practically all places, control over labour conditions and social equity protection has been relaxed. Both the proportion of those employed under harmful labour conditions and rates of industrial disease are increasing, and the rate of fatal industrial injuries remains high.

Groundless differences (i.e. without proper consideration for the quality and amount of labour) in the wage rates of employees in the context of professional groups, branches and regions are increasing.

The number of unemployed registered at employment services throughout the CIS countries is growing rapidly.

Professional orientation and vocational training services intended to promote the competitiveness of those seeking a job, the speeding up of the job search and the balancing of labour demand and supply in the professional context are working unsatisfactorily.

In the light of these conclusions, it is probable that tensions in the labour market will increase throughout the CIS countries. The deep economic crisis mentioned above will stimulate the flow of excess labour pushed out from enterprises into the labour market.

It is clear that forced migration will have a growing influence on employment and unemployment. The lack of intergovernmental regulations of the above processes results in the accumulation of refugees on limited territories, a sharp rise in population density in certain already over-populated regions, creating additional centres of social tension. The flow of refugees is both increasing quantitatively and widening geographically, leading to an acute shortage of skilled manpower in some regions and creating intractable problems of housing and employment in other regions.

It is expected that by the end of 1993 the number of registered unemployed in the CIS as a whole will reach nearly 1 million and the total number of unemployed (including those seeking a job without the assistance of employment services) will reach 4 million. [This prognosis proved to be correct. *Ed.*]

7

Towards a strategy of reform for systems of pay classification in countries in Central and Eastern Europe

J. KUX*

This chapter is an outline of the issues and questions concerning the system of remuneration which was used in the development of pay systems in Czechoslovakia and expected future trends. The system described below used to exist in most of the Central and Eastern European countries. Some countries still continue to follow this pattern.

DESCRIPTION OF JOB CLASSIFICATION AND SYSTEMS OF WAGE RATES

The origin of nation-wide effective pay regulations as a tool of the state for a strictly centralized control of wage policy dates back to 1948, i.e. to the beginning of the confiscation of private capital as well as the means of production at all levels of the economy of the former Czechoslovakia. As a result of intervention in natural property relationships, a gradual reduction and subsequent total liquidation of logical market relationships occurred, as simultaneously the economic consciousness of the nation disintegrated and the understanding of basic economic relationships was warped.

The principal changes in relationships, e.g. worker-job-pay or price of labour-pay, for a wide range of workers led, particularly in the 1950s, to significant apathy towards improving the workers' qualifications and a consequent lag in production.

In the early 1960s, in an attempt to deal with adverse impacts of the

---

* This chapter was originally given as a paper at the ILO Workshop on the Role of National Occupational Classifiers of the Central and Eastern European Countries in the Economic Restructuring, Geneva, December 1990.

new economic relationships on workers as well as to secure at least apparent relationships between wage and price levels, it was necessary to create a pay system which would be based upon logical evaluation and grading of jobs according to a system of criteria determined by the qualifications required for jobs and the general working conditions as well as the individual conditions in which a job was done.

The pay system which came into being consisted of:

- *a system of rates* (tariffs), which is a system of tariffs and tariff scales graded (classified) according to criteria determining the quality and qualifications required for jobs as well as criteria determining general working conditions,
- *a system of 'wage forms'*, which covers a subsystem of bonuses, premiums, personal evaluation and additional pay (for working overtime, on night shifts, on Saturdays and Sundays, at heights, in hard and health endangering environments, priority projects, etc.) as well as a subsystem of actually applied wages, e.g. based upon hourly rates, piece rates, share and mixed wages.

As a whole, the pay system was further strictly divided into simultaneously applied systems of job evaluation and remuneration for 'manual workers', 'technical-economic workers' (i.e. non-manual workers) and workers in trade, while several autonomic systems of remuneration of workers in the non-productive (superstructure) sphere of the national economy were applied, i.e. in health services, education, culture and state administration.

Despite a rigid centralized wage policy, which was accompanied by a strict and irrational price policy, the system of rates preserved itself in the pay system as a more or less independent element based on the logical evaluation and classification of jobs. The same applies to its basic documentation in the form of the method of job evaluation for manual workers and professionals as well as catalogues of occupations and qualifications, which were all valid up to at least 1990.

Nevertheless, *the system of rates* as a system of evaluation and classification of jobs in terms of qualifications or demand for skills and general working conditions, including the systems of extras, has been construed with regard to conditions of big enterprises with a high grade of organizational complexity and a strictly defined division of labour. It follows that the influence of the system of rates upon other areas of production and, in particular, the non-productive sphere or superstructure is small and insufficient.

During the 1980s there were certain attempts at simplifying and liberalizing the pay systems. But all attempts to establish a rational relationship between employer and employee, between job and pay (wages) encountered the bureaucratic structure in the political and economic climate of that time. The first significant attempt (after some earlier unsuccessful reforms) was the programme 'Improvement of economic efficiency of pay systems', which was launched in 1980 and known as ZEUMS I and ZEUMS II, whose repercussions could be felt for at least ten years.

The continuous process of simplifying as well as rationalizing the pay system, the need for which was ever more pressing, was actually initiated by two regulations of the Federal Ministry of Labour and Social Affairs:

- a decree of reinforcement of competence and responsibility of enterprises for applying pay forms, by which the system of 'wage forms' ceased to exist by 1 January 1988,
- a decree to adapt the granting of pay preferences, which substantially reduced the subsystem of preference extras at the end of 1989.

Despite all endeavours to change the pay system substantially, the implemented adaptations and simplifications only negligibly affected the heart of the matter, i.e. the liberalization of wages and a really fair remuneration according to the demand for skill and qualifications of jobs as well as to general working conditions.

It was the 'velvet revolution' which opened the way to a change in proprietary relationships and to the creation of capital and the means of production as well as conditions for a way to a rational pay system, based upon the principle of collective negotiation of the 'social partners' (i.e. trade unions, employers and state). The result of this is a collective agreement at state or nation, industry branch and firm levels that contains a concretization of pay as well as the social aspects of the job done. The system of rates, as a result of a method with an analytical evaluation of jobs and general working conditions, can be claimed to form a logical part of the pay structure which is in principle correct and satisfactory.

The rigid application especially of the system of pay forms and preference extras has warped the whole structure. A number of politically motivated exceptions (e.g. wage preferences for enterprises and individuals working on orders for the army) caused further loss of efficiency in the system.

The present pay system principally classifies jobs into groups of manual work, technical work and services. The distinction is reflected in the method of job evaluation, which is divided into evaluation of manual workers' jobs, that of technical workers and other workers' jobs. The evaluation of jobs is detailed in sets of descriptions of jobs evaluated according to the demand for skill or qualifications as shown in qualification guidelines of manual workers' professions, technical requirements and service jobs. The distinction between jobs done by hand and by machine is reflected directly in the descriptions included in the qualification catalogues of manual workers' jobs.

The main conditions of a job beside pay are in the area of welfare and as such are not within the competence of the pay system. These are, for example, categories of retirement welfare, which divide the manual workers' jobs into three categories according to the risk to health. The categories form a differentiated basis used for calculation of retirement pensions, and at same time they form a precondition for premature retirement for those in the category with the top rate of risk.

The basis of a logical grading or classification of jobs within the pay system is the above mentioned *system of rates,*which separately classifies the manual workers' jobs into *nine tariff classes* and jobs in technical functions into *twenty-one tariff classes* according to the qualifications required for the jobs.

In accordance with criteria of general working conditions, the manual workers' jobs are subdivided into twelve tariff scales and the technical jobs into five basic scales which are then subdivided into scales 'a' and 'b', i.e. there are twenty-two tariff scales altogether.

The manual workers' jobs are divided into 601 trades according to industry branches, into twenty-nine qualification catalogues of manual workers' jobs which form representative sets of stated descriptions of jobs in a given branch of industry.

The *technical and other jobs* are divided into 108 technical and service functions which are divided into two nationally valid qualification catalogues, which also form representative sets of descriptions of jobs and functions in both categories of workers.

Individual rates are then assigned to tariff classes according to tariff scales. The system of rates is effective in all branches of production with the exception of some areas of non-productive work where specific pay regulations are being applied.

Evaluation and grading of jobs with the output in the form of qualification catalogues as stating the system of rates is secured by evaluation committees operating at national, industry, product or enterprise levels. The committees consist of groups of experts from individual enterprises and institutions. The committees provide for parity of evaluation at their respective level. The national committee is a consultative body of the Federal Ministry of Labour and Social Affairs which is responsible in this area.

The evaluation and classification of jobs at the national level is based upon the set of criteria for evaluation of complexity, responsibility and degree of skill required by jobs, upon 'analytic' method of evaluation of manual workers' jobs and analytic method of evaluation of technical workers' jobs.

The *analytic method of evaluation of manual workers' jobs* uses the following criteria:

- *professional theoretical training*, as shown in nine grades of professional theoretical knowledge needed for performing a job,
- *professional practical training*, as shown in seven grades of various time intervals needed for acquiring a certain level of craft skills and experience after finishing the theoretical training,
- *responsibility*, based upon the assumption that special competence and reliability is needed for the perfect performance of a job. Responsibility is divided into a material liability in six grades and a moral liability in four grades for the safety of co-workers while maintaining the legal requirements for safety and health at work,
- *difficulty (strain) of the job* divided into five grades of physical effort and four grades of neuropsychological and emotional strain,
- *risk of a mechanical injury*, presenting a risk permanently linked to the performance of a job while maintaining all legal regulations regarding safety and health at work,
- *special requirements*, determining other special capabilities required for performing certain jobs, divided into organizational capabilities and creative as well as artistic imagination.

The *analytical method of evaluation of technical workers' jobs* uses the following criteria:

- *professional theoretical training* divided into five grades according to the level of acquired education and five grades of further professional theoretical training, as for example professional courses, academic degrees, etc.
- *professional practice* divided into seven time intervals,
- *materials and moral liability*, divided into six grades according to the degree of liability for material damages which might arise as a result of work, process or a decision, and an ethical liability which is the responsibility for educational, economic and ethical results of an activity or a decision,
- *requirements of management and organizational complexity*, divided into four grades of demand for management according to the hierarchy of managing workers and into five categories relating to the size of the subordinated department or unit.

- *complexity and difficulty of job*, characterized in seven grades of mental and psychological strain required for performing the job,
- *working relations*, divided into five grades according to the level of intensity and importance of working relations within as well as outside of an organization,
- *moral qualities*, characterized in five grades according to the rate of ethical qualities required from technical workers,
- *special requirements*, characterized by an ability to effectively influence other people's behaviour via decision-making and logical decisions, by perfect knowledge of the issue in question etc., divided into two grades.

Both analytical methods of job evaluation are designed to be used at the national level for elaboration of nationally valid documents classifying jobs within the system of rates, i.e. for a nation-wide set of jobs as a basis for creating and approving catalogues of job qualifications.

At the level of each industry, product branch and enterprise, generally valid criteria of the analytic method are transformed into direct descriptions of complexity, difficulty and strain linked to jobs, which serve as representative examples of jobs in qualification catalogues and which form a basis for a 'global' comparison within separate industry branches, product branches or enterprises. Such comparisons are the responsibility of the respective committees at the level of industry, product branch or enterprise.

The main problem of the now disappearing pay system, which is thus a system of actual pay classification of jobs, is the separation of the systems used for the evaluation of the jobs of manual workers and that of technical workers which results in the creation of an unnatural relationship between these two categories of workers with respect to their wages.

Another problem is the considerable complexity of the system used for evaluation of general working conditions in twelve tariff scales which, due to its subjectivity, creates a precondition for an excessive pressure towards granting of higher tariff scales in enterprises or departments concerned with the production of goods.

Social partnership was being formed only gradually by increasing the activity of trade unions and their confederation in Czechoslovakia. The first working contacts between the Federal Ministry of Labour and Social Affairs and the trade unions' central office as well as the individual trade unions dealing with the pay system gave rise to proposals and suggestions aiming at a reduction in the complex system of tariff scales and some of the pay extras for work in difficult or health endangering environments.

Along with a state proposal of a pay reform comprising, among other things, an amendment of the system of analytic evaluation and classification of jobs, issues have been raised which take a broader view of the problems on both theoretical and practical levels of professional qualification or training of workers and the principle of its conclusive evidence in practice.

The first job grading, i.e. the first tariff classification, is determined by pay regulations for remuneration of all categories of workers with a direct link to the level of the acquired qualification or training. Further job grading in another firm, or after some time within the same enterprise, depends on the length of professional training which is then needed being recorded on a 'credit sheet'. Further job grading depends also on actual abilities of the worker or, as the case may be, on acquiring higher qualifications within a certain period, as well as on whether the manufacturing programme of the enterprise requires jobs in a higher tariff rate (as laid down in the relevant qualification catalogue).

Labour mobility was hampered in the past by provisions of the Labour Code regarding the 'protective time-limits' used when cancelling contracts or giving notice. These limits were against the interests of workers in times of apparent surplus of labour resulting from a non-competitive environment. Labour mobility was further damped by a system of preference extras (geographical weightings granted in certain regions and industrial agglomerations, and 'technological' extras in mines, metallurgy and energy industries, or both). The rise of a competitive environment both among enterprises and among workers along with applying the amendments to the Labour Code and other regulations frees the natural labour mobility.

RELATIONSHIPS BETWEEN JOBS, WAGE SCALES AND WAGE-FIXING SYSTEMS

The level of job grading of an individual worker depends on classifying a given range of jobs done into a tariff class according to the relevant qualification catalogue (within evaluation and classification of jobs as mentioned above). A wage rate is assigned to each tariff class, depending on the tariff scale according to general working conditions of the job done. This system of job grading is uniform and valid at all levels of the remuneration system.

At the central level, basic kinds of extras are being fixed, i.e. for working overtime, on Saturdays and Sundays, on night-shifts, at heights over 50 metres, in difficult or health-endangering environments, in highly hazardous conditions and for emergency duty. The enterprise decides on the application of other pay extras.

At the firm level, the actual system of the 'pay forms', i.e. bonuses, premiums, personal evaluation, etc. is being applied as well as the basic kind of pay (based on hourly rates, piece rates, shares, mixed wage etc.), which is entirely the responsibility of the enterprises, of course in cooperation with trade unions.

The system of rates, i.e. tariff classes and tariff scales with actual tariff rates, has always formed a basis for the construction of total pay in the sense of the nominal wage. Expected wage increases have been determined by comparison of nominal wages and price levels.

The term 'minimum wage' did not exist in the Czechoslovakian economy in the past. But later, negotiations between the state and the trade unions were held in order to determine a minimum wage. The basis for minimum wage determination was the minimum wage rate for the stated evaluation of the job with the least complexity, difficulty and strain.

The mechanism of wage fixing depended directly on classifying jobs according to the above-mentioned criteria, which, along with wage rates, formed part of the mechanism of wage-rate fixing. Other components of the wage (bonuses, premiums, personal evaluation, etc.) were more or less calculated on a percentage basis according to the wage rates. The only exceptions to this were pay extras.

At the central level, wage rates forming the basis of tariff wages were fixed. The real increase in wages at the firm level depended to a certain degree on growth in the 'above-rate' wage (bonuses, premiums, shares in the economic results of the enterprise), which were, when a certain limit had been exceeded, centrally controlled by a system of wage regulation.

PAY CLASSIFICATION AT THE FIRM LEVEL

So far, the possibility of changing the grading of a job as well as the wage structure of an individual worker was implemented in particular via comparisons of the worker's qualifications and the length of professional training to the descriptions of job tasks (mentioned in the qualification catalogues) assigned to tariff classes, i.e. within the system of rates. The upgrading of a job and thus a wage increase, depended on whether jobs in a certain tariff class already existed within a firm. If they did, the other prerequisite was a sufficient planned wage fund in the firm. If it was overdrawn, the worker would have to wait until later. The participation of the firm's trade-union organization was rather formal in this process.

There were in principle no differences between national and enterprise pay classifications, i.e. in the number of tariff classes, in expressing criteria and in documents used (catalogue or set of jobs). The only difference was in the level of wage rates in particular tariff classes which was determined by a tariff scale that was approved by the centre to be used by the enterprise according to the level of general working conditions. A metallurgical firm, for example, was entitled to the sixth tariff scale, i.e. in the tariff classes 1 through 9 the rates are somewhat higher than in an enterprise that produces knitwear, which is entitled to the third tariff scale.

Job evaluation schemes applied for all enterprises and institutions at all levels with the exception of 'small organizations' to whom a six-grade system of evaluation and classification of jobs, common to all categories of workers, had been applicable since 1989. Four tariff grades were used for manual workers and six tariff grades for technical workers. The evaluation in principle was the same in this case, too, and was based upon a global comparison of jobs with a set of representative descriptions of jobs included in the set of jobs displayed in an appendix to the pay regulation decree. Tariff ranges are assigned to particular tariff grades. The same applied, from May 1990 on, to private enterprises employing, as a rule, up to 200 workers (small businesses), with the exception of tariffs for individual grades which formed the minimum basic wage.

The central system of analytical job evaluation is being transformed when applied to job evaluation at the level of industry, product branches or enterprises, into the 'global comparison', whose basis is the qualification catalogues of jobs, or as the case may be, the sets of examples of jobs at the enterprise level.

The qualifications of new recruits were compared to the qualification prerequisites for performing certain jobs mentioned in the qualification catalogue.

The wage rates in particular tariff clauses were used as the basic wage and, of course, as a hiring wage, too. Other relationships between wage rates and the total wage have been described above.

In general, the career path of an individual was a result of a natural professional development characterized by the length of professional training. A career was nevertheless partly dependent, too, on the existence of actual jobs needed to implement the programme of an enterprise or an institution. A career developed without central intervention, with only a few exceptions where promotion was granted because of accumulated years of seniority.

Previously, the enterprises as well as non-productive institutions were given limits on staff numbers. At present, these limits are only used in state-owned institutions or in other institutions financed by the state.

A worker can request his personnel department (department of labour economics) via his superior to re-evaluate his professional qualification because he has just finished a professional course, training or other form of education, i.e. when he has improved his professional qualification and thus has a possibility of a higher job and wage grading. The worker has this opportunity also when he is in doubt about the correctness of his grading. In this case, he consults the relevant trade-union organization in the enterprise.

CONCLUDING REMARKS

The state proposal for pay reform in Czechoslovakia included in particular the tripartite collective negotiation of social partners, i.e. employer, unions and state, at three levels:

- national–general agreement,
- industry–industry agreement,
- enterprise–enterprise agreement.

Questions concerning wages development, the level and conditions of applying wage rates, the creation and application of job catalogues, the system of pay extras, minimum wages and other conditions of remuneration were to be among the issues of these negotiations. It was proposed to reduce the system of tariff scales to two or three scales for general working conditions.

The analytic point-rating evaluation of jobs used for inter-branch comparisons according to the above-mentioned criteria, the result of which was the national classification of jobs, was to be transformed in the creation of nationally compatible catalogues by criteria typical of particular branches. The examples of jobs included in the catalogue and its parts for particular branches will be more concrete in content and scope, and their classification will correspond to the traditional professions and functions. The job catalogues are presumed to be a part of the tripartite negotiation of social partners and a basis of the wage negotiations at the general industry as well as enterprise levels.

By enhancing the function of wages as a price of labour and a tool of social justice, pay will function as an important factor in the development of the market economy. In the future, the incentive and distributive function of pay will be exclusively the responsibility of an enterprise or an organization.

8

Hungarian labour statistics in transition

A. KELETI*

In order to understand the necessary steps that those in charge of Hungarian labour statistics have undertaken in the transition to a market economy, we first have to review the past.

PAST PRACTICE AND ITS PROBLEMS

In past decades Hungarian labour statistics were based primarily on exhaustive data collection from enterprises; nevertheless, for the annual compilation of the labour force balance other data sources were used as well, such as agricultural surveys, population censuses and the social security register.

Firms, co-operatives, other organizations and institutions classified into the so-called 'material' branches (manufacturing, mining and quarrying, electricity and gas supply, construction, trade, transport and communication, financial services, agriculture and forestry) reported data on employment, wages and earnings to the Central Statistics Office (CSO) monthly or quarterly depending on the branch.

The inquiry into detailed labour characteristics was conducted in the frame of a so-called unified annual 'labour census' covering all firms, organizations and institutions with a legal entity and supplied detailed statistics on point-of-time employment, labour force turnover, earnings and loss of working hours. Due to the high organizational concentration of the Hungarian economy, the reporting units were large organizations

* This chapter was originally given as a paper at the Third Joint ECE/ILO Meeting on Labour Force Statistics, Geneva, February 1991.

with a statistical administration able to satisfy all government information needs.

The restructuring of the Hungarian economy in the 1980s presented a challenge to the traditional labour statistics data collection system in two respects.

– The birth of thousands of new small ventures and the dissolution of big organizations resulted in a dramatic growth in the number of firms, which made the annual labour census virtually impossible. The new small enterprises have neither the discipline nor the skills required to fill out statistical forms. The growing number of the self-employed is an additional problem since they are not included in the coverage of the traditional labour statistics data collections as the majority of them are unincorporated.
– New phenomena have emerged on the labour market (for example unemployment), which cannot be measured through enterprise or establishment surveys.

The magnitude of the problem we face in the growing number of statistical units is well illustrated by the following figures. The number of units with a legal entity has risen from 7,816 in 1985 to 26,702 in 1990. The respective figure was 15,169 in 1989 which means that the number of statistical units almost doubled in a year.

The majority of firms have just a few employees so their weight in employment is relatively low. Since 1988 a lower limit of 50 employees (20 in construction) has obtained for the labour census and the level of required response has been differentiated according to the size of the firm in all labour statistics inquiries.

MAJOR PLANS FOR THE FUTURE

Measuring wages and employment

In future our labour statistics data collection should obviously use representative sample surveys of enterprises instead of censuses. We shall have censuses only every three or five years.

We conducted our first enterprise sample survey in 1990. In this survey, in which the sample was stratified by size of enterprise, we enquired about the number of employees in certain earning brackets.

The introduction of sample surveys raised several problems:

– The growing private sector - the process of privatization and subsidy cuts for state enterprises cause very high enterprise birth and death

rates which made a sample rapidly outdated even during the sampling period.
- Organizational and institutional changes made the measuring of economic output and employment by industries quite difficult.
- A business register had to be set up to include not only enterprises with a legal entity but all enterprises to provide a sampling frame with appropriate coverage.

Measuring unemployment

For ideological and political reasons unemployment as such did not exist in the past. Accordingly, no statistical programmes were designed to measure it.

The first attempt to measure unemployment according to the statistical concept of unemployment was undertaken in the 1990 population census. This approach did not alter the existing system of definitions and classifications, it simply introduced a new concept (such as the unemployed seeking work) in addition to the existing ones. This solution was proper for the comparability of data in time series, but it also had many conceptual and technical shortcomings. A major conceptual problem was the treatment of pensioners and students, who were classified automatically as economically inactive. From a technical point of view the information required proved to be too complex for a census questionnaire and we concluded that the 'skip pattern' for establishing economic activity needed a separate questionnaire and a separate survey.

Based on this experience and on the study of international recommendations and national practices, the Hungarian CSO planned to start a monthly household Labour Force Survey with quarterly estimates in 1992. The pilot survey for testing the questionnaire was to take place in January 1991. The experimental survey for testing the survey design and the estimating methods were to be implemented in the second quarter of 1991. During the second half of 1991 the experience of the tests were to be analysed and preparations made for the implementation of the regular Labour Force Survey starting in January 1992.

The Hungarian CSO has an operating infrastructure of household surveys (USHS, unified system of household surveys) for conducting the household expenditure survey, the household income survey and all other household surveys which will be able to encompass the LFS. The conceptual and methodological framework of the Hungarian LFS is outlined in Figure 8.1, and Annex 3 at the end of this volume.

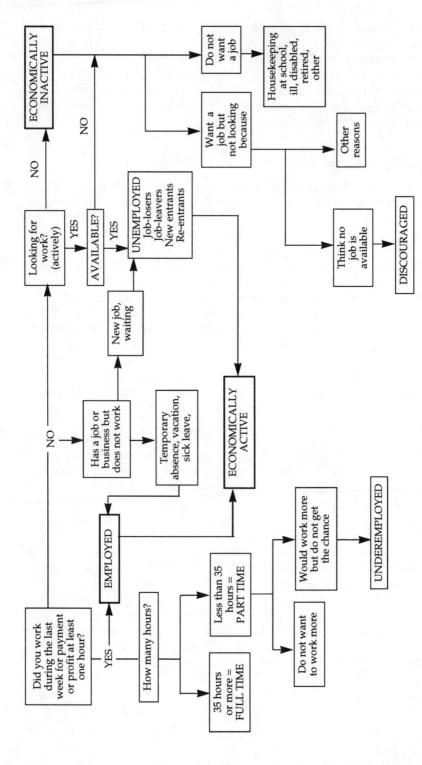

Fig. 8.1 Flow chart of the questionnaire for determining labour force status of population aged 15 years and over

Adjustment of classifications

Our transition efforts naturally included the revision of the major economic classifications. By 1992 it was expected that the Hungarian classification of economic activities would be compatible with that of the European Community (NACE). In close connection with Hungarian design efforts for the LFS we revised our occupational and status-in-employment classifications. The old occupational classification was based on the 1970 census and its structure was more or less incompatible with that of the International Standard Classification of Occupations (ISCO-88). We see ISCO-88 as a model for our new occupational classification. Accordingly, it will reflect only the kind of work pursued irrespective of industry, organization and status in employment. The old status-in-employment classification was based on the concept of a class structure and it had some ideological implications. We plan to revise it as well.

Annex 4 (Conceptual and technical outline of the Hungarian Labour Force Survey) is to be found at the end of this volume.

Part II

Labour force, employment and unemployment

9

International standards on the measurement of economic activity, employment, unemployment and underemployment

R. HUSSMANNS*

Statistics of the economically active population, employment, unemployment and underemployment serve a large variety of purposes. They provide measures of labour supply, labour input, the structure of employment and the extent to which the available labour time and human resources are actually utilized or not. Such information is essential for macro-economic and human resources development planning and policy formulation. When collected at different points in time, the data provide the basis for monitoring current trends and changes in the labour market and employment situation, which may be analysed in connection with other economic and social phenomena so as to evaluate macro-economic policies. The unemployment rate, in particular, is widely used as an overall indicator of the current performance of a nation's economy.

Statistics of the economically active population, employment, unemployment and underemployment are also an essential base for the design and evaluation of government programmes geared to employment creation, vocational training, income maintenance, poverty alleviation and similar objectives. The measurement of the relationships between employment, income and other socio-economic characteristics provides information on the adequacy of employment of different subgroups of the population, the income-generating capacity of different

* This chapter was originally prepared as an article for the *ILO Bulletin of Labour Statistics*, No.1 (1989). It is based on various chapters of the following ILO publication: *Surveys of economically active population, employment and underemployment: An ILO manual on concepts and methods*, written by Ralf Hussmanns, Farhad Mehran and Vijay Verma (Geneva, ILO, 1990).

types of economic activities, and the number and characteristics of persons unable to ensure their economic well-being on the basis of the employment opportunities available to them. Information on employment and income, disaggregated by branches of economic activity, occupations and socio-demographic characteristics, is needed for collective bargaining, for assessment of the social effects of structural adjustment policies on different subgroups of the population, and for the analysis of race, sex or age inequalities in work opportunities and participation and their changes over time.

So as to provide guidance to countries in developing their national statistical programmes and promote international comparability, the International Labour Organization promulgates international standards on the various topics of labour statistics. These standards are set by the International Conference of Labour Statisticians (ICLS) which convenes about every five years. The standards currently in force concerning statistics of the economically active population, employment, unemployment and underemployment have been adopted by the Thirteenth ICLS in 1982 (ILO 1983).

The present chapter is intended to describe one by one the basic concepts and definitions laid down in the 1982 international standards. Where relevant, particular issues are discussed that may arise in survey applications concerning measurement problems and the appropriate statistical treatment of particular categories of workers, such as self-employed persons, unpaid family workers, casual workers, seasonal workers, apprentices and trainees, persons on lay-off and persons engaged in production for own and household consumption, who sometimes are at the borderline between labour force categories.

THE CONCEPT AND BOUNDARY OF ECONOMIC ACTIVITY

A clear understanding of the concept and boundary of economic activity is a fundamental requirement for the correct application of the definitions of the economically active population, employment and unemployment in labour force surveys. The exact boundary between economic and non-economic activities is a matter of convention, but unless a precise dividing line is drawn, the statistical treatment of many situations encountered in practice remains ambiguous and will raise questions about the reliability of the resulting statistics.

The concept of economic activity adopted by the Thirteenth ICLS (1982) for the measurement of the economically active population is defined in terms of the production of goods and services as set forth by the United Nations System of National Accounts (SNA). The international standards specify that 'the economically active population comprises all persons of either sex who furnish the supply of labour for the production of economic goods and services, as defined by the United Nations systems of national accounts and balances, during a specified time-reference period'. Thus, persons are to be considered as economically active if (and only if) they contribute or are available to contribute to the production of goods and services falling within the SNA production boundary. The use of a definition of economic activity which is based on the SNA serves to ensure that the activity concepts of employment statistics and production statistics are consistent, thus facilitating the joint analysis of the two bodies of statistics.

SNA production boundary

According to the SNA (Rev. 3, 1968),[1] the production of goods and services comprises:

(a) the production of goods and services normally intended for sale on the market at a price that is designed to cover their costs of production;

(b) the production of other goods and services which are not normally sold on the market at a price intended to cover their cost of production, such as government services and private non-profit services to households, domestic services rendered by one household to another and other items;

(c) specified types of production for own consumption and fixed capital formation for own use.

The latter include:

(c1) the production of primary products (e.g. milk, cereals, fruit, cotton, wood) for own consumption;

(c2) the processing of primary products by their producers to make such goods as butter, flour, wine, cloth or furniture for their own use, whether or not they sell any of these products on the market;

---

[1] The SNA has meanwhile been revised. The revised version (SNA, Rev.4, 1993) entails, among other changes, some modifications in the delineation of the production boundary. In particular, the production boundary has been extended to include the production of all *goods* for own final use (own final consumption or gross fixed capital formation), provided the amount of a good produced for own final use is quantitatively important in relation to the total supply of that good in a country. Regarding *services* produced for own final consumption, the production boundary includes only the following: housing services produced by owner-occupiers of dwellings, and domestic or personal services produced by employing paid domestic staff. All domestic or personal services provided by unpaid household members remain excluded.

(c3) the production for own consumption of other goods and services only if they are also produced for the market by the same households;

(c4) the production of fixed assets for own use, such as own-account construction of dwellings, farm buildings, roads, tools and similar items which have an expected life of ·use of one year or more;

(c5) the total rent of owner-occupied dwellings (representing an imputed monetary value rather than an activity, this item has no relevance for employment statistics).

For convenience, the activities corresponding to (a) and (b) may be designated as market activities or market production, and those corresponding to (c) as non-market economic activities or non-market production. The aggregate constitutes the scope of economic activity for the measurement of the economically active population. All other activities are called non-economic activities.

Market activities

Though market production and non-market production are defined in terms of the end use of the product rather than on the basis of the paid or unpaid nature of the production, market activities typically involve some form of remuneration to those who participate in them. Such remuneration may be in the form of pay or profit. Pay includes cash payment as well as payment-in-kind, whether they are received in the same period where the work is done or not. Cash payment includes wages or salaries at time or piece rates, fees or tips, bonuses or gratuities, etc. Payment-in-kind may be in the form of food, fuel, housing or other goods and services. Payment-in-kind as the sole means of remuneration is not uncommon in some countries, e.g. for agricultural workers receiving a share of the harvest or for apprentices and trainees working in exchange for board and lodging.

Profit refers to the remuneration for activities performed by persons who operate their own farm, business enterprise or service undertaking with or without hired employees. An activity may be undertaken for profit even if currently no profit is made during the reference period of the survey. Work for profit also includes the activities of family members undertaken in connection with the operation of a household enterprise producing for the market, even though these persons typically work for family gain and do not receive any direct payment for the work done. Similarly, market activities include also work performed for productive purposes on the basis of an exchange labour arrangement between households, and the production of goods and services for barter among households, even when no cash payment is received.

Non-market economic activities

The rationale for the inclusion of certain types of non-market production in the 1968 SNA definition while excluding others lies in the importance of the activities for the subsistence of the population in many countries, and in the frequent existence of close market parallels, i.e. identical or very similar goods and services are usually also available on the market. Throughout the world, the production and processing of primary products of agriculture, hunting, forestry, fishing, mining and quarrying for own use represent a major part of consumption for many persons and their families.

Similarly, in a number of countries construction of houses, wells and other items to be considered as investment goods is undertaken to a significant extent on an own-account basis. Furthermore, since a shift may take place from production for own consumption to market production as economic development proceeds, it is essential to account for both types of activities, so as to obtain a comparable measure of the economically active population at different periods or for different countries.

There are also practical considerations involved in the delineation of the SNA production boundary. So as to cover market production completely, it is necessary to include some non-market production as well, as it is in practice often impossible to measure the market component separately when the same persons are engaged in both types of production. A similar argument applies for the inclusion of processing of primary products for own consumption which cannot be separated from the production of such products when carried out by the same households. This is the main reason why the 1968 SNA considered processing of goods for own consumption an economic activity only if it involved the processing of *primary* products and was carried out by the producers of such items. Thus, using cotton fabric (a processed product) to make clothes was excluded just as spinning cotton fibres (a primary product) bought at the market was excluded, whereas spinning cotton fibres produced by oneself was included.

Non-economic activities

Being based on the SNA definition of production of goods and services, the concept of economic activity for the measurement of the economically active population excludes production for own consumption of items other than those mentioned above under (c), such as the processing of primary products by those who do not produce them, the production of other goods and services by households who do not sell any part of them in the market, and current repairs and maintenance of constructions, etc., carried out by households for themselves.

Moreover, the SNA production boundary excludes volunteer services rendered to the community or private non-profit organizations, and unpaid domestic activities such as teaching and nursing of own children or cooking food and washing clothes for one's own household. The fact that such activities fall at present outside the boundary of economic activity does, however, not mean that such activities, which are mainly carried out by women, should not be statistically measured at all, as it is widely recognized that they provide a major contribution to the welfare of populations and the development of countries. In fact, the 1982 international standards contain a provision to identify persons engaged in unpaid community and volunteer services, and other persons engaged in marginal activities which fall outside the boundary of economic activities, separately from the population not economically active.

Measurement

In measuring the economically active population in household surveys, it is essential that careful attention be paid in questionnaire design and interviewer instructions so as to translate the notion of economic activity into appropriate questions, because the interviewers' and respondents' own subjective understanding of economic activity may differ from what the concept intends to include. This requirement is fundamental, as it sets the frame for all subsequent information collected in the course of the interview. A misunderstanding of whether or not certain activities are to be considered as economic may thus have irremediable impacts on the entire interview and on the survey results. Such problems may particularly arise in situations where a substantial part of the economically active population is engaged in activities other than regular full-time full-year paid employment or self-employment, such as part-time employment, casual work, work remunerated in kind, home-based work, unpaid family work and production for own consumption. In such situations, additional probing questions or an activity list may prove useful to reduce underreporting.

THE CURRENTLY ACTIVE POPULATION

The 1982 international standards distinguish between two measures of the economically active population: the currently active population (labour force), measured in relation to a short reference period such as one week or one day, and the usually active population, measured in relation to a long reference period such as a year.

The currently active population (or the labour force) comprises all persons above a specified minimum age (e.g. 15 years) who, during a specified brief period of one week or one day, fulfil the requirements for inclusion among the employed or the unemployed as described in later sections of this chapter. The currently active population is the most widely used measure of the economically active population. Being based on a short reference period, it is used for measuring the current employment and unemployment situation of the economy and the current employment characteristics of the population. When measurement is repeated at sufficiently frequent intervals, current changes over time can be monitored.

Labour force framework

The measurement of the currently active population is based on the labour force framework. The essential feature of the labour force framework is that individuals are categorized according to their activities during a specified short reference period by using a specific set of priority rules. The result is a classification of the population into three mutually exclusive and exhaustive categories: employed, unemployed and not in the labour force (or not currently active). The first two categories make up the currently active population (or labour force), which gives a measure of the number of persons furnishing the supply of labour at a given moment in time.

Priority rules

So as to ensure that each person is classified into one and only one of the three basic categories of the framework, the following set of priority rules is adopted. The first step consists of identifying, among persons above the specified minimum age, those who, during the specified short reference period, were either at work or temporarily absent from work (the 'employed' category); the next step is to identify among the remaining persons those who were seeking and/or available for work (the 'unemployed' category). The third category (persons not in the labour force or not currently active), i.e. those without work who were not seeking and/or nor available for work, then falls out residually. Persons below the age specified for measuring the economically active population are added to the population not currently active. In this scheme, precedence is given to employment over unemployment and to unemployment over economic inactivity. A person who is both working and seeking work is classified as employed, and a student who is attending school and also seeking work is classified as unemployed. One corollary of the priority rules is that employment always takes precedence over other activities, regardless of the amount of time devoted to it during the reference period, which in extreme cases may be only one hour. A related feature of the labour force framework is that the concept of unemployment is limited to the situation of a total lack of work.

Activity principle

Another characteristic of the labour force framework is that a person's labour force status should be determined on the basis of what the person was actually doing during the specified reference period (activity principle). The purpose of the activity principle is to make measurement of the labour force as objective as possible. Thus only persons who were engaged in an economic activity or who were seeking and/or available for such an activity are to be considered for inclusion into the labour force. There are only few exceptions to this activity principle, such as the inclusion among the employed of persons temporarily absent from work, or the inclusion among the unemployed of persons without work who are not seeking work because they have already found a job to start at a date subsequent to the reference period.

Applicability of the labour force framework

The labour force framework is best suited to situations where the dominant type of employment is regular full-time paid employment. In these situations, a working person falls unambiguously in the employed category, a person seeking and/or available for such employment falls into the unemployed category, and others fall outside the labour force. In practice, however, the employment situation in a given country will to a greater or lesser extent differ from this pattern. Some deviations may be unimportant or can be handled by proper application of the underlying concepts and definitions, but others may require more elaborate considerations. For example, there might be situations falling at the borderline between labour force categories (e.g. persons on temporary layoff, unpaid family workers during the off-season, persons on training schemes), raising questions about their appropriate statistical treatment. Others, while clearly falling into one category or another, contribute to the heterogeneity of that category, thus raising difficulties in the interpretation of the resulting statistics and calling for further differentiations (e.g. distinction between adequately employed and inadequately employed). There may even be situations which raise questions about the very meaningfulness of categories, such as the virtual non-existence of unemployment in the sense of total lack of work in certain countries.

Some of these issues will be discussed along with the definitions of employment, unemployment and underemployment in later sections of this chapter.

The current activity measurement provides a snapshot picture of the economically active population at a given point of time. In situations where the dominant pattern of employment is year-round, with little or no seasonal variations and relatively few movements into and out of the labour force or its main components, such a snapshot picture is probably sufficient to provide an adequate representation of the employment situation for the whole year. However, where significant seasonal patterns of activities or substantial labour force movements exist, the employment picture obtained for one short reference period may not be representative of others. In such situations, measurement should be made over a longer period of time, either by repeating or staggering the current activity measurement over time so as to cover the desired longer period, or by using the longer period itself as the reference period for measurement. In principle, the two approaches will give different results, due to differences in measurement concepts and methods. The first approach requires increasing the frequency of labour force surveys or spreading the sample over time, while the second approach calls for retrospective measurement on the basis of a long reference period with an appropriate conceptual framework. A framework introduced in 1982 as international standard is that of the 'usually active population'.

THE USUALLY ACTIVE POPULATION

The usually active population comprises all persons above a specified age (e.g. 15 years) whose main activity status as determined in terms of number of weeks or days during a long specified period (such as the preceding 12 months or the preceding calendar year) was employed or unemployed. Residually, the population not usually active comprises all persons whose main activity status during the reference period was neither employed nor unemployed, including persons below the age specified for measuring the economically active population.

The measurement of the usually active population is based on the activity status of individuals, assessed on the basis of a 'main activity' criterion over a long reference period, as opposed to assessment of activity status on the basis of the priority criterion used for measurement of the currently active population in the labour force framework. Another fundamental difference between the two measurement frameworks concerns subdivisions. In the usual activity framework, individuals are first classified as usually active or not usually active, and then the usually active may be further subdivided as employed or unemployed according to the main activity during the active period. In the labour force framework, however, individuals are first identified as employed or unemployed, and then the two categories are summed to obtain the currently active population.

Illustration

To illustrate the usual activity framework, consider the example of a person who, during the course of a year, was employed for 13 weeks, unemployed for 18 weeks and not economically active during the remaining 21 weeks. This person would first be classified as usually active as the extent of economic activity over the year (31 weeks) exceeded the extent of inactivity, and would then be classified as unemployed as the extent of unemployment exceeded that of employment. This is despite the fact that among the three activity statuses 'employed', 'unemployed' and 'not active', the person was not active for the largest number of weeks. The example shows that, for the measurement of the usually active population and its components, data on the duration of employment and unemployment over the year may also be needed. This is because the main activity status of individuals is to be determined on the basis of the amount of time that these individuals were employed or unemployed during the reference period, measured in terms of weeks or days of employment or unemployment.

Measurement

Accurate measurement of the usually active population and its components is in practice not a simple task. Unless panel surveys for statistical follow-up of individuals are used, it involves retrospective questioning on the employment and unemployment experience of individuals during a whole year. Since retrospective measurement over such a long reference period may be subject to substantial recall errors, particularly in situations of frequent changes in activity status, it is important to adopt measurement procedures to reduce these errors to the extent possible. This may be done, for example, by structuring the reference year in terms of calendar months or jobs held.

The definitions of one week or one day of employment or unemployment should, in principle, be the same as those used in the labour force framework. This provides a conceptual link between the definitions of the usually active population and the currently active population. In survey applications, however, the procedure for measuring weeks or days of employment or unemployment will be somewhat different from the measurements in the current activity framework because of practical limitations due to the use of a long reference period.

EMPLOYMENT

The international definition of employment, as given in the 1982 standards, is formulated in terms of the labour force framework, i.e. with respect to a short reference period. The definition distinguishes between paid employment (including apprentices and members of the armed forces) and self-employment (including members of producers' co-operatives, unpaid family workers and persons engaged in non-market production). It provides separate criteria for the measurement of these two types of employment. According to the definition, the 'employed' comprise all persons above the age specified for measuring the economically active population (e.g. 15 years) who, during a specified short period of either one week or one day, were in the following categories:

(a) paid employment:
  (a1) *at work*: persons who, during the reference period, performed some work (i.e. at least one hour) for wage or salary, in cash or in kind;
  (a2) *with a job but not at work*: persons who, having already worked in their present job, were temporarily not at work during the reference period and had a formal attachment to their job;
(b) self-employment:
  (b1) *at work*: persons who, during the reference period, performed some work (i.e. at least one hour) for profit or family gain, in cash or in kind;
  (b2) *with an enterprise but not at work*: persons with an enterprise (which may be a business enterprise, a farm or a service undertaking) who were temporarily not at work during the reference period for any specific reason.

The concept of work for the measurement of employment corresponds to the concept of economic activity as derived from the United Nations System of National Accounts. This means that the notion of 'work for pay, profit or family gain' in the definition of employment should be interpreted as any activity falling within the SNA production boundary.

The one hour criterion

For measuring the number of persons employed, employment is broadly defined in the labour force framework. The international standards stipulate that, for operational purposes, the notion of 'some work' should be interpreted as work for at least one hour during the reference period. This means that engagement in an economic activity for as little as one hour is sufficient for being classified as employed on the basis of the labour force framework. There are several interrelated reasons for the use of the one hour criterion in the international definition of employment. One is to make this definition as extensive as possible, in order to cover all types of employment that may exist in a given country, including short-time work, casual labour, stand-by work and other types of irregular employment. Another reason is to ensure that at an aggregate level total labour input corresponds to total production. This is particularly needed when joint analysis of employment and production statistics is intended. The one hour criterion is in line with the priority rules of the labour force framework which gives precedence to any employment activity over any other activity, and which defines unemployment as a situation of total lack of work. The definitions of employment and unemployment being inter-related in that framework, raising the minimum number of hours worked in the definition of employment would have the effect that unemployment would no longer only refer to a situation of total lack of work.

The one hour criterion has been reviewed by the Fourteenth ICLS in 1987 and, while agreeing to retain it, the Conference emphasised that the resulting employment data should be further classified by hours of work (ILO 1988). Such additional information permits distinction among different subgroups of the employed and is helpful to a sound interpretation of the statistics. The broadness of the definition of employment emphasizes also the importance of the recommendations of the 1982 international standards on the measurement of underemployment and the analysis of the relationships between employment and income.

Temporary absence from work

The international definition of employment includes among the employed certain persons who were not at work during the reference period. These are persons who were temporarily absent from work for reasons such as illness or injury, holiday or vacation, strike or lock-out, educational or training leave, maternity or parental leave, temporary reduction in economic activity, temporary disorganization or suspension of work due to bad weather, mechanical or electrical breakdown, shortage of raw materials or fuels, etc., or other temporary absence with or without leave. In general, the notion of temporary absence from work refers to situations in which a period of work is interrupted by a period of absence. This implies that persons should only be considered as temporarily absent from work (and thus as employed) if they have already worked at their present activity and are expected to return to their work after the period of absence. However, there could be exceptional cases where persons might be considered as being temporarily absent from work even though they have not yet worked in their job, e.g. persons who happen to be sick at the day when they are to start a new job.

Temporary absence from paid employment

The international definition of employment specifies certain criteria for assessing temporary absence from work which differ between paid employment and self-employment. In the case of paid employment, the criteria are based on the notion of 'formal job attachment', to be determined in the light of national circumstances according to one or more of the following criteria: (i) the continued receipt of wage or salary; (ii) an assurance of return to work following the end of the contingency, or an agreement as to the date of return; and (iii) the elapsed duration of absence from the job, which may be that duration for which workers can receive compensation benefits without obligations to accept other jobs. This third criterion implies that the absence should be of a fairly short duration to be considered temporary, although the international standards could not specify any precise time limit that would meaningfully apply to all types of absences.

Regarding absence from work, a borderline situation may be that of persons temporarily laid off, i.e. persons whose contract of employment of whose activity has been suspended by the employer for a specified or unspecified period. They should be considered as temporarily absent from work and classified as employed only if they maintain a formal job attachment. Persons laid off without formal job attachment should be classified as unemployed or not economically active, depending on their job search activity and (or) current availability for work. Borderline situations may also arise in the case of non-regular employees. Casual workers working on a daily or weekly basis for an employer do not have a formal job attachment and, when not at work during the reference day or week, should not be classified as employed. Other non-regular employees, such as seasonal workers, should be classified as employed when not at work, if they have a formal job attachment during the reference period.

Temporary absence from self-employment

Given the large diversity in working patterns of self-employed persons, the notion of temporary absence from self-employment is less elaborate than that for paid employment. According to the international standards, persons with an enterprise, who were temporarily not at work during the reference period for any specific reason, should be considered employed. A parallel to the criterion of formal attachment for paid workers does not exist in the case of self-employed persons. In practice, the decision as to whether or not a self-employed person is to be considered absent from work (and therefore as employed) should be based on the continued existence of the enterprise during the absence of its operator. The decision as to whether the absence is to be considered temporary or not could be based on its duration, to be determined according to national circumstances.

For casual own-account workers, such as side-street shoe-shine boys or itinerant newspaper vendors, it may be assumed that their enterprise does not continue to exist when they are away from work. Thus, casual own-account workers when not at work should not be considered as 'with an enterprise but not at work' and should not be classified as employed.

Regarding employers and own-account workers engaged in seasonal activities, one may assume that, during the busy season, the enterprise itself continues to exist when the operator is absent, and in this case the operator should be classified as employed when temporarily absent from work. During the off-season, however, one cannot always assume that an enterprise continues to exist. For example, enterprises like fruit kiosks, ice-cream shops and beach restaurants are generally not in operation during the off-season, and therefore the operators of such enterprises should not be classified as employed when they are not at work during the off-season. There are, however, other enterprises which continue to exist during the off-season, e.g. farms which are operated all year round though the bulk of their activities are carried out seasonally. In such cases, a self-employed person not at work during the off-season could be classified as employed (with an enterprise but not at work) provided the duration of absence from work falls within an acceptable limit.

Unpaid family workers, though participating in the activities of a family enterprise, are not considered to have an enterprise of their own. Accordingly, unpaid family workers cannot be 'with an enterprise but not at work'. Therefore, unpaid family workers not at work should not be included among the employed. They would be considered as unemployed or not economically active depending on their search or availability for work during the reference period.

Particular groups

The international standards refer explicitly to some particular groups of workers to be included among the employed: unpaid family workers at work, persons engaged in the production of goods and services for own and household consumption, paid apprentices, working students and homemakers, and members of the armed forces.

Unpaid family workers. An unpaid family worker is a person who works without pay in an economic enterprise operated by a related person living in the same household. Where it is customary for young persons, in particular, to work without pay in an economic enterprise operated by a related person who does not live in the same household, the requirement of 'living in the same household' may be eliminated (UN 1980). In the previous international standards, adopted at the 1954 ICLS, unpaid family workers were required to have worked at least one-third of normal working hours to be classified as employed. This special provision was abandoned at the 1982 ICLS, so that according to the present international standards unpaid family workers at work are to be considered as employed irrespective of the number of hours worked during the reference period, the same as other categories of workers. Referring to countries that, for special reasons, prefer to set a minimum time criterion for the inclusion of unpaid family workers among the employed, the international standards specify that they should identify and separately classify those who worked less than the prescribed time.

Persons engaged in non-market production. Another category of unpaid workers to be considered for inclusion among the employed are persons engaged in the production of goods and services for own and household consumption, if such activities fall into the production boundary of the SNA. The international standards mention, however, that these persons, should be considered employed if such production comprises an important contribution to the total consumption of the household. This provision conforms to the practice in many countries of excluding negligible non-market economic activities from national accounting statistics. Though its implementation in labour force surveys may be difficult, the important contribution provision also serves to exclude from the economically active population persons who may, for example, be growing some vegetables in their backyards but whose subsistence does not significantly depend on it.

Apprentices and trainees. Concerning apprentices, the international standards state explicitly that those who receive pay in cash or in kind should be considered in paid employment and be classified as 'at work' or 'not at work' on the same basis as other persons in paid employment. Regarding apprentices who are not paid, no specific statement is made in the international standards, and the appropriate statistical treatment should therefore follow from the general principles.

Apprentices who fulfil the conditions for inclusion among unpaid family workers should be classified as employed when at work for at least one hour during the reference period. In the case of other unpaid apprentices, their inclusion among the employed may be determined on the basis of whether or not they are associated with the productive activities of an enterprise. If such apprentices contribute to the production of goods and services, they should be classified as employed. Otherwise, they should be classified as unemployed or not economically active, depending on their job search activity or availability for work.

In addition to apprenticeships, there are various other types of training schemes, organized directly by enterprises to train or retrain their staff, or subsidized by the government as a way to promote employment. Such training schemes are so varied in nature, modalities of contract, modes of payment, duration of training, etc., that specific guide-lines on the classification of the trainees into labour force categories cannot be formulated. The appropriate statistical treatment should be determined on a scheme-by-scheme basis. Having discussed the issue, the Fourteenth ICLS agreed on the following general guide-lines (ILO 1988).

In principle, trainees can be classified as employed if their activity can be considered as work, or if they have a formal job attachment. When training takes place within the context of an enterprise, it can be assumed that the trainees are associated with the production of goods and services of the enterprise, at least for one hour during the reference period. In that case they should be considered as 'at work' and be classified as employed, irrespective of whether or not they receive a wage or salary from the employer.

When the training does not take place within the context of an enterprise (e.g. training outside the enterprise, or inside the enterprise but without association with the production activity of the enterprise), the statistical treatment should depend on whether or not the trainees were employed by the enterprise before the training period (including cases classified as employed as mentioned above):

(a) If employed by the enterprise before the training period, the trainees should be considered as employed but not at work while on training, if they maintain a formal job attachment. An example are training schemes where periods of training in a specialized institution alternate with periods of work in the enterprise. To establish whether or not a formal job attachment exists, the criterion of 'assurance of return to work' (to be interpreted as assurance of return to work with the same employer) should be considered to be the essential one. In situations where such assurance of return to work does not exist, formal job attachment should be assessed on the basis of the criterion of 'continued receipt of wage or salary'. This criterion should be considered as satisfied if the employer paid directly all or a significant part of the wage or salary. The third criterion, 'elapsed duration of absence', might also be used in particular situations, e.g. in connection with long-term training schemes.

(b) If the trainees were not employed by the enterprise before the training period, they cannot be considered as 'with a job but not at work' and the notion of formal job attachment does not apply. Consequently, if the training scheme provides a definite commitment to employment at the end of the training, the statistical treatment might follow that of persons who have made arrangements to take up employment at a date subsequent to the reference period, and who are to be classified as unemployed if currently available for work (see the following section). Otherwise, the trainees should be classified as unemployed or not economically active depending upon their job search activity or availability for work.

Students, homemakers, etc. With respect to other groups particularly mentioned, the 1982 international standards specify that students, homemakers and others mainly engaged in non-economic activities during the reference period, who at the same time were in paid employment or self-employment, should be considered as employed on the same basis as other categories of employed persons (and be identified separately, where possible). This is fully in line with the priority rules of the labour force framework.

Members of the armed forces. Another group of persons singled out in the international standards for inclusion among the employed are members of the armed forces. The statistics should include both the regular and temporary members of the armed forces as specified in the most recent revision of the International Standard Classification of Occupations (ISCO). It follows logically that persons performing civilian services as an alternative to compulsory military services, wherever such possibility exists, should also be classified as employed.

UNEMPLOYMENT

The international standard definition of unemployment is based on three criteria which have to be met simultaneously. According to this definition the 'unemployed' comprise all persons above the age specified for measuring the economically active population who during the reference period were:

(a) 'without work', i.e. were not in paid employment or self-employment as specified by the international definition of employment;
(b) 'currently available for work', i.e. were available for paid employment or self-employment during the reference period; and
(c) 'seeking work', i.e. had taken specific steps in a specified recent period to seek paid employment or self-employment.

In formulating these criteria, the international standards do not refer to any institutional or legal provisions, such as the receipt of unemployment insurance benefits or the registration at a public placement office. The international definition of unemployment is intended to refer exclusively to a person's particular activities during a specified reference period.

Without work

The 'without work' criterion serves to draw the distinction line between employment and non-employment and to ensure that employment and unemployment are mutually exclusive, with precedence given to employment. Thus, a person is to be considered as without work if he or she did not work at all during the reference period (not even for one hour) nor was temporarily absent from work in the sense described in the previous section of this chapter. The other two criteria of the standard definition of unemployment, 'current availability for work' and 'seeking work', serve to distinguish among the non-employed population those who are unemployed from those who are not economically active.

Seeking work

In accordance with the activity principle of the labour force framework, the seeking work criterion is formulated in terms of active search for work. A person must have taken specific steps in a specified recent period to obtain work for being considered as seeking work. A general declaration of being in search of work is not sufficient. This formulation of the criterion is meant to provide an element of objectivity for measurement. The recent period specified for job search activities need not be the same as the basic survey reference period of one week or one day, but might be longer, such as one month or the past four weeks. The purpose of extending the job search period somewhat backwards in time is to take account of the prevailing time-lags involved in the process of obtaining work after the initial step to find it was made, time-lags during which persons may not take any other initiatives to find work. This may particularly be the case of persons who can only apply for employment with one potential employer (e.g. judges) and are awaiting the reply to their application.

The examples of active steps to seek work listed in the international standards include: registration at a public or private employment exchange; application to employers; checking at worksites, farms, factory gates, market or other assembly places; placing or answering newspaper advertisements; seeking assistance of friends or relatives; looking for land, building, machinery or equipment to establish own enterprise; arranging for financial resources; applying for permits and licences, etc. Some of these examples refer to rather formal methods of seeking work (e.g. registration at an employment exchange), while others are more informal (e.g. seeking assistance of friends or relatives). Concerning 'registration at a public or private employment exchange', the Fourteenth ICLS specified that this should be considered an active step to seek work only when it is for the purpose of obtaining a job offer, as opposed to cases where registration is merely an administrative require-ment for the receipt of certain social benefits (ILO 1988).

Note that the examples given above cover steps referring not only to paid employment but also to self-employment. This is because the notion of seeking work is independent of the type and duration of employment sought, including self-employment, part-time employment, temporary, seasonal or casual work, and, in general, any type of work considered as economic activity.

Seeking self-employment

The notion of seeking self-employment requires particular attention, as for self-employed persons the dividing line between seeking work activi-ties and the self-employment activities themselves is often difficult to draw. In many situations, activities such as looking for potential clients or orders, or advertising the goods or services produced, are an essential component of the self-employment activity itself. One may also need to clarify, when new enterprises are set up, at what point the process of seeking self-employment turns to become a self-employment activity itself. For example, it is not obvious whether the activities of buying an initial stock or acquiring the necessary equipment for opening a shop should still be regarded as a search activity or already as self-employed work. Having discussed the subject, the Fourteenth ICLS noted that the distinction between seeking self-employment and the self-employment activity itself could be based on the point when the enterprise starts to exist formally, e.g. when the enterprise is registered. Thus, activities taking place before the registration of the enterprise would be regarded as search activities, while activities after registration would be considered as self-employment itself. In situations where enterprises are not necessarily required to formally register in order to operate, it was suggested to draw the dividing line at the point when the enterprise is ready to receive the first order, when financial resources have become available, or when the necessary infrastructure is in place (ILO 1988).

Current availability for work

According to the international standards, persons should be available for work during the reference period to be considered unemployed. Availability for work means that, given a work opportunity, a person should be able and ready to work. When used in the context of the standard definition of unemployment, a purpose of the availability criterion is to exclude persons who are seeking work to begin at a later date. Such may be the case of students who, at the time of the survey, are seeking work to be taken up after completion of the school year. In this situation the availability criterion serves as a test of the current readiness to start work. The availability criterion also serves to exclude other persons who cannot take up work due to certain impediments, such as family responsibilities, illness, or commitments to community services.

While the availability criterion is formulated in the international standards as availability during the reference week or day of the survey, in practice many countries prefer to use a slightly longer period, e.g. the two weeks following the interview. This is to account for the fact that not everyone who is seeking work can be expected or is expected to take up a job immediately when it is offered. Persons may be temporarily sick at that moment, or may have to make arrangements concerning child care, transport facilities, etc., before being able to start work. Furthermore, it may be usual practice that enterprises do not expect newly recruited employees to start work before the forthcoming first or fifteenth of the month.

Future starts

The international standards specify one particular category of workers for whom an exception is made from the general rule that all three criteria (without work, currently available for work, seeking work) have to be satisfied simultaneously for being considered as unemployed under the standard definition. These are persons without work who have made arrangements to take up paid employment or undertake self-employment activity at a date subsequent to the reference period ('future starts'). Such persons, if currently available for work, are to be considered as unemployed, whether or not they continue to seek work. Between the alternative of considering them as unemployed or employed (with a job or enterprise but not at work), the international standards have opted for unemployment. This is because these persons, being currently available for work, would presumably already have started work had the job begun earlier and as such form part of the currently under-utilized labour resources. Furthermore, their classification as temporarily absent from work would not be in line with the requirement that a person temporarily absent from work must have worked already in the job in question.

Relaxation of the standard definition of unemployment

Seeking work is essentially a process of search for information on the labour market. In this sense, it is particularly meaningful as a definitional criterion in situations where the bulk of the working population is oriented towards paid employment and where channels for exchange of labour-market information exist and are widely used. While in industrialized countries these conditions are largely satisfied, this may not be the case in many developing countries where most workers are self-employed, often in household enterprises, and where labour exchanges and similar institutional arrangements are not fully developed and are often limited to certain urban sectors or particular categories of workers. In rural areas and in agriculture, because of the size of the localities and the nature of the activities, most workers have more or less complete knowledge of the work opportunities in their areas at particular periods of the year, making it often unnecessary to take active steps to seek work. Even in industrialized countries and in urban labour markets of developing countries, there may exist similar situations in which particular groups of workers do not actively seek work because they believe that no work corresponding to their skill is available in their area or at particular times of the business cycle.

Relaxation of the seeking work criterion

Because it was felt that the standard definition of unemployment, with its emphasis on the seeking work criterion, might be somewhat restrictive and might not fully capture the prevailing employment situations in many countries, the 1982 international standards introduced a provision which allows for the relaxation of the seeking work criterion in certain situations. This provision is confined to situations where 'the conventional means of seeking work are of limited relevance, where the labour market is largely unorganized or of limited scope, where labour absorption is at the time inadequate, or where the labour force is largely self-employed' (ILO 1983).

Formulating a definition of unemployment under the relaxation provision does not necessarily mean that the seeking work criterion should be completely relaxed for all categories of workers. The relaxation may be only partial. One would then include among the unemployed, in addition to persons satisfying the standard definition, certain groups of persons without work who are currently available for work but who are not seeking work for particular reasons.

An example of partial relaxation of the seeking work criterion, explicitly mentioned in the international standards, refers to persons temporarily laid off by their employer without maintaining a formal job attachment, i.e. to lay-offs not to be classified as employed (with a job but not at work). Under the standard definition of unemployment, such persons should be considered unemployed only if they are currently available for work and seeking work. For countries which, depending on national circumstances and policies, prefer to relax the seeking work criterion in the case of persons temporarily laid off, the international standards contain a provision to include such persons, if currently available for work but not seeking work, as a separate subcategory among the unemployed. Other examples, not specifically mentioned in the international standards, would be seasonal workers awaiting the busy season and the so-called 'discouraged workers'.

Availability for work under the relaxation provision

Where the labour-market situation justifies the relaxation of the seeking work criterion, unemployment would be defined, for the persons concerned, in terms of the remaining two criteria, i.e. without work and current availability for work. The availability criterion, in particular, becomes then a crucial element for measurement and should be fully tested.

Where the seeking work criterion is relaxed, a person without work would be considered unemployed if, given a work opportunity, he or she is able and ready to work. The meaning of the conditional element 'given a work opportunity' is more ambiguous when the seeking work criterion is relaxed than when it is not. When the seeking work criterion is applied, the conditional element is linked to the type of work sought by the jobseeker, as most active steps to seek work imply that the jobseeker has some idea of the type of work he or she has been looking for. However, when the seeking work criterion is relaxed, this link is cut and the notion of 'given a work opportunity' is much less clear. The context to which current availability refers should then be specified by indicating the particulars of the potential work opportunities in terms of remuneration, working time, location, occupation, etc.

The international standards recognize that apart from special circumstances (e.g. school attendance, family responsibilities, infirmity or disablement) availability for work depends essentially on the nature of potential work opportunities. They recommend that in

The application of the criterion of current availability for work, especially in situations where the 'seeking work' criterion is relaxed, appropriate tests should be developed to suit national circumstances. Such tests may be based on notions such as present desire for work, previous work experience, willingness to take up work for wage or salary on locally prevailing terms, or readiness to undertake self-employment activity, given the necessary resources and facilities.

UNDEREMPLOYMENT

Unemployment is defined in the labour force framework as an extreme situation of total lack of work. Less extreme situations of partial lack of work are all embodied within the concept of employment, broadly defined as engagement in an economic activity for at least one hour during the reference period. It is for identifying such situations of partial lack of work and for complementing the statistics on employment and unemployment that the concept of underemployment has been introduced. According to the international standards, underemployment exists 'when a person's employment is inadequate, in relation to specified norms or alternative employment, account being taken of his or her occupational skill (training and working experience)'.

The measurement of underemployment has particular relevance in developing countries, notably in agricultural activities. In many developing countries, because of high prevalence of self-employment, limited coverage of workers by unemployment insurance or social security systems and other reasons, the level of measured unemployment is consistently low. This has been explained by the fact that only few people can afford to be unemployed for some period of time, whereas the bulk of the population must engage themselves in some economic activity, however little or inadequate that may be. In such circumstances, the employment situation cannot be fully described by unemployment data alone and the statistics should be supplemented with data on underemployment.

While the measurement of underemployment has mostly been

recommended for describing the employment situation in developing countries, its relevance for industrialized countries is also increasingly felt. This is because in many countries, due to the recent changes in the employment situation and the rise of various forms of precarious employment, new situations have emerged that can be regarded as underemployment. In fact, the 1987 ICLS agreed on the usefulness of the concept of underemployment in relation to the employment situation of participants in certain categories of employment promotion schemes, though mentioning that the concept may need further elaboration in this context.

Visible and invisible underemployment

The international standards distinguish between two principal forms of underemployment: visible underemployment and invisible underemployment. Visible underemployment reflects an insufficiency in the volume of employment and is thus a statistical concept which is directly measurable by surveys. Invisible underemployment is primarily an analytical concept reflecting a misallocation of labour resources or a fundamental imbalance between labour and other factors of production. The characteristic symptoms of invisible underemployment, as indicated in the international standards, might be low income, underutilization of skill, or low productivity.

A comprehensive study of invisible underemployment involves analysis of a wide variety of data, including income and skill levels (disguised underemployment) and productivity measures (potential underemployment). Data requirements for the measurement of invisible underemployment are thus very demanding and involve a number of unresolved difficulties (e.g. evaluating the quality of jobs against the skills of the incumbents, linking data on the productivity of establishments to data on the characteristics of individual workers). Recognizing the formidable measurement problems involved, the 1982 international standards state that 'for operational reasons, the statistical measurement of underemployment may be limited to visible underemployment'.

Visible underemployment

The international standards consider two elements in the measurement of visible underemployment: (a) the number of persons visibly underemployed and (b) the quantum of visible underemployment. The first element gives results in terms of number of persons, and the second element is measured in terms of time units such as working days, half-days or hours.

Persons visibly underemployed

According to the international standards, persons visibly underemployed comprise 'all persons in paid or self-employment, whether at work or not at work, involuntarily working less than the normal duration of work determined for the activity, who were seeking or available for additional work during the reference period'. Thus, the definition sets forth three criteria for identification of the visibly underemployed: (i) working less than normal duration; (ii) doing so on an involuntary basis; and (iii) seeking or being available for additional work during the reference period. For considering a person as visibly underemployed, all three criteria must be satisfied simultaneously.

The concept applies to all employed persons, not only to persons in paid employment but also to persons in self-employment, and not only to those currently at work but also to those temporarily absent from work. The underemployed being a subgroup of the employed, the concept does not apply to the population not economically active. By definition, an economically inactive person cannot be underemployed.

Working less than normal duration

Assessment of this criterion involves comparing the number of hours worked by a particular worker during the reference period with the number of hours that workers normally work in the corresponding activity. Visible underemployment being a characteristic of a person and not of an activity, special provisions have to be made for multiple jobholders so as to account for all of their activities.

There are essentially two approaches for identifying work of less than normal duration in a survey. One approach is to ask respondents directly whether or not they worked less than normal duration. The other approach is to obtain information on both normal and individual hours of work and compare the two. The first approach may be suitable where the working hours of the bulk of the population are contractually regulated and survey respondents know about these regulations. Otherwise, the second approach should be used.

Determination of normal duration of work

The international standards specify that, for the purpose of classifying persons as visibly underemployed, normal duration of work for an activity should be determined 'as reflected in national legislation to the extent it is applicable, and usual practices in other cases, or in terms of a uniform conventional norm'. Assessment of normal hours of work in surveys raises certain difficulties. In its strict sense, the notion is essentially limited to regular paid employees, whose working time is regulated by national legislation, collective agreements or at least by a written or verbal employment contract. However, such regulations may vary from one branch of economic activity to another, and even for a given branch they may differ among establishments or according to the occupation, age and other characteristics of the worker. This means that normal hours of work would have to be assessed on an individual basis.

Moreover, similar provisions for casual workers, multiple jobholders and self-employed persons do not generally exist, so that in such cases the normal duration of work would have to be determined on the basis of usual practices. Even this may, however, be difficult in cases where the hours of work usually spent in a given activity are highly variable among workers. This may particularly be the case in agricultural and seasonal activities.

The international standards suggest therefore, as an alternative method, to use a uniform conventional norm (e.g. 30, 35, 40 hours) for the normal duration of work. Such a norm is to be defined in the light of national circumstances, and to be applied to all activities and all categories of workers. In assessing visible underemployment, special provisions have then to be made for workers who, though reporting working hours below the uniform norm, are nevertheless to be considered as fully employed, since full-time work in their activity does not involve more hours of work (teachers, judges, etc.).

Involuntary nature

Once identified that a person is working less than normal duration, one has to assess whether this situation is involuntary or not. This may be determined in surveys by asking for the reason why a person worked less than normal duration. The importance of this second criterion of the international definition of persons visibly underemployed results from the fact that there are many different reasons for work below normal duration. In certain situations, persons are forced to do so because of economic reasons, i.e. they are faced with a slack period, material shortages, etc., or they cannot find more work. However, there are also situations where persons decide voluntarily to work less. This is the case of many working women with children, young persons combining studies with employment, or elderly workers voluntarily participating in phased retirement schemes. Moreover, for the purpose of measuring visible underemployment, the notion of 'involuntary reason' should be interpreted in the sense of 'due to the economic situation' so as to exclude other involuntary reasons like illness, disablement, etc.

Seeking or available for additional work

Finally, to be considered as visibly underemployed, a person involuntarily working less than normal duration must be seeking or available for additional work during the reference period. The purpose of this criterion is twofold. First, the criterion serves to reinforce the probe on the involuntary nature of short-time work; second, it is used to maintain consistency within the activity principle embedded in the labour force framework.

The notion of additional work should be interpreted in a broad sense. It is meant to refer to all work arrangements and types of work that could increase a person's total working hours. Additional work may thus mean: (a) working more hours at the present job; (b) obtaining another job of the same or a different type in addition to the present one; (c) replacing the present job by another one of the same or a different type, but with more hours; or (d) combinations of these. In the case of self-employment, additional work should be interpreted so as to cover not only an increase in the number of working hours but also an increase in the number of clients or orders.

Quantum of visible underemployment

According to the 1982 international standards, quantum of visible underemployment refers to the aggregate 'time available for additional employment during the reference period in respect of each person visibly underemployed . . . computed in units of working days, half-days or hours as may be convenient in national circumstances, depending on the nature of the data collected'.

The international standards particularly mention two methods for measuring the time available for additional employment, without excluding other possibilities. The first method is based on a direct inquiry on the duration of work sought, i.e. on the number of additional days, half-days or hours of work sought or available for during the reference period up to the normal duration of work. Difficulties may, however, arise in the case of workers not remunerated on time rates, such as many self-employed persons, piece-rate workers, home-based workers and workers remunerated by the task. Such persons may not think in terms of duration of work sought but rather in terms of the amount of extra orders they could accept, the number of additional clients they could cope with, etc.

The second method, called labour time disposition, is more precise but also more complex. It consists of compiling, on a day-by-day basis, for each person concerned, a balance sheet of the total labour time potentially available, broken down into time employed (or, more precisely, time worked), time available for employment and time not available for employment during the reference period. When compiled for all persons in the labour force, the labour time disposition approach also permits derivation of a composite estimate of the quantum of current unemployment and visible underemployment. It should also be mentioned that the approach offers many other possibilities for data analysis. In particular, many different work patterns can be revealed, e.g. full-time/full-week, full-time/part-week, part-time/full-week and part-time/part-week employment.

EMPLOYMENT AND INCOME RELATIONSHIPS

Inadequacy of employment may result from a number of different factors, among which insufficient volume of employment (in terms of time worked) and low remuneration are the two most obvious ones. Statistics on unemployment and visible underemployment provide insight only on the first of these factors. They do not provide any information on the adequacy of the incomes obtained from employment and on related social aspects. The limitation of the concepts of unemployment and visible underemployment becomes evident, for example, in the case of persons who, though fully employed in terms of hours, have low earnings and therefore seek extra or different work. Another example applies to the situation of self-employed persons, where a lack of demand may result in low intensity of work and low income rather than in a reduction of time spent at work. This is because there is a tendency for such persons to spread their work over time rather than to work short-time when the demand for their products or services is low. Such situations are as important for employment policies as are unemployment and visible underemployment.

So as to indicate the need for supplementing statistics of employment, unemployment and invisible underemployment with statistics that would provide insights on the income aspect of employment inadequacy, the 1982 international standards recommend that countries develop data collection programmes for the analysis of the relationships between employment and income. In particular, data should be compiled for the purpose of (a) analysing the income-generating capacity of different economic activities; and (b) identifying the number and characteristics of persons who are unable to maintain their economic well-being on the basis of the employment opportunities available to them. However, the relationships between employment and income are complex, and up to now relatively little national or international experience exists regarding statistics on these topics. Thus, there is still much work to be done in the future.

REFERENCES

Hussmanns, R.; Mehran, F.; Verma, V. (1990): *Surveys of economically active population, employment, unemployment and underemployment: An ILO manual on concepts and methods*, ILO, Geneva, 1990.

International Labour Office (1983): 'Thirteenth International Conference of Labour Statisticians, Resolution concerning statistics of the economically active population, employment, unemployment and underemployment' (text also in French and Spanish), *Bulletin of Labour Statistics*, ILO, Geneva, 1983-3, pp. xi-xv.

International Labour Organisation (1988): *Fourteenth International Conference of Labour Statisticians, Geneva, 28 October-6 November 1987, Report of the Conference*, (ICLS/14/D.14), ILO, Geneva, 1988.

United Nations (1968): *A System of National Accounts, Studies in Methods*, Series F, No. 2, Rev. 3 (ST/STAT/SER.F/2) Rev.3, New York, 1968.

United Nations (1980): *Principles and Recommendations for Populationand Housing Censuses*, Statistical Papers Series M No. 67 (ST/ESA/ STAT/SER. M/67), New York, 1980.

10

Satistical study of employment and unemployment in the Repulic of Belarus

K. KISELEVA*

The transition to a market economy and the development of a labour market require the creation of new methods of accumulation and analysis of statistical data. Under the centralized management and planning system, statistical work had to reflect the implementation of the plan indices. At present the programme of transition to market relations is being carried out in the Republic, which involves the following new elements: leasing enterprises, joint stock companies and economic associations are being established; the process of the privatization of state property has begun. Due to these developments, the problem of bringing existing labour statistics closer to international standards has become one of the utmost urgency. This applies first of all to employment and unemployment indices.

Statistical monitoring of employment and labour remuneration is still carried out by means of collection and processing of statistical data from all enterprises and organizations of the Republic. In recent years, the State Committee on Statistics and Analysis of Belarus has introduced a number of important alterations into labour statistics. Due to the rapid changes taking place in the labour market, monthly statistical monitoring of all governmental enterprises and organizations was adopted in 1992. This enables the following of the dynamics of the number of employed and their intra-industrial redistribution, the availability of vacant jobs, and the scale of forthcoming redundancies. The reports of employment services provide information on the unemployed

---

* This chapter was originally written as a paper for the Joint ECE/ILO/OECD Work Session on Labour Statistics and Issues of Concern for Transition Countries, Paris, December 1992.

and on their placement in employment. Statistical monitoring over development of the new market structures has been organized.

The State Committee on Statistics and Analysis (GOSKOMSTAT) uses the balance method of employment study in its statistical practice. The balance sheet of Labour resources is drawn up annually on the basis of population statistics' data, reports of enterprises and organizations of all forms of property, and on the tax inspection data. The balance of labour resources report consists of two sections. The first one reflects the availability and structure of labour resources, the second their distribution in accordance with forms of employment. The labour resources concept includes those citizens who have the ability to work (men of 16–59 years of age, women of 16–54), those employed in the national economy or able to work but not working due to some reason, as well as teenagers and persons of pension age who are actually working, excluding invalids of the I and II groups, granted a privileged pension. The following groups of population are defined in the system of measures, characterizing the labour resources' distribution according to the fields of employment:

- employed in the state sector of the economy;
- employed in the collective farm and cooperative sector (farms, private production, individual labour, private enterprises);
- students who are able to work, studying at schools, vocational, secondary specialized and higher education institutions;
- citizens who are able to work, but are not employed in the national economy (housewives; women with children up to 3 years of age who are on child-care leave; citizens in the military service; unemployed and other categories).

Upon the adoption of the Property Law, the data on the number of employed in enterprises and organizations of various forms of property (state-owned, collective, private and combined) were included into the labour force balance.

The transition of the national economy to multi-structural economic development is accompanied by changes in the employment structure and increased labour force turnover among enterprises of various branches of the economy and forms of property.

There has been labour force flow from the branches of material production to the non-production fields. However, the share of employment in these branches is still high and accounts for 74 per cent of the total number of employed. In the course of the market economy formation, the services industry of the Republic, which at present accounts for 29 per cent of the employed population, will require more and more employees.

State property prevails in the Republic; nevertheless, the process of formation and development of other forms of property and management methods are being observed more and more. At present 67 per cent of employees work in state enterprises and organizations, and 33 per cent in new market structures (leasing, joint stock companies, economic associations and cooperatives). There are signs of development in the agricultural sector also. On 1 January 1992 there were 757 farms in Belarus, 2.6 times as many as on 1 October 1990. The process of state property privatization has begun in Belarus and it applies to all branches of the national economy. At present 161 enterprises with 60,000 employees have been privatized.

The transition from a planned economy to a market one is accompanied by the growth of redundancy. It results in the increase of the number of unemployed and non-working citizens.

The Employment Law came into force in the Republic from 1 July 1991. This law determines: the concept of employed population; the status of the unemployed; the major principles of the governmental employment policy; the state's guarantees to the Republic's citizens of free retraining, assistance in finding a job and legal protection of the right to labour; social guarantees and compensations to the unemployed etc.

The collection of employment and unemployment statistics is a duty of the employment services created by the State Labour and Social Protection Committee. The employment services study labour force demand and supply, carry out registration of the unemployed and of vacant jobs, and organize both vocational training and retraining of the unemployed.

The state statistical bodies receive quarterly and monthly data on the number and movement of the unemployed (classified by sex, place of permanent residence), on their employment placement, retraining, and on the number of unemployed receiving unemployment benefits.

In order to monitor the number of non-working and unemployed citizens we use only the reports of employment services. However, the actual number of citizens redundant from enterprises and organizations is considerably higher.

The problem of redundancy will become more serious and the number of unemployed will increase; 'hidden' unemployment may increase too. For these reasons, there is an urgent need to have accurate statistical monitoring of employment and unemployment. In this respect we need the experience of other states.

Within the framework of the State Programme of Transition to a System of Statistical Accounting and Reports (a system of the national accounts), as accepted in international practice, we are carrying out preparatory work on bringing labour measures in line with international standards.

It is planned to develop methodological techniques to measure labour force, employment and unemployment indicators in accordance with the ILO international recommendations. Preparatory work will then be carried out for a sample household survey for the purposes of employment and unemployment study.

We have no experience in this field but we know that the ILO Bureau of Statistics, other international organizations and countries with a market economy have accumulated a great deal of experience in this area. International seminars, training of our specialists and consultations with international organizations will be extremely useful to us in the speedy creation of an up-to-date labour statistical system in the Republic of Belarus.

It is planned to revise existing classifications in order to bring them closer to those applied in international practice. In particular, it is necessary to revise the existing classification of the national economy branches in accordance with the wording of the International Standard Industrial Classification. We have set ourselves the task of transforming the existing All-Union Classifier of Workers' Professions, Positions of Office Workers and Tariff Rates, as well as the Rate-qualifying Directories, into the Uniform Classification of Occupations according to the main principles of the International Standard Classification of Occupations (ISCO-88), providing for common occupational definitions. The changes taking place in the labour market require classification of the employed by their status in employment.

11

The Labour Force Survey in Czechoslovakia

B. MEJSTŘÍK and J. KUX*

The traditional system of family surveys (general household surveys, income surveys, family budgets) is now being supplemented with a new type of survey – a labour force survey – which was not used in the past. The reason for introducing this new type of survey is the gradual collapse of the former and virtually the only source of information, which was based on enterprise reporting, as the result of the establishment of the small-business private sector. There is a lack of reliable information on employment in small businesses, on the number of self-employed workers, on the 'grey', informal economy, and on links between economic activity or inactivity and demographic indicators, qualifications and the like. Data on hours worked are insufficient, and statistical information on unemployment – a phenomenon unknown before – is completely missing. For the time being, administrative sources – the files of labour offices on job applications, which are affected by frequently changing national administrative regulations – are being used for such purposes. These were the main reasons why Czechoslovak statisticians considered various possibilities and international experiences, and then prepared this new type of survey.

It has to be emphasized that the direct incentive to design these surveys was provided by the seminar that the ILO and the UN Statistical Office organized in Moscow in the autumn of 1990. Of great help to the Czechoslovak statisticians in designing the surveys were, above all, experts from the United Kingdom's Department of Employment and the

* This chapter was originally written as a paper for the Joint ECE/ILO/OECD Work Session on Labour Statistics and Issues of Concern for Transition Countries, Paris, December 1992.

Office of Population Censuses and Surveys, who rendered assistance in compiling a comprehensive concept for design of the surveys. Significant contributions were also made by the United States Bureau of Labor Statistics, the United States Bureau of the Census, INSEE of France and Eurostat. Without their help, Czechoslovak statisticians could not have prepared these surveys successfully.

THE CONCEPTION OF THE CZECHOSLOVAK LABOUR FORCE SAMPLE SURVEYS

At the very beginning, three options were considered:

- to design the first Czechoslovak survey as a sub-set of the 1992 Microcensus then under preparation (an approach similar to that taken in the Federal Republic of Germany) and decide on further steps later on;
- to start with yearly labour force sample surveys (as initially done in most developed market economies);
- to begin immediately with the target solution of quarterly surveys.

Even though the first two options might have seemed less costly and organizationally intensive, a detailed analysis clearly showed the third option – to begin immediately with the target solution of surveys on a quarterly basis – to be preferable. The principal reason was the urgent need to provide missing data as soon as possible and with a periodicity which would permit the rapidly changing situation in the labour market of Czechoslovakia to be monitored flexibly. Consequently, the government authorities concerned were persuaded to provide sufficient resources for these surveys.

Contents of the surveys

Data on the extent and structure of employment, unemployment, economic inactivity, underemployment, hours worked, second or multiple jobs, and incomes from employment and other sources will be surveyed (at least within the pilot test). The questionnaire is split into two parts: part A concerns all members of the household in general (10 questions altogether) and part B deals with the economic activity of all members who are 15 years of age and over (no upper limit has been fixed, and it includes about 60 questions in total). A specimen of the questionnaire is presented in Annex 5.

Scope of reporting households

The sample is assumed to include approximately 40,000 reporting households (which translates into about 0.8 per cent of the total households) and is to be reduced when experience has been gained. The 1991 population census is used for the sample frame. Each of the households will be called upon five times in subsequent quarters and then be removed from the sample. The rotation of the sample in each quarter will thus be 20 per cent.

Organization of the survey

The survey will be run through personal interviews taking the form of personal calls. Future interviews will be conducted by telephone, if mutually agreed upon. Laptops or notebooks (CAPI or CATI) are expected to be gradually used for the survey. No specific date will be fixed for the survey in a particular quarter – the survey will be run throughout the quarter for reasons of capacity: the sample will be split into 13 segments corresponding to the thirteen weeks of the quarter and each week one-thirteenth of the sample will be visited. The quarterly results will thus be a total of individual results arrived at during thirteen weeks. (A similar procedure was taken for the shift from yearly to quarterly surveys in the United Kingdom.)

The Dutch software program BLAISE will be used to enter and check the data (its advantages will be enjoyed after the shift to CAPI in particular); the data are assumed to be processed on PCs and a main-frame, and cooperation concerning the database mode is now under discussion with Quantime, U.K., which operates the Eurostat database and assisted in introducing surveys in the United Kingdom, Greece and other countries.

Time schedule of implementation

Despite the original estimate of 18–24 months from decision to implementation for Czechoslovakia and the warnings made by foreign experts that the preparation of LFS is quite time consuming, the time schedule for the preparation inevitably had to be shortened for Czechoslovak conditions. The whole concept of the project was approved in early December 1991 by the managements of the three statistical offices (Federal, Czech and Slovak). In February 1992, executives of the three statistical offices attended a training course (1-2 weeks) in London. Workers employed by the regional administrations of the Czech and Slovak Statistical Offices, who were to organize the survey in their regions (twelve in total) as supervisors, received a training course, held in Czechoslovakia in November 1992, and experts of the United States Bureau of Labor Statistics and Bureau of the Census participated in it. The first pilot test in the Czech Republic was made in June–July 1992 for a group of selected households; the second was run in September 1992 and covered selected households in all Czech districts. The technical project of data collection, processing and publishing and the interviewer's manual were finalized in December 1992. In the Slovak Republic, the pilot test was conducted in the fourth quarter of 1992. Routine surveying was to start at the beginning of 1993. However, as the whole set would not be completely filled up due to the rotation until the third round or so, the first two rounds might only be experimental in nature because of lower representativeness, and full-value results might only be available in the second half of 1993.

EVALUATION OF THE LFS PILOT TESTS RUN IN THE CZECH REPUBLIC

The design of the LFS was verified by the Czech Statistical Office by means of two pilot tests, the objectives of which were especially:

- To verify the methodological appropriateness of the designed materials (especially of the designed questionnaires),
- to establish the requirements of the LFS in terms of time and money,
- to check the programmes for input data acquisition, checking and processing for function,
- to ascertain respondents' attitudes to the LFSs under preparation,
- to give the workers of the state statistics bureau entrusted with the LFSs a practice run on the routine activities to be carried out later.

The first pilot test was run in nine chosen administrative districts of the Czech Republic from 8 to 28 June. In each of the districts, fifty dwellings were selected in a specified manner (a total of 450 dwellings for the whole Czech Republic).

Based on the results derived from the first pilot test, the Czech Statistical Office organized the second pilot test. This pilot test, which was conducted from 14–25 September (reference weeks from 7 September or 14 September), was conducted virtually in all districts of the republic and based on a random sample of dwellings in the individual districts. As in the first pilot test, the second pilot test also used preliminary results of 3 March 1991 population and housing census for the sampling frame.

Selected in the first phase were census districts in the administrative districts. The method of stratified systematic sampling with probabilities proportional to the number of dwellings in the census districts was chosen. The probability of selection was proportional to the number of permanently inhabited dwellings established by the 1991 census. To achieve representativeness within the districts, the dwellings from selected districts were chosen so that their number was the same for each of the districts. Hence, in each administrative district four census districts were selected, and in each of the selected census districts nine dwellings were selected. The sampling interval varied for the individual districts, depending on their size. In the districts included in the first pilot test, interviewers partially repeated their June calls and partially called at the new dwellings selected. The sample under survey already amounted to almost 3,000 dwellings.

For the pilot tests, instructions were given for the checking and processing of data by regional statistical bodies. Besides the definition of the survey extent and the way of sampling the dwellings, these instructions also included the interviewer's tasks involved in the preparation and implementation of the survey. Each of the interviewers was supposed to make a survey plan of the selected dwellings and, if feasible, notify the household of his/her call. For this purpose, a letter from the President of the Czech Statistical Office was written to the selected households. The instructions also incorporated principles to be adhered to in interviewing and a detailed explanation concerning the individual questions in both questionnaires.

The instructions described in detail the interviewer's tasks to be fulfilled during the pilot test and the closing work, with stress placed on the necessity for keeping to the time schedule of the survey so that accumulation of work would be avoided at the end of the period specified for the pilot test. Other documents were also prepared for the pilot test – the interviewer's diary and the weekly summary of the survey results.

The regional coordinators (supervisors) had to become acquainted with these basic materials, as did their deputies who in turn instructed interviewers of the district statistical administrations concerned. At least one interviewer was in charge of the second pilot test at the district level. In some of the districts, however, two workers engaged in statistical work called at the selected households. The regional coordinators (eight in total) cooperated with the interviewers where organization and methodology were concerned, checked that the schedule was adhered to and verified that the questionnaires were filled in correctly.

The software for acquiring data from the questionnaires was also verified. The Central Bureau of Statistics of the Netherlands provided BLAISE software free of charge to the Czechoslovak statisticians and also included its supporting software, ABACUS, MANIPULA and

BASCULA. All three statistical offices each received one authorized copy and the software was installed. The Federal Statistical Office prepared the application of BLAISE to the collection of data from the questionnaires used in the first and second LFS pilot tests run by the Czech Statistical Office.

The results of the pilot tests revealed a relatively large degree of citizen cooperation. The proportion of the dwellings surveyed in the first pilot test was 78 per cent on average for the whole Czech Republic and ranged in individual districts from 72 per cent (Prague) to 86 per cent (rural districts). The first data available from the second pilot test confirmed the comparatively high acceptance of the survey by the population, but there were signals indicating that the willingness to cooperate has dropped in some households (especially in those also chosen for the second pilot test). In general, the percentage of the surveyed households is likely to be slightly lower compared with the first pilot test. Better cooperation was obtained from respondents in rural parts of the districts, whereas the situation in Prague and bigger municipalities was more difficult. It can be expected that the second pilot test, which involves more interviewers, will show bigger differences in their findings.

The findings and comments obtained vary in nature. The comments on the methodological and organizational preparation highlight various aspects of the interviewer's work and the limited opportunity to call at households in the morning or later at night. However, the experience of interviewers was not identical. Generally, they point out the problem of finding the addresses of sampled dwellings due to the difficult orientation in cities, towns and villages (wrong house numbers, frequent changes in the names of streets) and to the difficulties involved in contacting the dwellings situated in housing estates or historical parts of cities and towns where the blocks of flats are generally locked.

The population census data used for the sampling frame becomes out of date quickly and the lists of dwellings in the selected census districts have to be updated frequently. Another problem is the high proportion of dwellings inhabited by the retired. Incorporation of these dwellings into the survey reduces, to a certain extent, the validity of the survey especially in Prague and rural areas. The comments on the questionnaires resulted primarily from the heterogeneity of the types of respondents. The area and sequence of questions for some respondents should be made more precise – this applies, for instance, to women on maternity leave. Furthermore, the method of surveying children over 15 who have not yet completed their education is unresolved. It is necessary clearly to define the number of digits for the classification of economic activities (which respects the classification NACE) and the classification of occupations (based on ISCO). Moreover, the range of questions explaining overtime hours for some occupations (medical doctors, policemen, soldiers, etc.) should be extended.

As far as the unwillingness to respond to some questions is concerned, this was sometimes observed in the questions concerning income levels (this was the case for private entrepreneurs in particular). Partial findings indicate that it would be more appropriate to ask questions about income brackets and not about absolute incomes, which had been already tested in the first pilot test. Similarly, it was recommended by the coordinators and interviewers that the questions evaluating the financial conditions of households, which were omitted in the second pilot test, be incorporated into the questionnaires again.

There were frequent comments on the time demands of the survey and transport. The time demands are high, with considerable differences existing between municipalities and rural districts. More detailed analyses reveal that to survey fifty dwellings in the first pilot test required approximately 117–124 hours of work, but the actual inter-viewing (including the filling-in of the questionnaires) only called for 25–29 hours of work. Much time was consumed by travelling to respondents (38–55 hours) and time losses (waiting for means of transport, looking for the address, and waiting between individual appointments) which amounted to 5–11 hours. Approximately 27 hours were needed for completing the questionnaires (particularly for coding according to the classification of activities and that of occupations).

The preliminary data of the second pilot test indicate the average time needed to survey one household to have further increased by approxi-mately 10–20 per cent, which may be explained by the fact the second pilot test covered rural municipalities and villages in a representative manner.

The second pilot test indicates that it is most appropriate to call at households between 15:00 and 19:00 on Mondays through Thursdays, especially since a number of municipal households do not spend their weekends where they reside. The time demands of the survey require that the transport problem be solved. One means of eliminating time lost, improving the coverage of households in rural areas and increasing the mobility of the interviewer, would be to use private cars. This is, however, conditional on the funds of the CSO budget.

Comments on the PILOT.EXE programme prepared by the FSO emphasized some problems arising from the fact that the BLAISE software was only received just before the start of the first pilot test and the program had to be made in a very short time. For the second pilot test, the program was modified in accordance with some alterations in the questionnaires, and its application to this test already uses the system texts translated into Czech.

It has been recommended by the regional statistical bodies that the individual cities, towns and villages concerned be informed about a survey in advance and that local councils be asked to cooperate with interviewers as the latter can provide important information at the stage of updating selected census districts (data on new construction, on demolitions, etc.) which may facilitate the conduct of the survey.

The two pilot tests organized by the Czech Statistical Office provided a number of findings which would be utilized in the final questionnaires, data acquisition and processing software and organizational and financial issues. The LFS questionnaire used in the above pilot surveys is shown in Annex 5.

CONCLUSIONS

The course of the preparatory work has been favourable so far. The results of the first pilot tests where both the interviewers and particularly the selected households took a very active part in the survey are especially encouraging. The willingness of the Czechoslovak households to cooperate in the survey is satisfactory, compared with the original pessimistic expectations. Hence, the extent of the non-response is not likely to exceed 20 per cent. Although there is a minor delay in preparing the survey in the Slovak Republic, substantiated assumptions exist for launching routine surveying at the beginning of 1993. [Both Czech and Slovak Republics successfully launched their respective full-scale Labour Force Surveys in 1993. *Ed.*]

Annex 5 (Labour force sample survey for Czechoslovakia) is to be found at the end of this volume.

12

The Hungarian Labour Force survey, 1992: Reference Manual

HUNGARIAN CENTRAL STATISTICAL OFFICE

The transition of the Hungarian economy from a centrally planned system to a market economy necessitates fundamental changes in Hungarian labour statistics.

Among the basic changes, one of the most important was the introduction of a regular Labour Force Survey on a household basis, started after a pilot survey in January 1992.

The main purpose of the LFS is to obtain timely and accurate information on the labour force status of the Hungarian population, thereby enabling labour force trends to be monitored. The quarterly household survey classifies the civilian, non-institutional population aged 15–74 years according to labour force status. The major data items can also be cross-classified with variables such as age, sex, occupation, industry, etc. The survey definitions follow the concepts and recommendations of the ILO.

The data for the survey are collected monthly by paper-and-pencil interviews, and take place in the week which contains the 19th day of each month. In 1992 a minority of interviews were carried out using laptop computers.

The LFS sample is a two- and three-stage stratified probability sample of housing units. There are approximately 30,000 households (i.e. about 50,000 persons) to be interviewed in each quarter (i.e. 10,000 households a month). The overall sampling fraction is 0.8 per cent. Each sample household provides information on employment for a period of six consecutive quarters, then leaves the sample for ever. One-sixth of the sample is changed on each occasion.

An estimate is prepared for every quarter by averaging the data of the three months surveyed. The figures are adjusted for non-response and recently also to allow for changes in demographic distributions.

The interviews take place in the week which contains the 19th day of every month. Throughout the questionnaire, questions refer to 'last week'. This is the reference week, which runs from Monday to Sunday and contains the 12th day of the month.

The Hungarian Labour Force Survey uses the following two sets of questionnaires:

- *Social-Demographic Data* – relating to social-demographic data of the members of the households
- *Economic Activity Questionnaire* – concentrating on economic activity of individuals and comprising nineteen questions, seventeen of them relating to economic activity

INSTRUCTIONS FOR INTERVIEWERS

On the first page of the Social-Demographic question every member of the household is listed, but the rest of the questions refer only to people between 15–74 years old.

From the entries in items 1–7, we classify the civilian non-institutional population between 15–74 years old into the following groups:

EMPLOYED
- persons working during the survey week
- persons not working who had a job or business from which they were temporarily absent for the whole of the survey week

UNDEREMPLOYED
- persons working less than 36 hours during the week for an economic reason, i.e. slack work, full-time work not available, starting or ending a job during the week
- persons not working because of temporary lay off

UNEMPLOYED
- persons not working who have looked for work during the past four weeks and were available for work during the survey week
- persons who were waiting to start a new job within thirty days

NOT IN THE LABOUR FORCE
- persons neither employed nor unemployed

Passive unemployed (discouraged workers): persons who want a job but did not look for work because they
　　(a) believe no work is available in line of work or area
　　(b) could not find any work (there are too many unemployed)

(c) lack necessary schooling, training, skills or experience
(d) think they are too young or too old

The *economically active population* includes everyone available for work at the reference week, i.e. employed, unemployed and underemployed.

NOTES ON THE ECONOMIC ACTIVITY QUESTIONNAIRE

1. Did . . . do at least one hour work for pay or profit last week?

Definition of work: a person can work for wages or salary, profit, pay 'in kind', profit expected in the future or without pay on a family farm or business.

Do not consider as 'working' unpaid work for another household, volunteer work without pay for organizations, building or renovation of a house or flat, housework and work around the house.

2. How many hours did . . . work last week?

Ask actual work, include overtime and exclude time off. For wage earners, include hours worked without compensation in connection with their jobs. Mealbreaks should be included (maximum half an hour).

Main work: means *actual* work on the reference week. When a respondent has more than one job, let him/her decide which job is to be considered as the main work. Where a respondent cannot decide, the main work should be the one in which the greatest number of hours were worked in the reference week.

Persons engaged in the production of economic goods or services should be considered as self-employed if a significant proportion of the production is intended for sale in the market.

3. For persons who worked less than 36 hours at all jobs last week, ask whether the person usually works 36 hours or more. Two entries are required. Then ask what is the reason . . . worked less than 36 hours last week or what is the reason . . . usually works less than 36 hours. Primary reason has to be marked.

'Slack work' means the following: reduction in economic activity, turnover reduced, lack of demand for product, shortage of materials, machine repairs, plant transformation, reorganization.

4. Does . . . have a gainful work from which he/she was temporarily absent last week?

This item is to be asked of and filled in for persons who did not work last week. Do not count child-care leave as employment, only maternity leave, which is available for six months after childbirth. Mark 'No' if a retail dealer or a craftsman temporarily interrupts his/her activity and in the case of unpaid family members and seasonal workers out of season.

5. Why did not . . . work last week?

Mark illness for persons who have to take care of their child who is ill. Mark temporarily laid off for a person who is laid off but has been told to return back to work at a definite date or after an indefinite period.

6. Was . . . looking for work in the last four weeks?

7. What was . . . doing in the last four weeks to find work?

Last four weeks means up to and including survey week.

12. When did . . . last work in a job or business on a regular basis?

This question is asked of all respondents who did not have a job in the reference week. The question is not concerned with holiday jobs or casual work or business lasting less than two weeks.

13. Why did . . . leave this work?

This question refers to the last job mentioned in the Item 12.

17. Description of work

 – If the respondent worked last week (Item 1 = 1) ask about this job. If he/she had more than one job, ask about the main one.
 – If the respondent did not work last week (Item 1 = 2) but he/she has a job (Item 4 = 1) ask about the job from which he/she was temporarily absent.
 – If the respondent did not work (Item 1 = 2) and had no job (Item 4 = 3) or his/her job is to begin within thirty days (Item 4 = 2), ask about the last work.

17(d). How many hours does . . . usually work (or worked) each week in this job?

If the respondent does not know, two answers may be marked.
1. number of hours worked varies
2. this is not his/her regular job – mark this category for persons who have a regular job, but last week he/she was temporarily absent from this one or worked for some reason more in his/her second job.

People who work only as a seasonal worker should be asked the hours when he/she worked.

18. Is . . . registered at the public employment agency as unemployed?

19. Does . . . receive unemployment benefit?

Every respondent has to answer the above two questions.

Annex 6 contains the **Hungarian Labour Force Survey questionnaire** and is to be found at the end of this volume.

13

The Polish Labour Force Survey

J. WITKOWSKI*

The challenge facing Polish society in the early 1990s concerns virtually all fields of life. Polish statistics have to face it as well. It comes as no surprise, when one realizes that the aim of statistics is to describe socio-economic phenomena, which take place in every society, though on a different scale and with various intensity. The changes currently occurring in Poland enforce a modification of the statistical system to adapt it to the requirements of the market economy. The Central Statistical Office has met the challenge and systematically perfects the range and methods of gathering information.

The labour market is one of the areas of reality which undergoes particularly dynamic changes. During a very short period of time, a complete transformation of the rules operating on the Polish labour market took place, from those governed by a constant lack of manpower to those characterized by massive unemployment. These are not the only features typical of the latest tendencies on the labour market. We also observe significant changes in the level and structure of employment, the increasing importance of self-employment and a more important role for the private sector in creating new work places. However, not all the events on the labour market may be seen as desirable and profitable. This creates an obligation to monitor the labour market changes constantly and to review the supporting processes counteracting unfavourable tendencies.

* This chapter was originally written as a paper for the Joint ECE/ILO/OECD Work Session on Labour Statistics and Issues of Concern for Transition Countries, Paris, December 1992.

One of the most important problems of the current Polish labour market is undoubtedly the phenomenon of unemployment. It raises the greatest interest and anxiety, and at the same time most controversy. In the early 1990s unemployment has become more than just an economic problem. To a greater and greater extent, it has become the basic social and political issue of the end of this century. There is no doubt that a systematic analysis and evaluation of the changes on the labour market are indispensable from this perspective as well.

New informational needs connected with the necessity of analysing previously unknown phenomena,with more frequent and detailed observation of fundamental events occurring on the labour market and with a new role for statistics as a decision-making tool rendered the former system of collecting information insufficient for a multi-level analysis of the Polish labour market. An urgent need appeared to create a modern system of information on the labour market.

The Central Statistical Office has undertaken attempts to construct, gradually, such a system of information on the labour market; their first result is a Labour Force Survey conducted for the first time in Poland in May 1992.

THE CONCEPT OF THE SURVEY

The Labour Force Survey is to be one of the main sources of an integrated information system on the labour market, which should be available in Poland in the mid 1990s. Thus, it should meet the requirements of a long-term study, becoming part of a future system of labour market research and undertaking problems relevant not only for the present but also for the future. It is also important that the study opens up possibilities of limiting traditional information collecting methods in the form of statistical reports as far as employment is concerned.

Keeping in mind these aims, while preparing the concept of the survey, we made use of the experience of Western countries, which have conducted such surveys for a long time and we took into consideration the requirements of the International Labour Organization. This explanation is important, for many methodological solutions and definitions of basic labour market categories used in the market economy countries are different from those applied so far in Poland. Reaching for the experience of other countries seemed rational because of lack of such experience in conducting this type of survey in our country and because of the necessity to adapt our statistics to international standards.

Looking for inspiration in international solutions does not mean literal application of the survey methodology used in another country. It must

be stressed that methodologies used in different countries for a Labour Force Survey vary significantly, and it was only lately that Eurostat made any attempt to unify them even in the EC countries. Moreover, the particular situation of our country as far as the labour market study is concerned has forced us to use other countries' experience with caution. Consequently, in the concept of the labour force survey, the assumption of keeping unified notions and definitions was made, which secured the possibility of international comparisons, but at the same time the necessity of adapting them to Polish needs and conditions was recognized. Thus, the final concept was formulated, according to which the survey is:
– national,
– representative,
– realized on households, whose members aged 15 or over, are covered,
– panel, i.e. repeated over at least a year on the same sample of households,
– quarterly, i.e. conducted every three months,
– covering current economic activity, which in practice means that the observation concerns the situation in a selected week of a three-month period (the 15th day of the middle month),
– comparable to similar studies in other countries.

   In the labour force survey, features of individuals constitute the object of observation and features of households are considered only in passing. Because of the aim of the survey, information about the individuals' position on the labour market is most important. It allows us to distinguish three categories of population: the employed, the unemployed, and the professionally inactive (not in the labour force). Following our assumptions, we should have the criteria of this classification comparable with the solutions applied in international statistics. In international statistics, work constitutes the basic criterion of population division and it is applied first. This means that the category of the employed is distinguished first, then the category of the unemployed, and finally that of the professionally inactive. This sequence of population classification guarantees that each person belongs to only one category.
   Following the International Labour Organization recommendations, among the employed we shall include:

– persons who, during the week of the survey, earned money working for at least an hour, i.e. were employed or self-employed in agriculture or outside agriculture (services, workshops, shops, companies, etc.),

- persons who, during the week of the survey, temporarily did not work (e.g. because of illness, leave, studies, interruption in the enterprise activity etc.), but formally were employed or self-employed.
- persons who helped in a family farm or family enterprise without pay.

Next, among the unemployed we shall include persons who meet the following three conditions:
- during the reference week, they did not work (according to the criteria mentioned above),
- they actively searched for employment, i.e. they undertook particular action to find a job,
- they were ready to take a job in the week of the survey or the following one.

Persons not included in either of the two categories form a group of the professionally inactive (not in the labour force).

THE SIZE AND METHOD OF SELECTING THE SAMPLE

The representative character of the survey assumes a choice of the examined population that would allow for generalization of the results. The choice of method of sample selection depends, among other things, on the aim of the study, the type of features examined and the level of detail in the generalized preparation of the results of the survey. In many countries, the costs and organization of the survey are very important factors in the criterion of sample selection. All these elements were taken into consideration in preparing a sampling scheme for the labour force survey.

Taking into consideration accessibility of basic information about the general population and the requirements concerning the constructed survey, we decided that the sample would be based on the so-called register of census districts as well as on the lists of apartments found in individual districts. The lists had been prepared on the basis of the population census in 1988 and were updated annually on the basis of reports on building construction. At the same time, the register of districts were also updated. In fact, that was the only possible solution in the case of the Labour Force Survey.

Census districts were accepted as primary sampling units. These are units including at most 1,000, and not fewer than 350 apartments on average. The regions were divided into voivodships, and within them into groups distinguished according to the size of the villages. The number of such groups was different in different voivodships because of their local specificity and ranged from three (a village and two urban areas) to six. In the whole country 194 strata were distinguished. In each such stratum an appropriate number of statistical regions was drawn proportionally to the number of apartments. In this way, 1,238 statistical regions were drawn during the first stage.

In the second sampling stage, apartments for the study were drawn directly. Initially, the number of apartments to be drawn from each region was 15. This number had been agreed upon on the basis of an experimental study, to ensure that all interviews could be conducted by one interviewer during one week in the district. The number then had to be modified in accordance with the probability of the district being chosen for the sample, so that the eventual apartment sample was automatically balanced with the probability of an individual apartment being selected equalling 1/606. In effect, the number of apartments drawn in a district ranged from 10 to 18.

Following the above scheme, 18,437 apartments were drawn in the whole country. In the May Labour Force Survey, 16,940 apartments were covered, which constituted 91.8 per cent of the sample apartments. As far as completeness is concerned, conducting the survey was much more difficult in urban areas (90 per cent of drawn apartments were examined) than in rural areas (the percentage was 95.5 per cent). There were also spatial differences in the completeness of the survey. In highly urban areas, the percentage of examined flats was much lower than in other voivodships. In some voivodships, completeness of the survey reached 99 per cent.

The study held in May covered 18,736 households all over the country, including 11,913 households in towns. In every household all persons aged 15 and more were interviewed, which resulted in 44,968 individual data-files, including 26,658 in towns.

EMPLOYMENT AND UNEMPLOYMENT IN THE LIGHT OF THE LFS

The most comprehensive measure for the evaluation of the participation of human resources in the labour process is the activity rate (labour force participation rate). It defines the proportion of the economically active part of the population to the population in general or to a chosen age category. In this particular case the population aged 15 years and over was examined.

According to the definition used in international statistics, the economically active population (labour force) contains employed and unemployed persons. These two groups together form a category of the labour force. In May 1992, the economically active population constituted over 61 per cent of the population aged 15 and more. The level of economic activity is higher in the male and rural population. The results of this survey cannot be directly compared to the data coming from the population census conducted in 1988 (so far this was the only source of information on economic activity of the population), because different definitions of a working person were used in these studies.

Table 13.1. Level of economic activity of population in Poland, May 1992

Area	Labour force participation rate (activity rate)			Employment participation rate		
	Total	Men	Women	Total	Men	Women
Poland	61.4	69.9	53.7	53.5	61.6	46.1
Urban	59.0	67.4	51.6	50.1	58.1	43.1
Rural	65.6	74.2	57.3	59.3	67.4	51.4

In the LFS, 'working person' was a person who worked for at least 1 hour in the reference week. The definition used in the census (1988) was based on different criteria. Despite the differences it is worth noticing that in May 1992 the labour force participation rate was lower than at the end of 1988 in all categories. An important decrease of economic activity can be noticed in the category of people aged 45 and more, especially among people about to retire. These are the results of a difficult labour market situation – quite a big number of persons took the opportunity of early retirement.

If we want to evaluate the actual participation of the population in the process of labour activity, the rates are not precise enough. A great part of the labour force is unemployed. Table 13.1 contains additional information on employment participation rates. The proportion of working persons to the total number of population aged 15 years and more is 53 per cent (for women living in urban areas, only 43 per cent). It shows how big the unused reserves of labour force are, especially among women in urban areas.

When the labour market situation deteriorates and particularly when mass unemployment appears, it is very common in many countries to work part-time. According to the results of the LFS, 1,722,000 persons are employed part-time in Poland, which constitutes 11.3 per cent of the total working population. Part-time work is more common in the rural (14.6 per cent) than in urban areas (9.1 per cent). Some of the rural population is certainly redundant from the point of view of demand for labour in individual farms, which indicates hidden unemployment (labour hoarding) in the rural area.

In the labour market situation of 1992, the most difficult and alarming problem was unemployment. According to the data available from the local labour offices, the level and dynamics of unemployment were very high. Now, we may verify these data on the basis of the LFS.

Table 13.2. Part-time workers in Poland, May 1992

Area	Part-time workers in thousands	%	% of total number employed
Poland	1,722	100.0	11.3
Urban	817	47.4	9.1
Rural	905	52.6	14.6

Table 13.3. Unemployment in Poland according to the LFS, May 1992

Area	Number of unemployed in thousands	Unemployment rate	
		As % of total labour force	As % of persons of working age
Poland	2,254	12.9	13.4
Urban	1,597	15.1	15.1
Rural	657	9.6	10.6

When we try to compare the results of the survey with registered unemployment we must remember the different methodology and definitions used in the two sources of data. According to the LFS, the number of the unemployed in Poland amounted to 2,254,000 persons. This number is higher by 25,000 than the number of the unemployed registered in the labour office. There is also a difference in the unemployment rate; according to the study it is 12.9 per cent while according to records it is 12.3 per cent. If we take into consideration only the persons of working age (in Poland: 18–60/65), the unemployment rate according to the survey is 13.5 per cent not only because of a greater

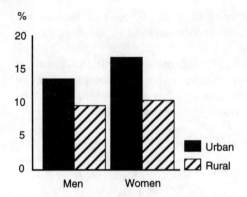

Fig. 13.1 Unemployed rate by sex and place of residence

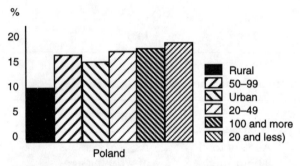

Fig. 13.2 Unemployed rate by place of residence

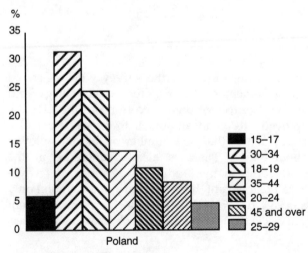

Fig. 13.3 Unemployed rate by age

number of unemployed persons but also because of a smaller number in the labour force. We maintain that the unemployment rate calculated on the basis of the labour force survey is more precise. According to the results of our survey, a much more difficult situation on the labour market occurs in urban areas, where over 15 per cent of labour force is out of work, while in the rural area the unemployment rate amounts to 9.6 per cent. The evaluation of the actual labour market situation can be different in the rural areas, if we take into consideration a comparatively high percentage of part-time workers.

What is the very important in the current labour market situation is the unequal risk of unemployment suffered by different groups of the population. The biggest differentiation is by age and by sex. The LFS shows that women are in a much worse position than men. This is demonstrated by the unemployment rate which is much higher for women than for men. It is also beyond doubt that young persons are in the most difficult situation. In the category of youth aged 18–19, the unemployment rate amounts to 34 per cent, in the age group of 20–24 it is 27 per cent. The threat of unemployment decreases in older groups of the population. In the age group of 45 and over, 7 per cent of the labour force is out of work. In this category the risk of unemployment for men and women is very similar. Young women, however, are much more often unemployed than young men.

Table 13.4. Unemployment rate in Poland by sex and age, May 1992

Age	Total	Men	Women
Total	12.9	11.9	14.1
Up to 24 yrs	26.3	24.4	28.5
25-44 yrs	12.9	11.4	14.7
45 and over	7.4	7.4	7.2
Working age	13.5	12.3	14.9

The results of the LFS show important changes, which have taken place on the Polish labour market during the economic transformation. One of the most important findings of the study is – at the current stage of analysis – the confirmation of a high rate of unemployment, which influenced different groups of people to a different extent.

14

The Labour Force Survey: a means of statistical investigation of the Romanian labour market

I. VANTU*

REFERENCE POINTS IN THE DEVELOPMENT OF A LABOUR MARKET IN THE TRANSITION PERIOD

The emergence and functioning of the evolving labour market in our country is a major, complex, sensitive and long-term process in Romania's transition towards a market economy. The specific nature of the resources circulating in this market clearly differentiate it from the others. It also grants it an important role in providing and maintaining macroeconomic balances, social and political stability.

The reconstruction of the former economic system in Romania depends to a great extent on the reaction of the people. They are affected by the dramatic shift from a command economy, where unknowns and risks were as low as incomes, to a new one approximating to perfect competition. While in the last century the market economy developed quite naturally against a background of favourable circumstances that promoted capitalism as a normal stage in the historical evolution of society, in 1992 unemployment caused by psychological unrest and capital scarcities may lead to unpredictable responses.

Therefore, ensuring employment equilibrium is an issue requiring an impressive number of policy guidelines, not only in the economic, legislative, organizational, educational and training fields, but also in information and statistics as well. Realistic monitoring and forecasting of economic phenomena, with such profound social implications, require

* This chapter was originally written as a paper for the Joint ECE/ILO/OECD Work Session on Labour Statistics and Issues of Concern for Transition Countries, Paris, December 1992.

the sound interpretation of labour force needs and resources in respect of their levels, structures and trends.

Some laws passed in the early 1990s promoted small enterprises, self-employment and family businesses, created the preconditions for extensive privatization, produced land reform, and recognized, among others: free determination of prices and wages, freedom to hire and fire workers, the introduction of collective bargaining, the right to strike, unemployment benefits and training, etc.

As a result of this upheaval in the organization of society, there have been changes in unemployment policy and practice, making room for labour market forces and mechanisms. Thus, graduates are no longer automatically provided with employment, neither are people of working age compulsorily allocated to jobs and forced to quit them at the legal retirement age, staff levels and structures in enterprises are no longer determined by branch ministries, the rights of both employers and employees to decide and to select are recognized, the government has ceased to plan and allocate labour and acts more like a regulator. At the same time, the state has gradually reduced subsidies to its enterprises, which in their turn, in order to keep labour productivity above a certain level and to survive, are induced to shed redundant workers.

In this very dynamic context, the Romanian National Commission for Statistics, lacking experience in meeting the challenge of these changes and suffering from many technical and budgetary limitations, did not use the most efficient methods for collecting information on employment and unemployment, so as to identify what was happening in the labour market in 1989–92, a period crucial for the restructuring process. Unfortunately, we still had to rely on traditional statistical methods. Though reshaped and updated, they were based on quite exhaustive surveys in mainly state-owned enterprises, and on administrative sources. As to carrying out a regular household-based labour force survey (LFS), resource constraints forced its programme to be spaced out over a period of two years (1992–94). A methodological constraint resulted from the timing of the 1992 Population and Housing Census data, which would act both as a benchmark and as a sampling frame.

CONCEPTUAL FRAMEWORK OF THE LABOUR FORCE SURVEY

In order to correctly reflect the evolution of complex, multidimensional phenomena, specific to the labour market, and to clear the confusion of ideas surrounding them, the strategy has been to diversify the concepts and the connected statistics, on one hand, and to keep the definitions under a rigorous control to ensure the stability in time and space of the survey proceedings, on the other hand.

To this end, two main objectives are given an overwhelming importance at the present stage:

- meeting the international recommendations;
- ensuring stability and comparability with other statistical sources.

Most of the European countries were anxious to adapt the ILO and/or SOEC conventions to their former nationally specific ones. This required more or less significant revisions of their statistical systems. Apparently, compared to their situation, our condition, of having to redesign the whole labour force statistical apparatus entirely, places us in a favourable position. We are supposed to take advantage, first, of the unitary system of international standards, which is finished to a great extent and conceived in order to ensure clarity and objectivity. Secondly, we may make use of the practical knowledge of possible errors and ways to avoid them that the foreign experts who have provided us with technical assistance generously shared with us.

In fact, even when treading in somebody's footsteps one may face some unforeseeable obstacles if only because 'translating' the international recommendations, however general, into the national language is not a mere nothing. Moreover, another major impediment to choosing the best solutions seems to be the budgetary factor. Thus, better options may be rejected in favour of some that are less costly, or deadlines may be delayed.

Under the impact of international conventions

Adopting the ILO recommendations primarily means that some approaches and classifications will allow comparisons in time and space, freed from the national administrative regulations. Accurate specifications of all the concepts and definitions required by the survey (see Annex 7) will be the basis of the content and order of questions in the survey questionnaires.

The persons covered by the survey are 14 years and over, which is the minimum age allowing comparisons both with our census and with SOEC data collections. In order to classify them according to their activity status into the three main population categories – employed, unemployed, and non-active – and to allow certain refinements for persons marginally attached to the labour force, the following three principles have been granted special attention:

(i) An extensive investigation of the economic activity, which goes before any other status. Employment during the reference period takes precedence over other activities, regardless of the amount of time spent on it.

(ii) Considering *de facto* situations, it is what the person was actually doing during the specified reference period, no matter what his/her legal status is, that matters. This factual approach, compared to the institutional one, will principally influence the definition of the unemployed group, but also that of the groups on the fringe of the labour market, such as underemployed or discouraged workers. As a consequence, ILO unemployment is defined by a combination of criteria and not by the spontaneous statement of the respondents, or by their legal situation.

(iii) Instantaneity of the situation. A person is to be classified only in compliance with his/her status during the reference week, namely the week preceding the interview. Exception will be made, for pragmatic reasons solely, in the case of the job search period (the preceding month), or the availability period (the following 15 days).

Another main concern, associated not only with conducting this survey, but with the complete reformation of the Romanian statistical system, was the adoption of internationally consistent classifications. Consequently, starting with the 1992 Census, a new occupational classification based on the 1988 International Standard Classification of Occupations (ISCO-88) has been used. Yet another version of the Romanian Occupational Classification, compatible to the EC version of ISCO-88 (ISCO-88 COM), is being prepared. Similarly, good progress was made with the introduction of the National Classification of Economic Activities (CAEN), based both on the International Standard Industry Classification (ISIC Rev. 3) and on the new European Community Classification of Economic Activities (NACE Rev. 1). A new Romanian Classification of Status in Employment based on the International Classification of Status in Employment (ICSE) was adopted as well.

Consistency

In January 1992, amid conditions of political and economic disruption and uncertainty following the revolution, the National Commission for Statistics conducted Romania's first housing and population census since 1977. The targets set were to carry out a 100 per cent enumeration of the population, and to produce final results by the end of 1993. Preliminary results were available in September 1992.

There is a feed-back connection between the planned LFS and the

Population Census, which emphasizes the need to harmonize the definitions, the classifications and the registration methods used.

In the course of 1993, Census results relating to labour force topics (economic activity, occupation, status in employment, level of education, industrial sector, place of work, etc.) will allow a keen scrutiny of the labour market. It is not only *per se* that these results are interesting. They are intended to be used as a standard for the representativeness checks later on, and in the estimation and adjustment procedures.

The Census Post Enumeration Survey, taken in a systematic probability sample of 520 census enumeration areas, served as a basis for the selection of a two-stage master-sample of about 2,500 enumeration areas, or 250,000 households, which will be used to provide a frame for selection of future survey samples. The master-sample was drawn by geographically stratified and cluster probability methods, designed to ensure representativeness, both at the national and at the county levels.

By its method and object, this LFS is expected to act as a microcensus, assuming intercensally the part of a national reference. That is why stability is the cornerstone of the survey. Comparability in time should be eased in order to assemble new and very homogenous series. As is well known, the slightest modification operated between two censuses over concepts, definitions, and implicitly questionnaires, is full of undesirable consequences. Therefore, thorough investigation and a great deal of judgement in selecting the theoretical and technical instruments for the achievement of this survey are necessary prerequisites for its stability until the next population census.

OTHER ISSUES OF CONCERN IN THE PREPARATION FOR THE FIRST LFS

The main constraint, the optimization of the costs/benefits ratio, with the assumption of a minimal numerator, caused a range of decisions to be taken, some of them diverging from the international recommendations or from the actual practice of the industrialized countries.

(a) Periodicity is to be annual. As a result, we shall get a rather specialized survey, providing structural information. However, a continuous one, producing immediate data, would perhaps have been more desirable.

(b) Certain topics, even though of interest, have been avoided, on the assumption that they are sensitive in the present social, political and economic climate, and would suffer from a high non-response or inaccurate response rate. Such questions as those on income, wages, multiple jobholding and on hours actually worked at secondary jobs have temporarily been left out. Nevertheless, it is still possible, as the survey gains ground in future years, that its confidentiality will be proved, and, as users of its results (governmental, commercial, academic) become more active, demanding and sophisticated, that the pressing demand for such information will be met.

(c) Some difficult problems, where we could use the technical support of foreign specialists, given our lack of expertise in the field, are those connected to techniques best suited to achieving good results in the following activities:
  - updating the survey subsample, especially with regards to newly constructed housing units;
  - extending results;
  - estimation of sampling errors;
  - adjustment of survey results (non-responses, coverage, seasonal variations).

(d) Data collection techniques will not be strikingly modern. Due to the substantially lower costs involved, we prefer the traditional paper questionnaires, and interviewers to collect the data by directly interviewing, if possible the same person, every year, namely the reference person, despite all the advantages offered by CATI or CAPI techniques.

(e) Simultaneously meeting two requirements: quality and rapidity in data processing, will be followed by developing an efficient data processing system. Considering the present and future technical equipment, two stages are contemplated:
  (i) decentralized, at local level, using microcomputers for data entry, for preliminary validation checks, for coding (possibly by means of computer-assisted coding systems), for imputations;
  (ii) file transfer on the Bucharest main-frame with a view to centralized processing (final validation checks, aggregate codings, adjustments, weighting, tabulations).

PRECONDITIONS FOR IMPROVED LABOUR FORCE STATISTICS

As it is conceived, the Romanian LFS with its present questionnaires, with its sample design and with its periodicity, shows a range of obvious additional advantages in comparison with the sources formerly used.

(a) Annual provision of reliable statistics on active population, employment and unemployment. According to the national practice up to 1992, complete statistics on the structure of both active population and employment were obtained only on the occasion of population censuses. Unemployment, previously considered as non-existent, was formerly recorded exclusively on the basis of local employment office registrations. Consequently, applying the current national legislation gives significantly different results to those which would have been produced by applying the ILO unemployment definition.

The survey results will thus permit future preparation of a wide range of cross-classifications and tabulations. Distributions of employed and unemployed persons according to different characteristics, the activity and unemployment rate calculated at the national level (total and by age groups, occupation, sex, etc.) are absolutely necessary, both for an *ex post* analysis of the labour market, and in adopting *ex ante* optimum decisions on economic and social issues.

(b) Presenting regular data on other particular groups. Being organized at long time–intervals, the survey allows the use of a large and sophisticated individual questionnaire, by means of which it will be possible to determine and study in detail complementary groups at the borderline between labour force categories (underemployment, lay-offs, discouraged, seasonal and occasional workers), as well as the usually active population, which will be interesting to compare with the Census.

We are especially preoccupied by the choice of criteria delineating visible underemployment as accurately as possible, particularly in the agricultural sector.

(c) Complementary surveys. As the Romanian statistical staff gains experience, and as new requests for additional statistics appear, it is possible that complementary surveys will be added, using the yearly excluded third of the rotational sample. These supplementary surveys would study in depth topics of potential interest (i.e. working conditions, youth activity, women's activity, the situation of the unemployed persons).

(d) Monthly statistics. There is a tendency in all countries to publish the ILO unemployment rate monthly, regarded as a short-term indicator of the labour market. As the LFS is the only source able to provide such information and its frequency is annual, we shall consider developing a methodology to estimate ILO unemployment monthly. An adjustment of the monthly statistics on registered unemployment in accordance with annual survey results will probably be contemplated.

[A pilot Labour Force Survey was successfully conducted in November 1993. *Ed.*]

Annex 7 (Conceptual outline of the planned Romanian Labour Force Survey) is to be found at the end of the volume.

15

The guidelines for the transition of Russian Federation statistics for the study of employment and unemployment through Labour Force Surveys

T. GORBACHEVA*

Economic reform aimed at the development of market relations in the Russian Federation has been accompanied by vital changes in the area of employment.

Until recently the employment structure in the former Soviet Union was fairly homogeneous – practically all working people were employed in the state sector or by collective farms. Other kinds of economic activity were represented only by domestic and handicraft trade and by collective farmers' private production, which accounted for 1 million out of 75 million people employed in the national economy in 1986. Under such conditions the system for the collection of statistical data on employment was based exclusively on information obtained from industrial enterprises, state institutions and organizations on an overall basis.

Collection of data on the number of those employed was carried out every quarter (from the beginning of 1992, monthly). The Balance Sheet of Labour Resources was drawn up annually. The structure of employment by education, sex, age, professional groups, position and other qualitative characteristics was studied on the basis of overall statistical accounting, carried out every 2-5 years. These sources of information, as well as population census data, enabled the labour resources situation to be assessed and covered practically all aspects of employment.

The transition to a multistructural economy has led to the appearance

* This chapter was originally written as a paper for the Joint ECE/ILO/OECD Work Session on Labour Statistics and Issues of Concern for Transition Countries, Paris, December 1992.

of new forms of employment, which lent themselves less to the usual methods of statistical accounting. Thus, starting from 1987, when the Cooperation Law was adopted, the new cooperative sector started to develop in the former Soviet Union. In December 1992 it had 2.1 million members. In the process of the land reform implementation a new social group – farmers – appeared, which grew to 250,000 by the middle of 1992. Other market structures were also developing: commodity and raw materials exchanges, firms, broking offices, commercial banks, etc. The possibility of enterprise 'privatization', available to employees and individual citizens, has enabled further development of the private sector. Some groups of the economically active population are playing a more and more prominent role in the labour market, deriving their income from informal kinds of activity which do not find any reflection in current statistical accounting.

At present the unemployment rate is not fully known either. The number of unemployed is determined only by registration with the Employment Service. In early September 1992, 295,000 were recognized as unemployed by the Federal State Employment Service of the Russian Federation. In fact, the number of unemployed who were seeking a job was much higher, but for various reasons a number of those unemployed remained unregistered. The problems connected with statistical accounting of all kinds of employment will become more and more acute during the process of economic reform.

Under existing conditions the plan for the development of employment statistics in the Russian Federation is based on the application of new methods and on new data sources. At present, work is being carried out on the register of enterprises in all kinds of property. It is based on the integration of accounting and statistical reports. The register will enable the systematization of data on the number of enterprises and employees in various sectors of the economy. This will create the necessary prerequisites for the transition to sampling methods of survey.

The major role in the expansion of employment data will be given to household sample surveys. The first Russian Labour Force Survey was conducted in November 1992. In the process of work on the programme and the instruments of survey, we took into consideration the necessity of further application of its results for supplementation and detailed processing of available statistical data, as well as for calculations on the labour market structure. International experience and the ILO international recommendations on this kind of survey were taken into account in order to ensure comparability of definitions and the computation of the economically active population and the unemployed with other countries.

The survey questionnaire's index system consists of the following sets of questions:

– demographic characteristics (sex, age, marital status, educational level);
– data on those employed;
– data on those unemployed.

The following categories of citizens will be considered as employed:

– those who performed paid work or had a paid occupation for at least several hours a week;
– those temporarily absent because of inability to work, or because of leave, training, halting of production due to a strike or other reasons;
– those self-employed, who performed unpaid work at a family enterprise or farm.

Questions to the employed cover the following subjects:

– kind of enterprise;
– field of economic activity;
– profession and position;
– informal activity;
– casual job;
– employment status
    including:
    hired labour,
    non-hired labour (self-employed, employers, members of producing cooperatives, persons who work free of charge for a family enterprise);
– additional work;
– working hours at principal and additional work;
– reasons and duration of temporary absence from principal work;
– forced underemployment;
– contentment with economic activity;
– search for other or additional work.

The block of questions on the unemployed population enables the distinction to be made between those who are unemployed and those who are economically inactive.

The number of unemployed is formed from the following categories:

– those who do not have a job, are ready to start work and are actively seeking it;

– those who do not have a job, are ready to start work, but who are not seeking one during the period of survey, because it was promised to them after this period;
– students and persons of pension age not employed in economic activity, seeking a job and ready to start it.

Data on the unemployed are classified according to the following indexes:

– duration of unemployment;
– profession or position at the previous job;
– reasons for the loss of job;
– desired character of future work;
– ways of seeking a job;
– registration at the Employment Service.

The economically inactive population consists of:

– students and persons of pension age, who did not have paid work or a profitable occupation during the surveyed week;
– unpaid workers of family enterprises, who were temporarily absent during the surveyed week and who were not seeking another job;
– persons without a job, wishing to find one but not seeking, because they had given up hope of finding a job;
– persons occupied with house-keeping.

In working out the survey programme for the classification of population according to educational level, employed and unemployed – by professions, or occupation – by branches of economic activity, the different national systems of classification have been applied.

It was planned to conduct the survey in all republics, territories and regions of the Russian Federation. The survey would cover about 230,000 families, numbering nearly 700,000 people, which amounts to 0.6 per cent of the total population between 15 and 72 years of age.

The selection was based on the population census data of 1989. Its dimensions are determined with regard for considerable differentiation of the Russian regions in the aspects of employment, as well as the need to obtain representative data at the republican, territorial and regional level.

The sampling procedure is founded on the search for the optimum version on eight variables: number of population (two groups – permanent population, population of 15–72 years of age); sex (two groups); age (eleven groups), number of members in family (seven groups), source of means of subsistence (ten groups), home ownership (three groups). The sample was created using a two-stage methodology.

At the first stage the enumerated sections of the survey were systematically selected on a regulated sampling basis. The sampling, formed at the first stage, was representative according to the structural correlations of the eight variables (fifty-one groups).

At the second stage a household was selected from the chosen enumerated sections. The selection of families was carried out on the basis of the two balanced combinative tables, each one of which represented a typified sampling basis, drawn up by combination of the structural correlations of the indexes above.

A household has been defined as the final element in the selection process, in which persons aged 15–72 will be surveyed.

The selection of households was carried out on the basis of the data bank of the computing centre of the Russian Federation State Committee on Statistics (GOSKOMSTAT). The lists of respondents to be surveyed were submitted to the territorial statistical bodies, which during the preparation period checked the existence of the residences, and if necessary informed the centre of any changes.

The survey will be carried out by specially trained interviewers visiting households and questioning those living there. It is planned to hire these interviewers from among the staff of statistical bodies, teachers and students of higher educational institutions, secondary school teachers and those unemployed with the necessary educational level. During the survey interviewers will be working under the supervision of instructors-controllers from the local statistical bodies.

In order to perfect the practical principles of the survey realization, as well as for the GOSKOMSTAT questionnaire approval, a pilot survey was carried out in the region of Orlov in June 1992. The survey covered 311 persons in 131 households.

As a result of the survey analyses, certain definitions were introduced into the questionnaire and the practical regulations on the full-scale survey in the regions were worked out.

The period from 26 October to 1 November 1992 was defined as the reference week for the full-scale survey.

At the beginning of September 1992 the staff of the republican, territorial and regional statistical bodies were given training on interviewing techniques and the checking and coding of questionnaires.

The questionnaires were processed at the GOSKOMSTAT computing centre.

[In November 1993, GOSKOMSTAT conducted the second round of the Russian LFS. *Ed.*]

Part III

Wage and labour cost

16

International standards of wage statistics: summary

R. RASSOU*

Standardization of wages and other labour statistics has been carried out by the ILO through the organization of International Conferences of Labour Statisticians (ICLS), fourteen of which have been held from 1923 to date. Several of these conferences adopted resolutions covering one aspect or another of wages statistics. The 12th ICLS (1973) adopted a comprehensive resolution concerning an integrated system of wages statistics, which is the recommendation currently in force.

DIFFERENT WAGE MEASURES

The term 'wages statistics' must be interpreted in a very broad sense. It is meant to cover different measures of wages reflecting different concepts: *wage rates* are considered as the price of labour, *earnings* as the income or the means of living of the employees and the family they support, *labour cost* represents the expenditure that employers incur in employing labour whether in the form of direct wages or fringe and supplementary payments, as well as expenditure on recruitment, vocational training, etc. It is also meant to cover *compensation of employees* (which is also a concept of wages as cost to the employer and data on this topic can be compiled as part of labour cost statistics), which is the wage measure used in connection with the national accounts. Another measure suggested has been that of *employee income*, provisionally defined as all receipts or benefits received by a worker by virtue of his current status as an employee, including non-wage receipts such as net

* This chapter was originally written as a paper for the ILO Workshop on Wage Statistics, Prague, November 1991.

current social security receipts from employers or the State. One derivative of employee income is *net disposable income*, which takes into account
the effect of direct taxation.

Table 16.1. Simplified relationship between different wage measures

---

A.   WAGE RATES

Wage rates (including statutory cost of living and other guaranteed
allowances, assuming time rates only) x time worked

= Basic wages for normal time worked

+ premiums, bonuses, allowances, etc.
+ remuneration for time not worked
+ bonuses and gratuities
+ payments in kind
+ housing and rent allowances

= Earnings

B.   EARNINGS

+ severance and termination pay
+ net current social security benefits from employers or the State

= Employee's income

C.   EMPLOYEE'S INCOME

– net current social security benefits from the State
+ employers' contributions to social security, pensions and related
schemes

= Compensation of employee

D.   COMPENSATION OF EMPLOYEE

+ cost of vocational training
+ cost of welfare services
+ other labour costs
+ taxes regarded as labour cost to the employer

= Labour cost

E.   LABOUR COST

TIME WORKED

A major variable relating to wages is time worked. The statistical concept of time worked includes three categories:

(i) normal hours of work, in excess of which any time worked is usually remunerated at overtime rates;

(ii) hours actually worked, which include overtime and other time spent at the workplace but exclude annual leave, paid public holidays, paid sick leave, meal breaks and time spent on travel from home to the workplace and vice versa;

(iii) hours paid for, which will include time for which wages are paid even for periods when no work is performed, such as paid annual leave, paid public holidays, paid sick leave etc.

SOURCES OF WAGES STATISTICS

Establishment surveys: surveys of employment, hours of work and earnings, occupational wage surveys, wage structure and distribution surveys, labour cost surveys, industrial censuses and surveys, agricultural censuses and surveys of holdings.

Household surveys: labour force sample surveys, household income and expenditure surveys.

Administrative sources: wage boards, arbitration tribunals, statutory orders, collective agreements, trade-union sources, social security returns, income tax returns.

FRAMEWORK FOR AN INTEGRATED SYSTEM OF BASIC WAGES STATISTICS

A wages statistics programme comprises:

(i) a current programme involving the regular compilation of essential information at short intervals in order to provide indicators of changes in the levels and trends of wages and hours of work for short-term needs;

(ii) an *ad hoc* programme for obtaining detailed and in-depth data for use in structural and causal analysis of the level and pattern of wages for long-term needs.

Within this programme, the agricultural sector is treated separately. The agricultural sector presents different and much more complex problems for statistics of wages and hours of work than does the non-agricultural sector.

The current statistics programme covers either: (i) statistics of average earnings and hours of work, or (ii) statistics of time rates of wages and normal hours of work, or both, depending on national needs and circumstances.

The occasional wages statistics programme comprises: (i) statistics of labour cost to provide reliable measures of the level, composition and evolution of the cost of labour to the employer; (ii) statistics of wage structure and distribution to highlight differences that exist from one region to another, between urban and rural areas, manual and non-manual workers, industries, occupations, establishments of different sizes, workers' personal characteristics such as sex, age, education, level of skill, length of service and type of employment.

In developing programmes of wages statistics, consideration has to be given to the requirements of a basic programme of labour statistics as defined by the ILO's Labour Statistics Convention, 1985 (No. 160) and Labour Statistics Recommendation, 1985 (No. 170).

17

Estabishment surveys: a review of national practices

M-T. DUPRÉ*

Statistical data collection by means of surveys is the most favoured instrument of statisticians who use their results to analyse and understand the economic and social aspects of a country, and their changes over time. They may concern individuals or households (labour force sample surveys, household surveys, income and expenditure surveys, etc.) or establishments or enterprises (industrial and commercial censuses and surveys, agricultural surveys, etc.). They constitute one of the basic sources of economic and social information.

This chapter deals only with surveys of establishments or enterprises. In some countries, the primary objective of these surveys is to provide data on the characteristics of establishments (such as output, value added, stocks, inventories, assets, etc.) and to estimate the gross and net output of industry. Their results are used for the study of the structure of the industry and the analysis of the various factors influencing its growth in the country. They may also provide for the collection of data on employment and conditions of work of employees (wages, hours of work, employee benefits, compensation of employees, etc.). In such cases, labour statistics are thus obtained as a by-product of industrial statistics. This is particularly the case in developing countries, where this type of survey often is the only source of information on the labour force.

In other countries, particularly in industrialized countries, statistical

---

* This chapter was originally written as a paper for the Joint ILO/EUROSTAT/StBA Seminar on the Use of Sampling Methods and Setting up of an Earning Statistics Survey System in Countries in Transition to a Market Economy, Berlin, February 1993.

inquiries are carried out which are especially designed for the purposes of compiling statistics of employment, earnings and hours of work, or statistics of labour cost, on a current and regular basis. They thus provide short-term indicators of economic activity and conditions of work.

Detailed information can be obtained from establishments surveyed on a complete enumeration basis. But this technique is a time-consuming and expensive operation. Thus, during the last decades, the use of sampling in the collection of economic and social data has been considerably developed throughout the world. Sample survey techniques provide an efficient means of obtaining monthly or quarterly information on employment, wages and hours of work from establishments.

This chapter is based on the preliminary results of an inquiry made in 1991/1992 by the ILO Bureau of Statistics, on the characteristics of establishment surveys which provide data on labour statistics, i.e. employment and conditions of work of employees (wages and salaries, hours of work, employee benefits, etc.). It relates to the replies received from some sixty-seven developed and developing countries, covering about a hundred establishment surveys grouped, where relevant, and distributed as shown in Table 17.1.

Table 17.1: Surveys covered by the ILO inquiry in 1991/92

	Number of countries	Number of surveys	Number of sample surveys
Africa	17	20	6
Americas	13	14	14
Asia/Oceania	19	34	23
Europe	18	29	22
Total	67	97	65

It should be noted that the coverage of this inquiry was not exhaustive. Some countries which did carry out establishment surveys had not replied; others provided us with rather sketchy replies which did not permit a thorough analysis of the survey methods. In addition, the present analysis does not describe the details of some specific occupational wage surveys (e.g. in Portugal), nor does it cover the methodology of labour cost surveys (such as those conducted in Australia, New Zealand, the European Community, etc.).

GENERAL CHARACTERISTICS OF THE SURVEYS

The scope and coverage of establishments surveys, as well as the methods used to conduct them, vary considerably from one country to another. It is therefore difficult to generalize with regard to national practices. Nevertheless, an attempt is made below to describe briefly the most important features of these surveys, with particular emphasis on the establishment frame and the use of sampling methods and estimation procedures.

Coverage

In most countries, establishment surveys cover the major divisions of economic activity. Agriculture is usually excluded, with the exception of some countries where it plays an important role in the national economy (this is particularly the case in some African and Asian countries). When agriculture is covered, information is usually collected from agricultural establishments duly registered in the formal sector (such as agricultural holdings, plantations, co-operatives, etc.).

Other most common exclusions are public administration and defence, and in all cases, household services. In developing countries, establishment surveys cover mainly the so-called modern or formal sector of the economy.

Geographical coverage is usually nation-wide, except in a few countries in Africa and Latin America where the surveys are limited to certain urban areas (e.g. Sudan, Chad, Honduras).

As regards the persons covered by the surveys, a distinction can be made between two types of surveys. Some surveys (about a third) are expected to provide a detailed picture of employment in the formal sector of the country (which is usually the case in developing countries). Therefore, they cover all persons engaged in the surveyed establishments, including working proprietors or partners. However, data on earnings and hours of work are normally collected for employees only. Other surveys are more specific and aim at analysing the level and changes in employment, wages and hours of work, of employees only. Their coverage is therefore restricted to this category of workers. Self-employed workers, domestic services and unpaid family workers are always excluded.

Enumeration unit

In most surveys, the source of the data, i.e. the unit of enumeration or investigation, is the *establishment* (i.e. an autonomous part of an enterprise engaged in one, or predominantly one, kind of activity at a single location, e.g. an individual farm, mine, factory, workshop, store or office). In a few cases, it is the *enterprise* (e.g. in Algeria, Benin, Japan, the Republic of Korea, Australia, Italy, Luxembourg) or the *local unit* (i.e. in New Zealand), or a combination of both (i.e. the establishment in the industrial sector and the enterprise in services, as is the case in several European Union countries). However, enterprises or firms may raise certain difficulties, in that they may operate two or more establishments engaged in distinct activities located at different sites. On the other hand, local units (or departments within an establishment) may not be in a position to give independent data in respect of significant labour topics. Thus, for most surveys, the establishment is adopted as the appropriate sampling and enumeration unit.

Payrolls form the source of information in these establishment surveys. Data on employment, earnings and hours of work are usually collected with regard to the total number of employees, or to the number of employees by category (wage earners, salaried employees, apprentices, etc.).

Only a few countries or areas collect data for individual employees in current and repetitive surveys. In such surveys, which are usually surveys providing detailed occupational employment and/or wages, the ultimate unit of observation is either the individual employee (as in the surveys conducted in Cyprus, Peru, the United Kingdom or Australia), or the occupation itself – in which case information is collected on the total number of employees engaged in the occupation and their characteristics (as in the occupational wage surveys conducted in the United States, Hong Kong, India).

Use of a threshold

In 53 per cent of the surveys, a lower threshold is set on the size of establishments to be covered. This threshold is usually expressed in terms of a specified number of employees – and establishments which employ fewer than that specific number of persons are omitted from the surveys. The minimum size of employment varies between 5 and 30 employees, depending on the country. In a few countries, this threshold is expressed in terms of industrial production and importance of the enterprise with regard to the national economy.

Periodicity

Regular surveys of employment, earnings and hours of work are conducted with various periodicities: approximately one-third are conducted on a quarterly basis, and another third on a yearly basis, while one-sixth only are carried out monthly. Other periodicities are bimonthly, half-yearly or, in very few cases, intervals exceeding a year.

Data collection method

In the great majority of cases (77 per cent of the surveys), data are collected by questionnaires mailed to the establishment/enterprise, and usually followed up by telephone or personal interview, either to remind non-respondents to return the questionnaire, or to obtain complementary information or clarifications from the respondents, or both.

Use of sampling

In two-thirds of the surveys analysed here, data are collected from a sample of establishments. The remaining surveys are based on a complete enumeration of establishments to be covered in the surveyed industries.

REGISTER OF ESTABLISHMENTS

All countries use a list of establishments which serves as a sample frame. Such lists of establishments are usually maintained by the National Statistical Office, on the basis of various sources, registers and directories kept by ministries or associations. In most cases, a combination of various sources is used to create and update the list of establishments. A distinction can be made between two types of sources: administrative records and directories, on the one hand, and official statistical sources, on the other hand.

The most important or frequent administrative sources used are listed below:

- business directories kept by the Ministries of Trade, Commerce, Industry, Agriculture, etc.;
- trading and transport licences;
- records kept by various government departments, such as the housing authorities, urban, rural and regional councils, water supply departments, construction departments, etc.;
- registers kept by the Chambers of Commerce, Trade, Industry, etc.;
- records kept by employers' and workers' associations;
- social security records;
- records from tax authorities;

and also,

- telephone directories, and
- newspaper advertisements.

Official statistical sources are also used both as the original source, and as a means of updating the statistical register of establishment. These are:

- the results of industrial, commercial or agricultural censuses;
- information collected from other economic surveys;
- field work and local enumeration (especially when the objective is to cover small establishments);
- postal enumeration using registration questionnaires (used to obtain complementary information on establishments recorded from administrative sources);

Updating of the statistical register takes place at least once a year and, in a growing number of countries, at more frequent intervals (for instance, quarterly or on a continuous basis), by register specialists. Regular and frequent updating is commonly found in countries where surveys are conducted at monthly or quarterly intervals. It is of particular relevance in countries and industries where a large number of small establishments represent an important proportion of the labour force or output, and where 'births' and 'deaths' of establishments, or changes in the employment levels, are frequent.

Depending on the source of information used, the register may cover all establishments, including those without paid employees (establishments owned or operated by self-employed persons, unincorporated companies, etc.), or include only establishments with paid employees, which is the case in the great majority of countries surveyed here.

SAMPLING METHODS

Survey design

As mentioned above, two-thirds of the surveys on which information was received are sample surveys. Not all sample surveys follow the same design. The choice of the sample design depends on many factors which include the objectives of the survey, the method of data collection, the availability of a sampling frame, etc., as well as institutional features such as the legal authority to collect data, the willingness of the respondents to provide information, etc. In addition, the resources available for the survey play an important role in the survey design.

Stratified sampling is used in the majority of sample surveys, since it gives better results than the simple random method. Indeed, the variance of changes in employment or that of average earnings is always smaller within a stratum than within the entire group of establishments to be surveyed in an industry group.

The sample design favoured by most countries is a *one-stage stratified sample*, whereby the list of establishments is divided into classes whose members are as homogeneous as possible, and each class (or stratum) is sampled separately. Various criteria are used for stratification, the most frequent of which are *economic activity* and *employment size*. Geographical location (region, state, etc.) is also frequently used, especially in large countries (India, the United States, Canada, etc.) and when one of the objectives of the survey is to obtain detailed information at the regional level. These three criteria are combined in twenty-two surveys.

Multi-stage sampling is generally used in occupational wage surveys, where the first-stage sampling unit is the establishment, and the second-stage sampling units are the employees to be included in the survey, who are selected systematically from payrolls.

Another characteristic of most sample surveys is the use of a *cut-off point*, i.e. the design provides for a complete enumeration of all large establishments (usually those with 100, 200 or 500 or more persons employed), combined with a sample of establishments below this size limit, stratified by size-groups. In most surveys using this method known as 'cut-off sampling', the cut-off point is the same for all the industries surveyed; in very few others (e.g. in Greece), it differs from industry to industry, depending on the concentration of establishments and the proportion of employment in these establishments.

Stratified cut-off sampling requires that for each industry, establishments be classified up to the 3 or 4-digit level and arranged in ascending order of number of employees. In countries where small establishments account for the major part of the employment in the industry, there are usually many classes with small ranges for the lower size-groups, and few classes with larger ranges for the upper size-groups (e.g. 5–9, 10–19, 20-49, 50-99 and 100 and above). The sample is then drawn by simple random technique, systematic sampling with a random start, or, more commonly, with probability proportional to size of strata (PPS).

Purposive sampling is adopted in very few cases (in Mexico and Switzerland, for instance).

In a few surveys (sixteen), a *rotation pattern* is applied, whereby part of the sample changes from one survey round to the next. When rotation is applied, the methods used differ according to the country or area. In the Canadian survey of employment, payrolls and hours, for instance, one-twelfth of the sample is rotated each month, while in Hong Kong, the sample is composed of eight replicates, four of which form part of each half-yearly survey round and three replicates overlap for two rounds; in Japan, two-thirds of the sampling units remain in the sample for two consecutive rounds, and the sample is completely renewed after eighteen months. In Spain and in Sweden, one-fifth of the sample rotates out every year, but in the United Kingdom there is a 75 per cent overlap of sampling units (employees) each year. Rotation may be applied to the whole sample, or only to the strata including the smaller establishments. Ecuador is an exceptional case where the rotation pattern is applied to the stratum comprising large establishments.

After selection of the sampling and stratification schemes, the next step is to decide on the *sample size and allocation*.

The determination of the sample size depends upon cost and accuracy considerations and on the sampling method to be used. In practice, the main determinant is the budget constraint and the objective is to develop a sampling design that will provide results of maximum accuracy for the funds available.

In theory, where probability sampling is used, the overall sampling fraction may be low. However, when the objective of the survey is to measure changes over time, larger sampling fractions are generally preferred. In practice, the sampling fraction varies widely between countries and surveys. Generally speaking, the overall sampling fraction is around 25 to 30 per cent of the universe. Notable exceptions are the United States, where the overall sampling fraction of the CES survey represents about 4.4 per cent of all establishments and the United Kingdom, where a 1 per cent sample of employees is selected.

In most cases, the sampling fraction varies with the stratum, i.e. with the size of establishments. Another common practice is to adopt a sampling rate which is in proportion to total employment in the stratum, or to the number of establishments in the size group. A few surveys are designed with a view to ensuring a constant coefficient of variation for each industry. In Canada, for instance, the total sample size is governed by the objective of a 3.0 per cent coefficient of variation for the estimate of employment at the province by industry division level. Hong Kong applies the method of optimum allocation, whereby a coefficient of variation of at most 2.0 per cent for employment statistics is set as the criterion for selected four-digit industry groups. In the United States, a specific form of optimum allocation, called allocation proportional to employment, is applied: i.e. the optimum number of establishments to be included in each industry/size stratum is determined by the ratio of the employment in each cell to the total employment in the industry.

Non-response is one of the problems to be dealt with when ensuring accuracy of sample survey results. Total non-response may be due to a variety of reasons: establishments which have gone out of business, changes of address, refusal to respond to the questionnaire, etc. Generally, every effort is made to follow-up on non-responding establishments, through reminders, telephone calls or personal visits. Where an establishment totally fails to respond to the survey, various techniques are applied:

(a) Over-sampling and substitution: over-sampling consists of the selection of additional establishments which may be substituted for those which fail to reply. Thus, the non-responding unit is replaced by another unit with similar known characteristics within the same stratum (i.e. economic activity, region, size, etc.). In some surveys, the non-responding unit is replaced immediately during the survey round, while in others the substitution is made at the next survey round.

(b) Imputation: if the non-responding unit has already been covered by previous survey rounds, the missing data may be estimated, either on the basis of the previous survey's results, assuming that such characteristics as employment, hours of work, etc. have not changed, or on the basis of the ratio of changes observed in similar responding units between the present survey round and the previous one.

Other methods are sometimes used, such as obtaining the missing information on non-responding units from other sources (e.g. as in the Bahamas and Canada).

Adjustments for non-response may also be made at the time of computation of estimates, by applying an adjustment factor (as in the Bahamas or in Germany, for instance).

Sampling error and precision of estimates

The calculation of sampling errors should be a common feature of sample surveys. However, in many cases, especially in African countries, sampling errors are simply not computed, either because the implementation of probability sampling methods was unsatisfactory, or for lack of resources.

In several surveys where sampling errors are computed, the standard error of estimates varies between 1 and around 5 per cent (e.g in South Africa (6 per cent), Nicaragua (4 per cent), Israel (from 0.1 to 0.4 per cent), Spain (around 5 per cent), the Republic of Korea (2 per cent for earnings), New Zealand (0.6 per cent for employment and 0.3 per cent for weekly and hourly earnings) and the United Kingdom (0.2 per cent for mean earnings).

In some countries, the sampling method is designed to keep the sampling errors within a fixed magnitude. For instance, in India, the sample design stipulates that the estimates should not differ from the true values by more than 5 per cent with 95 per cent probability; in Japan, the sampling method provides for the sampling error for 'contractual cash earnings' to be limited to 2 to 3 per cent for the national survey, while it can reach 7 to 10 per cent in the prefectural survey.

When the cut-off method is applied, the 'standard error' cannot be calculated as such. Some countries (e.g. Australia, the Philippines, Finland, the United Kingdom) compute the sampling variance of estimates. Canada uses the standard error of the survey estimates (or the coefficient of variation, when expressed as a percentage of the survey estimates) as a proxy to sampling error. The method used by the United States Bureau of Labor Statistics differs in that benchmark adjustments are made annually and the magnitude of the benchmark revision, which averages 0.2 per cent for total employment estimates, constitutes an indication of the standard error. Benchmark adjustments take account of sampling and response errors, as well as of changes in the industrial classification of individual establishments and other procedural processes. The method used to measure the reliability of the employment estimates is the 'root-mean-square error', i.e. the standard deviation adjusted for the bias in estimates.

ESTIMATION PROCEDURES

The computation of totals and averages, like the estimation of sampling errors, follows the sample design used for the survey. In all surveys where stratification is adopted, totals and averages are first calculated for each stratum and then combined to obtain the totals and averages for the industry as a whole. Two methods are most commonly used to gross up the survey results to national estimates. The first one is the use of appropriate weights, usually the inverse of the sampling fraction, in terms of number of employees, or number of establishments (such as in Japan, the Republic of Korea, the Philippines, New Zealand, Belgium, Spain, France, Ireland, Germany, etc.) or both (as in Thailand or the Netherlands).

The second method is the 'link relative' method, whereby the survey results are grossed up using the ratio of the previous round's estimates to the current round. This method is used for instance in Jamaica, Hong Kong, Israel, Japan, etc.

In some countries (in particular the Philippines, France, Ireland and the United States), adjustments are made to the estimates of employment by means of benchmark data on total employment obtained from other sources. However, benchmark adjustments are not made in respect of the estimates of earnings and hours of work.

18

Wage-fixing policy: consequences of wage data gathering

F. EYRAUD*

In this chapter, certain basic aspects of wage-fixing policies (whether implemented by governments, unions or employers) are presented and some conclusions reached on the type of wage statistics needed to help elaborate these policies. As such, the basic concern will be wage-fixing policies and not what seems feasible from a statistical point of view. The statistical needs are expressed in economic and social terms and it is left to statisticians to decide on what is possible and at what cost. It should be noted that the term 'wage' here refers to the remuneration of both manual and non-manual workers.

Any wage-fixing policy follows three main basic objectives: macroeconomic stability, efficient allocation of manpower and efficiency of production.

The system of wage determination is one of the determinants of a country's macroeconomic stability. The level of wages plays an essential role in maintaining the main macroeconomic equilibria: a low level of inflation (wages can combine with prices to feed an inflationary spiral); balanced growth (in which supply and demand increase at the same rate); and the equilibrium on the balance of payments (a consequence in particular of the two preceding equilibria).

The way in which wages are determined will have an influence on a country's ability to achieve a desirable allocation of manpower among the various sectors, occupations and regions of the economy. Relative

* This chapter was originally published as an article in the ILO *Bulletin of Labour Statistics*, No. 2 (1992), based on a paper presented to the ILO Workshop on Wages Statistics, Prague, November 1991.

wage levels will, along with other factors, bring about a movement of wage-earners from one enterprise (industry or region) where there is a surplus of manpower to another where manpower is in short supply. Similarly, occupational wage differential is one of the factors which induces occupational mobility. This sort of redistribution of manpower allows an overall improvement in labour productivity.

There is another category of issues regarding wage structure which must be analysed in more detail, namely low wage differentials between men and women. These are more policy-oriented as they are generally taken into account by specific governmental policies or collective bargaining devices. The ILO is particularly sensitive to these issues as they
relate to three of its major Conventions: Conventions Nos. 26 and 131 regarding minimum wage fixing and Convention No. 100 on equal pay.

Up to now, the objectives of wage policy have been examined at the countrywide level, but wage determination obviously plays an essential role in increasing efficiency of production within each individual enterprise. While wages do constitute a cost for an enterprise, that cost can be largely compensated for by the workers' contributions to production. A sound wage-fixing system could make employees take part more effectively in developing their company's production.

These various objectives, which will be dealt with in the following four sections, are certainly not easy to achieve. They may, moreover, enter into contradiction with one another. Thus, an attempt to bring about a better allocation of manpower, which would require raising certain wages, may interfere with the achieving of macroeconomic equilibrium. However, the stakes are so high that efforts must be made to overcome these difficulties rather than to avoid them, which is why all of the partners must be involved in the search for solutions. This stresses the importance of collective bargaining.

In every country in the world wages have always been a basic issue. There is one essential reason for this: wages are at the same time the main source of income for wage-earners and a major production cost for the enterprise. Naturally, these two inextricably connected features of wages can come into conflict. Since a worker and his family depend almost entirely on his wages to meet their basic needs for food, shelter and education, the worker will be especially concerned with maintaining (or increasing) his purchasing power. On the other hand, an employer will judge any growth in wages in terms of how it affects his enterprise's finances and position *vis-à-vis* its competitors. The concerns of wage-earners and of employers over wages are thus at variance, if not in opposition.

Therefore, the question of wages in which both government and social partners have legitimate and fundamental interests to defend is a highly sensitive one with a significant potential for conflict. The question of wages should thus be dealt with in such a way as to arrive at a some degree of consensus. Such consensus can be reached only through discussion and mutual agreement between the social partners concerned about any important decision regarding wage determination. It is apparent that the most effective method for this purpose is collective bargaining, which allows each party to express its own concerns and to see them in the context of the counterbalancing arguments of the other parties, thereby allowing each party to work out its position as knowledgeably as possible. As all the partners are involved in the final decision, they will be responsible for its implementation, thereby providing for a some degree of consensus. This question will be discussed in the penultimate section.

WAGE LEVEL AND ECONOMIC GROWTH

Where macroeconomic stability is concerned, there is no absolutely ideal wage level and development path that will ensure smooth economic growth.

If the level of wages is too low, then – in addition to a lack of equity due to the uneven distribution of national income – negative economic effects may be felt. When wages are too low, stimulation of the demand for local goods may, as a result, be insufficient, preventing the local economy from developing fully its potential. More generally, any wage determination system which fails to ensure some stability in the living standards of workers and their families runs the risk of eroding confidence in a money economy – the basis of economic development. If it is temporarily impossible to meet this condition on account of an unfavourable economic situation, the consequent sacrifices should be shared out equitably among the various segments of society. At a microlevel, wages that are too low will not motivate employees to give the best of themselves in their work.

On the other hand, if the overall level of wages is too high, it may contribute to a deterioration in the balance of payments as well as a fall in purchasing power by entering into a wage/price spiral. At the plant level, a general wage level that is too high may induce enterprises to limit their hiring, thus increasing unemployment. At the same time, a rise in labour costs reduces profits – and thus investment financing – by a corresponding amount.

The State has obviously a major role to play in striking a balance between these two potential tendencies of any wage-fixing mechanism. It is, however, absolutely fundamental that the objectives sought be precisely defined, so that there is no confusion between means and ends. Moreover, care must be taken not to set overambitious objectives or objectives that require greater means than are available. This is particularly so with restrictive income policies, where experience has shown that this manner of dealing with matters never solves the underlying problems. Blocking wages and prices has favoured a worsening of inequalities through the development of a parallel economy, and is usually followed by an explosion in wages and prices.

This pleads for good indicators of the average general wage level including non-wage labour costs. The indicators should be connected with other economic indicators including productivity trends and other variables which may have an effect on the general price level. Besides, the competitiveness of a country in an open economy depends to a large extent on what is going on in competing countries. From this point of view, any statistical data systems must endeavour to use concepts, definitions and a framework which are as comparable as possible to those in use in other countries.

WAGE STRUCTURE AND LABOUR MOBILITY

Wage structures indicate the wage differentials among workers according to their particular occupational situation: the kind of work they do, the sector, the region, the enterprise they work in, etc. Any action taken in this area should be aimed at keeping wage differentials within a framework that is considered legitimate by those concerned. Wage differentials will thus serve as a reward for the particular 'qualities' of individuals or groups or as compensation for the nature of the work they do. Relevant factors include differences in level of training and in working conditions, and everything else that either differentiates between workers' contributions to productive efficiency or else compensates certain workers for the negative particularities of their job. Used in this way, wage structures play a fundamental role, not only in bringing about a good social environment when they are perceived as fair, but also in increasing the efficiency of the economy in general. The 'compensatory' role of wage differentials should, in particular, permit the movement of workers from those regions, industries or occupations where there is abundant manpower to others where there is a manpower shortage because the jobs offered there are more difficult in terms of the qualifications required or as regards working conditions.

These considerations show that wage differentials cannot be measured according to a single variable. Employment composition explains to a large extent differences in average wage among sectors, as some require a more highly skilled labour force. Similarly, occupation, size of establishment, age and seniority affect the wage structure and their impact could vary according to sectors and, in a comparative perspective, according to countries. From this point of view, three main disaggregations are worth considering.

The geographical dimension is still an important area in spite of the fact that in several countries regional differentials tend to decrease due, in particular, to the development of wage collective bargaining at the national level, but it remains a variable which should not be neglected.

Of greater importance is the sectoral variable. To be fully relevant, it should cover more than the traditional medium- and large-sized industrial sector; small firms with less than ten employees should be included in one way or another, as they may well be a dynamic and expanding category in many economies. This applies to the service sector which, incidentally, includes a large proportion of small enterprises, and should be covered more fully than is generally the case in wage surveys.

Special consideration should also be given to the public sector. Here the State plays a similar role to that of any business concern. It needs to ensure that its 'products' provide good value for money, and therefore has obviously to control production costs, particularly wage costs. The public sector is often of central importance in the economy, for at least two reasons. Firstly because it sometimes employs a major part of the national wage-earning population; in this case, it has an essential role to play in the smooth development of a money economy. The second reason is that, even when the proportion of the working population employed by the public sector is relatively smaller, public sector wages may act as a reference point for the private sector. Here, there are two possibilities. Wages might be higher in the public sector,in which case private sector wages could try to close the gap. Alternatively, wages might be lower in the public sector, in which case there is a danger of the best public employees being drained off to private business. In either case, wage policy in the public sector is an essential element in the course taken by wages throughout the economy. For this reason, pay determination in the public sector follows quite a different pattern from that of the private sector. Besides, in many countries wage claims in the former sector have seriously challenged anti-inflation policies.

As regards occupational wage differentials, it is well known that this dimension is one of the main factors differentiating wages among employees. Information on this matter is of crucial importance for manpower planning as well as for determining a training policy, as greater occupational pay differential is supposed to induce greater investment in education and training which in turn should improve labour efficiency. A valid occupational classification is thus necessary for data-gathering purposes.

Therefore, some of the main disaggregations which would help to monitor the efficiency of labour allocation in relation to wage differentials are quantitative information on wage rates and earnings relating to the individual employee with reference to characteristics such as sex, age, education, level of skill, length of service, nature of employment and occupation as well as certain characteristics of the establishment in which he or she is employed.

WAGE STRUCTURE AND AN EQUITABLE WAGE

The concept of an equitable wage which is used here refers to one of the major objectives that any wage-fixing policy should pursue, namely equity in wage determination. The concept of equity is at the heart of any successful wage policy. Its pursuit will help to establish a balance among the diverse and often contradictory demands made of wage determination. Several features of the concept of equity in wages can be listed. The most important is a better distribution of income – one that will permit the reduction of inequalities, according to the principle of equal pay for equal work. (This principle should be applied with due regard to differences in contribution made to production, and the method of assessing those differences should be made clear.) The improved distribution of income should also attempt to raise the lowest wages.

The subject of a major ILO Convention, equal pay for work of equal value as regards men/women pay differentials, is of particular concern to most countries. An effective implementation of this policy requires statistical instruments which allow an assessment of the effectiveness of measures to reduce sex discrimination. For the comparison to be relevant, pay differentials for work of equal value must be taken; cross-tabulation breakdowns by sex and occupation and/or skill levels could be used as a proxy for work of equal value.

Another basic political issue concerns the way of assessing the level of statutory or agreed minimum wages relative to low wages, also the subject of important ILO Conventions.

The primary purpose of setting a minimum wage – a level below which it is prohibited to pay employees – is to ensure that wage-earners enjoy some basic protection, by preventing competition among enterprises from operating to the workers' detriment. While the principle of a minimum wage is simple, applying it requires that a number of questions be settled. The first of these is the choice of category of workers to be covered. Should the minimum wage apply to all workers or only to those in industries where wages are lowest and labour least well protected? The advantage of extending it as widely as possible is that it will then cover employees of small businesses, where protection is generally weak, whatever the sector of activity. The advantage of a sector-by-sector system is that the decentralization of decision-making makes it easier to reach tripartite decisions on setting minimum wages.

Another point to be settled is the criteria which should be used to establish the level of the minimum wage. Two considerations should be taken into account: satisfying the basic needs of individuals and their families, and the enterprise's ability to pay. A difficult balance needs to be found between these two sometimes contradictory factors. A third point to be considered concerns the procedures for setting and adjusting the minimum wage. Should automatic procedures be set up based on cost-of-living indicators or on growth indicators, or should less highly structured procedures be used? With what frequency should adjustments be made? Here again it is a question of striking a balance between keeping the lowest wages from falling and setting a pace for wage adjustments that will be compatible with the needs of production. Finally, the problem of application and enforcement needs to be pointed out. There can be increasing injustice between workers in sectors (urban zones, large enterprises) where authorities really check on the application of the minimum wage and zones (the informal sector in general) where such verification is practically non-existent.

While the purpose of minimum wages is to provide support for the lowest-paid wage-earners, the minimum wage is often considered as the bottom of the pay scale. A possible danger of this is that an increase in minimum wages will be carried over into the pay scale as a whole, thus leading to an overall increase in wage costs. For that reason, in certain countries negotiations are currently under way in some areas of the economy to devise a guaranteed annual remuneration, meant to disconnect support for wage-earners at the bottom of the scale from overall wage increases. An advantage of such a system is that it separates the protection of low-income wage-earners from the traditional practice of paying wages for a specific period of time.

When the minimum wage is paid on the same basis and with the same frequency as the employee's actual wage (daily, weekly, or monthly), it is often taken as a basic standard. In that case, if the minimum wage goes up, there is a danger that even employees who are earning more than the minimum wage will expect their wages to be increased. On the other hand, if the minimum wage is computed 'retrospectively' on an annual basis, there is no immediate comparison possible to wages in general. This procedure entails calculating the year's actual wages, comparing them to the minimum annual wage, and if the actual total wages for the year are the lower figure, making a payment for the difference. This way of disconnecting the usual frequency of wage payments from payment of the minimum wage has the advantage of making clearer to employees the distinction between wage increases and safeguarding the interests of low-paid wage-earners.

The implementation of any of these instruments supposes that reasonably accurate measures of low wages are available, which could pose certain difficulties. It is necessary to identify whether low wages are a permanent state for particular categories of employees or starting rates for new entrants in the firm. In this case, some kind of connection with age or seniority should be available. As small firms often offer low remuneration, this variable should be included in the wage surveys. Finally, atypical jobs frequently tend to be lowly paid, and are notably difficult to identify in wage surveys. These are some of the considerations which should be kept in mind in the elaboration of any wage statistics system.

WAGE SYSTEMS AND EFFICIENCY OF PRODUCTION

What has just been said about wage structures at the level of the overall economy also holds true, of course, at the level of the individual enterprise, since the individual enterprise has to classify its jobs hierarchically, possibly making use of job evaluation methods. It is at this level that a third dimension of wages comes specifically into play – pay systems.

If, as seen earlier, the level of wages is important, the way in which this level is arrived at is just as basic and as complex. In dealing with this problem an enterprise has to meet a triple objective: promoting high productivity, maintaining equity and controlling labour costs. The enterprise has available to it a wide range of methods of remuneration. Those methods can, moreover, be combined according to the objectives that the enterprise has set. Two aspects of this matter deserve special attention: linking pay to performance through payment-by-results (PBR) schemes and supplementary wage benefits.

With regard to the former, the most usual system consists of dividing pay into two portions: a portion that is fixed (the basic wage) and a portion which varies. It is extremely rare to find PBR systems where the entire wage varies. Some of the basic questions concerning PBR are the following:

– What is the unit whose performance will be measured: the individual, a small group of workers, a department, the plant as a whole, the company as a whole, or some combination of these units?
– By what criterion will performance be measured: the quantity produced, a decrease in the number of rejects, the rate of utilization of the machinery, or quality?
– Over what period of time will results be measured and rewards: a day, a week, a month, a quarter, a year?
– What portion of the wage will vary, and how will that portion be determined?

There are no set answers to these questions. In each case, individual characteristics need to be taken into account – those of the units of production, of the product manufactured, of the way in which it is manufactured (how work is organized, the types of machinery used), and those of the workers. Thus, in dealing with a kind of production that requires close cooperation among workers, it would probably be unrealistic to have pay systems based on the measure of individual performance. If production fluctuates greatly because of the particularities of the market, the period of time over which productivity is measured will need to be chosen accordingly. Further instances could be given. These examples are meant simply to emphasize the need for detailed analysis of the situation before any PBR system is devised. Various techniques can, moreover, be combined. However, there is one fact which cannot be overstressed: that when a pay system grows too complex, so that finally the workers can no longer understand it, it ceases to meet its objectives and quickly becomes unmanageable and counter-productive. Here again the advantages of consultation and agreement among the parties concerned are particularly valuable, since a pay system cannot serve its purpose unless it is accepted and understood by those it is applied to.

There are, in this perspective, a number of problems connected with any PBR system. Safety conditions may worsen as the pace of work increases. Quality standards may fall. If the system gets out of hand, wages may vary without justification or administrative costs may rise unduly (the rise in administrative costs may be increased still further by the settlement of conflicts connected with earnings fluctuations). Resistance to change may take the form of challenging the method used for measuring performance. These problems do not necessarily imply that a PBR system should be rejected, even if they have led some enterprises to prefer systems based on time (and such time-based systems, it should be noted, are rarely found in a pure form). It simply shows that because so much is at issue in the question of wages, it is never a simple procedure to set up a pay system.

As for supplementary wage benefits, there are two main types: direct payments and indirect benefits. The first category includes the extra payments made to remunerate various circumstances or attitudes, such as non-absenteeism, overtime, shift work, night work, etc. Extra payments of this sort are aimed at settling specific problems on a case-by-case basis. They thus allow wage structures to include a margin of flexibility. However, there is a danger that cash benefits of this kind may proliferate. They may even come to be considered as acquired rights to be maintained even if the original justification for them no longer exists. Furthermore, they may become so numerous as to make the wage structure meaningless. In other words, there is a danger that the system of remuneration may lose its rationale.

The second category, indirect wages, covers a number of benefits aimed at ensuring the overall social welfare of wage-earners. Such benefits might include guaranteed remuneration for time not worked (e.g. vacations, sick leave), social insurance (health, old age, unemployment), social services (meals, training allowances, housing), etc. Benefits of this kind tend to constitute an increasingly greater part of workers' total remuneration. This development is easily explained by the protection that indirect remuneration of this nature provides against the problems of sickness, unemployment and old age. Whereas traditionally enterprises gave this type of benefit in order to ensure the stability of their workforce – employees were not sure they would receive them if they changed enterprises – the tendency has been to guarantee this type of protection so widely that it has very often become an obligation for employers. Under these conditions, indirect remuneration of this kind, while remaining part of an enterprise's wage costs, becomes an instrument which the enterprise has difficulty in controlling. This is the reason why, although the principle of social welfare benefits is rarely questioned, there is much discussion today about making wage-earners more aware of their employer's role in paying for the social benefits they enjoy.

It does not necessarily follow that all these dimensions of wage systems should be collected by statistical surveys. What is pointed out, however, is the complexity and the economic and social importance of wage systems at the plant level. Therefore, it is very important for any wage survey to make available the following information: the types of payment systems, including the new ones; the types of regular premium and bonuses such as productivity bonus, merit pay or individualized pay increases; the range of benefits offered to employees including periodic bonuses not paid during the regular paid period and also deferred remuneration such as profit-sharing and possibly private health insurance or pension schemes.

As these benefits can become significant, it would be wise to make provision for them. From this point of view, the trend noticeable in Western countries (where there is an increasingly less straightforward relationship between wages and working time due to these deferred remunerations as well as flexible working-time practices) to collect associated information on a number of dimensions of remuneration and of working time, should perhaps be followed.

WAGE DETERMINATION THROUGH COLLECTIVE BARGAINING

Considering the divergence of interests that necessarily exists between employers seeking to maximize their company's profits and workers seeking to maximize their earnings, it may seem like a contradiction to propose that wages be determined on the basis of an agreement reached by these two parties through collective bargaining. In this case, it may be tempting to appeal to a supreme arbiter – the State, and, indeed, the role of the State should not be minimized. Nevertheless, in countries with free market economies, where it has become established as the primary method of wage determination, collective bargaining – in which the State may well take part – has shown itself to be a particularly useful tool for handling the question of wages. There are several reasons for this. The first is that collective bargaining was developed in order to bring back some balance into the relationship between the individual employee and his employer, as in this relationship the employer, by virtue of his position, enjoys an undeniable dominance. By structuring the relationship at the collective level, collective bargaining tends to create a balance of forces. The second reason is that collective bargaining puts into practice a solution that has been worked out mutually by the social partners. It is, therefore, fairly certain that they have sought a balance between economic and social needs – a basic condition for effective wage determination. Moreover, in signing an agreement, the social partners are making a formal commitment, which provides some guarantee that the rules thus agreed upon will in fact be put into operation. Finally, one other important advantage of this form of wage determination should be emphasized. Because of the flexibility with which adjustments can be made to collective agreements (as compared to laws), certain provisions can be quickly changed by mutual agreement and adapted to new situations.

The forms of collective bargaining can be highly diverse. This diversity is the result both of present-day social and economic conditions and of the historical conditions in which labour relations originated. The differences between the various forms of collective bargaining depend mainly on two questions: (1) which employees will be covered and (2) at what level will the collective bargaining take place? With regard to the first question, in certain countries, collective agreements cover all wage-earners. This is the case, for example, in the Scandinavian countries and Germany. In other countries, like Italy, France and the United Kingdom, a high proportion of wage-earners are included. Finally, there are some countries, for example North America and Japan, where only a particular part of the labour force is covered. These variations are connected, to some degree, with the second main question concerning collective bargaining – its level. Here also three main types of practice can be distinguished. Agreements may apply to the economy as a whole (often called the national level), or else to a single industry, or even to a single enterprise or plant. Intermediary levels also exist which subdivide the previous divisions – geographical zones, for example. (In the latter case, there could be, for instance, industry-wide agreements for a given region.) In certain countries, moreover, a combination of these different levels exist. One case in point is France, where negotiations are carried on at every level, and may or may not be interconnected.

If agreements are reached mainly at the national level, they are likely to cover all wage-earners. On the other hand, wherever company-level negotiations are predominant, only the employees of companies where there are trade unions will be covered by the agreements. This does not necessarily mean that other employees will have no protection at all outside government regulations. Other more or less informal negotiations exist which can provide favourable terms for non-unionized workers, even if those terms are less binding than when there is a union.

This system may appear very complex and hard to manage, but, in fact, these multifarious practices have the advantage of being more responsive to the needs expressed by the social partners themselves. This gives them great stability, since they correspond to the wishes of the participants, and at the same time keeps them flexible in case adjustments need to be made, since they can choose from a wide range of methods to deal with whatever type of problem may arise. According to one's objectives, it would be possible, for example, to restrict a particular provision of a collective agreement to the local level or, on the contrary, to make it more general, so as to reach the most effective arrangement.

There is no predetermined restriction on the subjects for negotiation in the area of wages. Here again, everything depends on what the social partners decide. In general, agreements in this area concern such matters as the level of periodic wage adjustments, the way in which these adjustments are distributed among the categories of employees, the forms remuneration will take – including the type and amount of extra pay, special incentive schemes and the setting of the minimum wage for each level of qualification.

The nature of the particular wage problem to be dealt with may of course determine the level at which the negotiation will take place. In general, the higher the level, the more likely it is that the agreements will lay down minimum standards for enterprises to follow, with the actual terms applied to employees being set at enterprise level. However, this is not a hard and fast rule. Everything depends on the particular combination of characteristics of the industry in question. Thus, when dealing with a branch of the economy that is homogeneous from the standpoint of company size, products manufactured, and characteristics of the labour force, it is perfectly conceivable for an industry-wide agreement to set terms that apply directly to individual companies. If, however, the above-mentioned features of the industry are very heterogeneous, the industry-wide agreement will tend rather to set minimum standards which will be extended and adapted according to actual conditions at the various workplaces.

It should be mentioned that the above two factors may be overshadowed by considerations of strategy. The employers' organization may seek to negotiate wage increases on an industry-wide level in order to keep them from being granted in a disorganized way within individual companies – a phenomenon which can lead to wage escalation. Similarly, if the unions feel in a position of strength at one or another level, they will be tempted to focus the negotiation on the point where the balance of forces most favours them.

When national economic situations worsen, wage negotiations – often encouraged by governments – have tended to take into account the need to limit wage increases. Attempts have also been made to maintain purchasing power without, however, making this into a hard and fast principle, since basically it would be preferable to protect the standard of living by limiting inflation. Mainly, it has been a matter of doing away with automatic wage increases – for example, by giving up the various systems of indexing wages to prices, or by modifying those systems and taking greater account of such factors as employers' ability to pay, productivity increases and labour market conditions.

The terms 'concession bargaining' or 'flexibility bargaining' have been used to describe the results of such negotiations. In exchange for concessions on wages from the unions, employers have committed themselves to offering compensations – shortening working hours, guaranteeing employment, etc. These agreements also cover other aspects of wages and may aim at improving the efficiency of production or adjusting to modified methods of production. One example of what it has been possible to negotiate along these lines is the simplifying of wage structures so as to facilitate the movement of workers within the company, as it is easier to make changes in jobs and responsibilities when wage levels and forms of wages are more homogeneous. Certain criteria for evaluating the qualities required of workers have also been modified. Physical requirements, for example, have been changed to mental capacity or ability to accept responsibility, so as to take account of new production needs.

The above discussion casts further light on the usefulness of collective bargaining for dealing with the question of wages. Since it means sharing the responsibility for decisions, collective bargaining makes it easier to settle problems peacefully, especially in periods of economic difficulty when decision-making becomes a more delicate but avoidable situation. In order for such methods of wage determination to be sound, the social partners should have reliable and up-to-date data on wages. In fact, this should be one of the priorities that any wage statistics system should endeavour to fulfil. As regards wage determination through collective bargaining as such, it would be extremely useful to gather information on wage bargaining levels, agreed wage increases, etc. if this wage-fixing method is the most used throughout the country.

CONCLUSION

The main objective of this chapter is to describe some of the principal wage issues of interest for economic analysis, for the formulation of governmental policy and for the purpose of collective bargaining. A few conclusions regarding wage data gathering have been reached but no detailed proposals have been presented on this matter. Bearing in mind the needs emanating from the role of wages in economic growth as well as social peace and equity, it is up to statisticians in consultation with users to define the kind of statistical indicators which may reasonably be elaborated from a technical and cost-appraisal point of view.

But whatever these indicators might be, a good wage statistics system should collect mutually consistent data corresponding to the various needs of information on wages and to the various concepts of wages. The system should provide for the possibility of measuring trends over time, for detailed structural analysis as well as for comparability with other countries. In this connection, the use of the international recommendations on wage statistics established by the ILO must indeed be encouraged.

19

Wage and labour cost statistics in Czechoslovakia

J. KUX*

Even if wage statistics in Czechoslovakia – based primarily on compulsory regular statistical reports from all registered enterprises but using some additional sources of information as well – were well developed, the new economic situation and conditions call for a transition in statistics as well. The main reasons for the transition are the creation and rapid development of a small private sector, where the enterprise reporting system can only provide data to a partial extent and where there is practically a complete absence of the data required, especially concerning total labour costs. The new data requirements resulted in the preparation of a special transition project which utilized the help and experience of developed countries, primarily INSEE in France, then the United States Bureau of Labor Statistics, and last but not least, of Eurostat.

Again, a very important step which initiated the preparation of the transition project on wage and related statistics was the workshop on wage statistics for transition countries which the ILO organized in November 1991 in Prague with the participation of experts from the United States, the United Kingdom, Sweden, Germany, Austria, Eurostat and experienced ILO experts. Individual Western countries informed the transition countries on the systems of wage statistics in their countries and on existing problems and further plans, which together with all the explanations provided by the ILO and Eurostat constituted a unique source of information for the countries in transition.

* This chapter was originally written as a paper for the Joint ECE/ILO/OECD Work Session on Labour Statistics and Issues of Concern for Transition Countries, Paris, December 1992.

All the papers of the Western and transition countries from that workshop (including the detailed Czechoslovak paper) are available from the ILO, and therefore the following section only provides a short summary of the existing wage statistics system in Czechoslovakia (for more detailed information, readers are referred to the papers of the ILO Prague Workshop on Wage Statistics).

THE SYSTEM OF WAGE STATISTICS IN CZECHOSLOVAKIA

The system in Czechoslovakia consisted of enterprise observations and household surveys.

(a) Enterprise observations (still the main source of information), comprising:

- monthly reports, which were organized in manufacturing, construction and transport enterprises with twenty-five or more employees only
- quarterly reports, which were organized in all branches of the economy, including the public sector (for smaller enterprises with up to twenty-five employees, a simplified questionnaire was used)
- annual reports with more detailed information, which were organized in all branches of the economy (but with a simplified questionnaire for smaller units with up to twenty-five employees)

Generally, the monthly, quarterly and annual reports included information on the total wage bill (with a simple breakdown by payment items) for the whole reporting period (not only for the selected reference week) and on total employment with a calculation of average earnings (in manufacturing and construction, for manual and non-manual workers separately).

- irregular surveys. These were usually organized every four years on the structure and distribution of earnings. The last two surveys in 1984 and 1988 were based on a sample of approximately 750,000 employees (a large 10 per cent sample) with some forty items for each individual which included demographic characteristics, education or skill, occupation, hours worked and the structure of earnings by payment items. The survey was not conducted through paper questionnaires, but by means of equipment such as magnetic tape recorders.

With the exception of the last survey mentioned above, all the enterprise observations were complete censuses.

(b) Household surveys (because of longer periodicity or a relatively small sample, they are considered as an additional source of information):

- microcensuses (income survey), which are organized every 3–5 years with a 2 per cent (100,000 families) sample, though in 1992 a smaller (1 per cent) sample was used
- family budget surveys: from 1991 on this was a quarterly survey, with a small sample of 6,000 families

In the 1991–92 period, following the Prague ILO Workshop on Wage Statistics, the following improvements were achieved:

- the contents of the regular surveys and observations and the definitions used in them were modified to respond more to the new data requirements and international recommendations (partial modification only)
- surveys were organized in the private sector as well, depending on the legal form and size of units: larger units with one hundred or more employees in 1991, and those with twenty-five or more employees beginning in 1992, with full reporting duty; smaller units with a reduced reporting duty; unincorporated (self-employed workers, not registered in the business register) had no reporting duty, but twice a year a 0.5 per cent sample was interviewed personally
- in connection with the implementation of SNA, enterprise surveys and observations were replaced by establishment surveys
- international industry and occupational classifications were adopted (NACE – Rev. 1, and a Czechoslovak modification of ISCO-88)
- earnings and income questions were included in the labour force sample survey questionnaire (at least for pilot-test purposes)
- a new household income survey for 1992 (microcensus 1992) was prepared.

PLANS FOR THE FURTHER DEVELOPMENT OF WAGE AND LABOUR COST STATISTICS

Czechoslovakia had plans to develop wage and labour cost statistics in a number of ways:

- further improvements to the contents and definitions of surveys, according to the experience of Western countries, national data requirements and international recommendations
- implementation of establishment sample surveys for smaller units

- implementation of new kinds of establishment surveys that have not yet been organized

  - a quarterly labour cost survey with constant weights (application of a European modification of the American Employment Cost Index EECI); preparation of the survey within the Eurostat Task Force on Short-Term Wage Indicators; in 1992, to complete the methodology of the survey; in 1993 to undertake experimental fieldwork; in 1994, planned implementation in Czechoslovakia (within the Task Force experiment, which would continue in 1994–95)
  - labour cost survey (in the framework of Eurostat's 1992 LCS); due to changes in the tax and social insurance system in Czechoslovakia beginning 1 January 1993, during 1993 work would be undertaken on the preparation of the survey and a pilot test, and Eurostat LCS 1992 would be implemented one year later (1993 or early in 1994)

- preparation of a new Survey of Earnings Structure and the Distribution of Wages
- implementation of Eurostat's Harmonized Household Income Surveys (after the processing of the 1992 Czechoslovak Microcensus, which would have meant beginning the Harmonized Survey in 1995 if Eurostat's plans had been adopted).

20

The Hungarian labour cost survey

HUNGARIAN CENTRAL STATISTICAL OFFICE*

In the year 1992 there were many changes in Hungarian Labour Statistics (i.e. the introduction of the Labour Force Survey, increased frequency of some other surveys etc.). One of these was the introduction of the measurement of labour cost in the Hungarian economy.

In countries with a developed market economy an urgent demand for information on the cost of employment arose from investors and other users in the early 1990s, due to the liberalized or in some cases free international flow of capital and labour. Hungarian aspirations to join the European Union in the future and the desire to participate in the international capital market have prompted demand for an objective and complete picture of the level and structure of labour cost in the Hungarian economy.

Because of changes in our information system, the only way to get reliable information on this item was to introduce a new establishment survey. In the work of identifying and describing the various components of wages and labour cost we used the ILO international recommendations adopted at the Eleventh International Conference of Labour Statisticians (1966, Geneva). In our terms the major part of labour cost comprises compensation of employees, while the remainder consists of employers' expenditure for vocational training and welfare services (such as canteens and associated services, educational, cultural and recreational facilities, and services, grants to unions or other social organizations and the cost of associated services for employees), the cost

* This chapter was originally written as a paper for the Joint ECE/ILO/OECD Work Session on Labour Statistics and Issues of Concern for Transition Countries, Paris, December 1992.

of recruitment and other miscellaneous items (such as work clothes, travel between the home and the place of work and vice versa, etc.) and taxes regarded as labour cost.

In the design of the survey we were supported by the detailed methodology and processing of the 1992 survey on labour costs being conducted by Eurostat. Accepting the Eurostat and ILO recommendations on labour cost statistics is not only a milestone in the transition of our statistical system, but will result in supplying the data requirements of international organizations in an appropriate way.

The main objective of our labour cost survey was to compile measures of the level, composition and evolution of labour cost to the employer.

The survey unit was the enterprise, traditional in our statistical practice. The survey covered enterprises involved in industry and services and employing more than twenty persons. The survey was conducted as a sample survey, all enterprises with more than fifty employees to provide data, but a stratified random probability sample was drawn from enterprises with up to fifty employees. It covered wage earners and salaried employees.

The survey began in 1992 and was planned to be conducted in every fourth year. Labour cost is to be computed in forints per capita per hour.

A committee of experts and research staff discussed the questionnaire, as well as the experiences of our staff who had tested the questionnaire. Preliminary data to be used as a benchmark for the following year's survey data were obtained from different administrative records, the sample was designed and plans were laid to process the data.

21

Wage statistics in the Republic of Lithuania

DEPARTMENT OF STATISTICS OF THE REPUBLIC OF LITHUANIA

Until 1991, wage statistics in the Republic of Lithuania were in no way different from wage statistics used in the former Soviet Union, i.e. the same methodology was used to calculate wage indices. Data were gathered and processed in accordance with a common programme. This procedure was necessary for the calculation of comparable indices for all the republics of the former Soviet Union (FSU).

Since 1991, the Statistics Department of the Republic of Lithuania has started to keep wage statistics separately and only exchanged information with the FSU's statistical organizations. One of the differences about the Lithuanian Republic's wage statistics is in the gathering of data on the average registered number of employees and the wage funds for individual branches of the Republic's economy. These data are used for comparisons between the rate of growth of consumer goods prices and the growth of average wages. Aggregate data from monthly reports are divided according to the productive and non-productive sphere, according to individual branches of these spheres and according to separate industries. The calculated average monthly wage (gross indicator) and the paid wage (net indicator) are reported separately. Furthermore, data are reported on the average wages' rate of growth on a monthly basis.

On 16 September 1991 the new Government regulations for wage funds and other sources of income of workers and employees were enacted, together with a new form of primary statistical reporting on wages. These regulations stipulate specific kinds of compensation

---

* This chapter was originally written as a paper for the ILO Workshop on Wage Statistics, Prague, November 1991.

(twenty-six in all), which are directly included in the means for compensation (the wage fund) and other kinds of payments which are not included in the means for compensation but are in fact other revenue for workers and employees. The regulations also define a new method of calculation of average wages and salaries as well as a new measure of average income.

The statistical form of primary reporting mentioned above consists of two sections:

- Number of works and employees and their wages and salaries.
- Workers' and employees' income and other monetary payments.

The first section includes such indices as the average registered number of employees (excluding employees with extra work contracts); compensation paid for consumer goods' price increases; number of registered shareholders at the end of the reporting period and their share revenues.

The second section specifies the following indices: the total assigned share dividends of company workers; total welfare and social payments; the total sum of revenues; reported separately is the amount of wages and salaries paid to workers and employees in the public sector. All data are published by individual branches of the national economy and by kind of activity.

Wage statistics in the Republic of Lithuania are oriented towards the solution of economic problems arising in the period of transition from a centrally planned to a market economy.

Part IV

Classification of occupations

22

The revised International Standard Classification of Occupations (ISCO–88)

E. HOFFMANN and M. SCOTT*

The Fourteenth International Conference of Labour Statisticians (ICLS) adopted in November 1987 a revised International Standard Classification of Occupations (ISCO-88) based on a proposal prepared by the Bureau of Statistics of the International Labour Office (ILO). This chapter describes the main features and purposes of occupational classifications in general and those of ISCO-88 in particular.

Founded in 1919 at the same time as the League of Nations, the International Labour Organization (ILO) is a specialized agency of the United Nations. One of its tasks is to develop international standards and guidelines to help countries improve their labour administration as well as the quality and reliability of their labour statistics, and to improve international comparability of statistical data. To these ends the need for an international standard classification of occupations was first discussed in 1921. However, it was only in 1949 at the Sixth ICLS that work to develop ISCO was initiated. As a result the Seventh ICLS (1949) adopted a provisional classification of nine major groups. In 1952 the ILO published the *International Classification for Migration and Employment Placement*, with detailed descriptions of 1,727 occupations based on the national classifications of eight industrialized countries. At the Eighth ICLS (1954) a provisional list of minor groups was approved and the Ninth ICLS (1957) completed the work by endorsing the major, minor and unit groups of the first ISCO. It was published in 1958 (ISCO-58) and included, in addition to the group definitions, descriptions of

* This chapter was originally written as a paper for the ILO Seminar on Social and Labour Statistics and Computerized Information System for Social Policy in Market Economies, Vilnius, August–September 1992.

occupational categories within each unit group. It was recognized at the Ninth ICLS that ISCO-58 would need to be revised after a certain time, and a new, revised edition of ISCO was published in 1968 (ISCO-68) with an expanded number of occupational descriptions. The result of the second and most recent revision of ISCO was published in 1989 as ISCO-88.

The purpose of this chapter is briefly:

(a) to outline the main user areas of an international standard classifi-
    cation of occupations;
(b) to present the main considerations and features of ISCO-88;
(c) to present the follow-up work on ISCO-88 carried out at the
    national level and by the Bureau of Statistics of the ILO.

In Annex 8 a brief description of each ISCO-88 major group is given with a list of sub-major and minor groups.

WHAT IS AN OCCUPATIONAL CLASSIFICATION?

An occupational classification is a tool for organizing all *jobs* in an estab-lishment, an industry or a country into a clearly defined set of groups. It will normally consist of two components:

– a descriptive component, which may be just a set of titles of occupations and occupational groups, but which usually consists of descriptions of the tasks and duties as well as other aspects of the jobs which
  belong to each of the defined groups. These descriptions can be said
  to constitute a *dictionary of occupations*;
– the *classification system* itself, which gives the guidelines on how jobs
  are to be classified into the most detailed groups of occupations and
  how these detailed groups are to be further aggregated to broader
  groups.

Occupational classifications can be compared to a system of maps for a country, say Switzerland: the top level of aggregation corresponds to a small-scale road map for the main motorways and highways; the next level corresponds to a set of larger-scale maps for, say, each of the main regions, also showing provincial and local roads; and so on. At the most detailed level will be the detailed technical maps used by the municipal engineers to plan sidewalks, traffic lights, road extensions, etc. The very detailed technical maps can be compared to the detailed job descriptions which are used by enterprises for their wage systems and which in many countries will not be the concern of the national authorities.

WHAT ARE OCCUPATIONAL CLASSIFICATIONS USED FOR?

National occupational classifications and dictionaries are usually designed to serve several purposes. Although the detailed occupational descriptions and the classification structure must be seen as parts of an integrated whole, different user areas have different degrees of interest in the various elements. *Detailed occupational descriptions* are used by those who need to know about the tasks, duties and working conditions of jobs, i.e. mainly by client-oriented users (i.e. those responsible for job placement, vocational training and guidance, migration control, etc.). The occupational descriptions should be designed primarily to meet the needs of such users, but should also include the descriptive elements necessary for applying relevant aggregation schemes. *The classification structure*, i.e. the grouping of the detailed occupations together in progressively more aggregated groups, should be designed mainly to facilitate the sorting of jobs and persons into groups, i.e. for matching job seekers and vacancies, or for statistical description and analysis of the labour market and the social structure.

Legislators and public sector administrators use occupational statistics in support of the formulation of government policies and to monitor progress with respect to the application of such policies, including those of manpower planning and the planning of educational and vocational training. *Managers* need occupational statistics for planning working conditions and deciding on manpower policies at the enterprise and industry level. *Psychologists* study the relationship between occupations and the personality and interests of workers. *Epidemiologists* use occupation in their study of work-related differences in morbidity and mortality. *Sociologists* use occupation as an important variable in the study of social differences in life styles and behaviour. *Economists* use occupation in the analysis of differences in the distribution of earnings and incomes over time and between groups. Depending on the purpose of the study, 'occupation' may be regarded as the main variable or it may serve as a background variable in the empirical analysis. Used as a background variable, it may serve as a proxy for other variables such as socio-economic groups or working conditions, or it may be used as one element in the construction of other variables, such as social class or socio-economic status.

ISCO is intended to facilitate international communication on the subject of occupations and occupational groups, narrowly or broadly defined, both for client-oriented and for statistical users. ISCO should therefore lend itself to different uses at the national level, while taking into account the special considerations which must follow from its international nature.

Internationally comparable statistics on occupational groups are used mainly to:

(a) compare the *distribution* of the employed population or some other variable (e.g. wages, hours of work, work accidents, income, consumption, reading habits) over occupational groups in two or more countries;

(b) compare data on broadly or narrowly defined *individual sets of occupations* in two or more countries, for example, to compare the average wages of computer programmers in country A with those in country B, or to compare the number of industrial designers in the two countries;

(c) merge data from different countries referring to comparable groups, for example, to obtain enough observations to study the incidence of particular work-related accidents or diseases among workers in broadly or narrowly defined occupational groups, believed to have similar exposure to particular working conditions or harmful substances.

Experience shows that at the international level, most users of occupational statistics need data at the higher level of aggregation – usually for type (a) descriptions. Important exceptions are international studies of earnings, work hazards and injuries and other conditions of work – such studies often require that detailed occupational groups can be defined consistently, sometimes in cross-classification with industry and/or status in employment.

It is important to note that while the statistical use of type (a) above requires that the occupational classification cover all types of jobs, the focus in other types of use (statistical or client-oriented) is on specific occupations or groups of occupations. The sum total of these users' interests could conceivably also cover all occupations, but they will in practice only cover a sub-set.

The main client-oriented applications of an international standard classification of occupations are in the international recruitment of workers and in the administration of short- or long-term migration of workers between countries. An internationally developed and agreed set of descriptions for detailed occupational categories which can serve as a common 'language' for the countries and parties involved in such programmes may greatly increase the effectiveness of the communication necessary for their execution.

When countries need a model as a basis for developing or revising their national classifications, or when a substitute for a national classification is needed in countries that have not developed their own, then an international standard classification may be a good alternative. These applications of ISCO have been kept in mind both in the original development of ISCO and in its subsequent revisions.

KEY CHARACTERISTICS OF ISCO-88

The recent revision of ISCO aimed to produce an international classification which would:

- have a firm and clear conceptual basis – to strengthen its usefulness as a descriptive and analytical tool and to make it easy to update with new occupations;
- reflect the labour markets of developing as well as of industrialized countries;
- better reflect women's position in the labour market;
- reflect occupational consequences of different technologies;
- incorporate new occupations and reflect shifts in the relative importance of occupational groups.

In the present context a *job* is defined as a set of tasks and duties which are (or can be assigned to be) carried out by one person. Most occupational classifications classify, i.e. group jobs together in *occupations* and more aggregate groups, by similarity of the type of work done. *Persons* are classified by occupations through their relationship to a past, present or future job. In ISCO-88 occupations are grouped together and further aggregated mainly on the basis of *the similarity of skills* required to fulfil the tasks and duties of the jobs. Two dimensions of the skill concept are used in the definition of ISCO-88 groups: *skill level*, which is a function of the range and complexity of the tasks involved, where the complexity of tasks has priority over the range; and *skill specialization*, which reflects type of knowledge applied, tools and equipment used, materials worked on, or with, and the nature of the goods and services produced. It should be emphasized that the focus in ISCO-88 is on the skills required to carry out the tasks and duties of an occupation – and not on whether a worker having a particular occupation is more or less skilled than another worker in the same occupation.

Only a few broad 'skill level' categories can usefully be identified for international comparisons. The International Standard Classification of Education (ISCED) has been used to define skill levels. This does not mean, however, that skills can only be obtained by formal education or training. Most skills may, and often are, acquired through experience and through informal training, although formal training plays a larger role in some countries than in others and a larger role at the higher skill levels than at the lower – see also below. For the purpose of the ISCO classification system, the decisive factor for determining how an occupation should be classified is the nature of the skills that are required to carry out the tasks and duties of the corresponding jobs – not the way these skills are acquired.

'Skill specialization' can be indicated both broadly and more narrowly and is related to subject matter areas, production processes, equipment used, materials worked with, products and services produced, etc. The words used to describe subject matter, production processes, etc. therefore have to be used as labels for the core sets of skills with which occupations are concerned. The same type of words is used to describe the groups in an industrial classification of production activities. For some workers it will therefore be possible to 'predict' the occupation in which they are working with a fairly high degree of success, knowing how they are classified by industry. This does not mean that ISCO is using industry as a classification criterion (except in a few cases where it is directly relevant): the reason is that skills in fact are linked to products, materials, etc., which are the determinants of the 'industry' of the establishment in which the work is carried out. The conceptual difference between the two types of classification should not be forgotten, even though it may be partly obscured by the correlation between them and by the terminology used.

ISCO-88 defines four levels of aggregation, consisting of:

- 10 major groups
- 28 sub-major groups (subdivisions of major groups)
- 116 minor groups (subdivisions of sub-major groups)
- 390 unit groups (subdivisions of minor groups)

Unit groups in most cases will consist of a number of detailed occupations. For example, as a separate occupation *Nuclear physicist* belongs to ISCO-88 unit group 2111 *Physicists and astronomers*, which belongs to minor group 211 *Physicists, chemists and related professionals*, which is part of sub-major group 21 *Physical, mathematical and engineering science professionals* of the major group 2 *Professionals*. The structure of ISCO-88 is shown in Table 22.1, and the major groups are briefly described in Annex 8.

Eight of the ten ISCO-88 major groups are delineated with reference to the four broad skill levels defined for ISCO, cf. Table 22.1. Five of the eight major groups, i.e. 4, 5, 6, 7 and 8, are considered to be at the same broad skill level and are distinguished by reference to broad skill specialization groups. Skill level references were not made in the definitions of the two major groups entitled *Legislators, senior officials and managers* and

Table 22.1: ISCO-88 major groups, number of sub-groups and skill level

	Major group	Sub-major groups	Minor groups	Unit groups	ISCO skill level
1	Legislators, senior officials and managers	3	8	33	–
2	Professionals	4	18	55	4th
3	Technicians and associate professionals	4	21	73	3rd
4	Clerks	2	7	23	2nd
5	Service workers and shop and market sales workers	2	9	23	2nd
6	Skilled agricultural and fishery workers	2	6	17	2nd
7	Craft and related workers	4	16	70	2nd
8	Plant and machine operators and assemblers	3	20	70	2nd
9	Elementary occupations	3	10	25	1st
0	Armed forces	1	1	1	–
	Total	28	116	390	

Armed forces respectively, because other aspects of the type of work were considered more important as similarity criteria, i.e. policy making and management functions, and military duties, respectively. As a result there are significant skill level differences within each of these two major groups. However, the sub-major and minor groups of major group 1 have been designed to include occupations at similar skill levels.

A distinction is made at the major group level between (a) occupations that are essentially craft-oriented (i.e. major group 6 *'Skilled agricultural and fishery workers'* and 7 *'Workers in crafts and related trades'*), and (b) occupations that are essentially oriented towards the operation of tools, machinery and industrial plants (i.e. major group 8 *'Plant and machine operators and assemblers'*) – to cope with the issue of different skill requirements for jobs with similar purposes, due to differences in technologies used.

Occupations which are craft oriented consist of skilled jobs *directly involved* in the production of goods or services, where the tasks and duties require an understanding of and experience with the natural resources and raw materials used and how to achieve the desired result. The workers in these jobs may also use more technologically advanced tools and machines, provided that this does not change the basic skills and understanding required. Modern machines and tools may be used to reduce the amount of physical effort and/or time required for specific tasks, or to increase the quality of the products. On the other hand the tasks and duties of jobs in *occupations which are oriented towards the operation of tools, machinery and industrial plants* require an *understanding of the machines*: how to operate them properly, how to identify malfunctioning and what to do when something goes wrong. The skills required are oriented towards the machines and what they are doing rather than to the transformation process as such or its results. Occupations where the tasks and duties consist of assembling products from component parts according to strict rules and procedures are considered to belong to the same major group as the machine-oriented occupations. Jobs which only require low or elementary skills and little or no judgement are classified to occupations in major group 9.

The Fourteenth ICLS decided that for international comparisons it should be possible to reflect in ISCO the important differences which exist between countries, and sometimes within a country, in the required skill levels of jobs which traditionally have been seen as belonging to the same occupational group. Such differences are linked to the actual tasks which are carried out as these, although similar in nature, may vary significantly in the degree of judgement, responsibility and planning required. These differences in tasks will have resulted in national differences in skill levels and qualifications required for entering the occupations. The Fourteenth ICLS therefore decided that ISCO-88 should make it possible for countries to classify some occupational groups either to major group 2 *Professionals* or to major group 3 *Technicians and associate professionals*, depending on national circumstances. This possibility was created for primary, pre-primary and special teaching occupations, nursing and midwifery occupations, social work occupations and some artistic occupations.

The Fourteenth ICLS also decided that, as in ISCO-68, jobs in the armed forces should be classified in a separate major group 0 *Armed forces*, even if the jobs involve tasks and duties similar to those of civilian counterparts.

All occupations which consist of jobs in which the workers have mainly legislative, administrative or managerial tasks and duties should be classified to major group 1 *Legislators, senior officials and managers*. In ISCO-68 they were partly classified to major group 2 (*Administrative and managerial workers*) and partly to other major groups.

'Working proprietors' are to be classified according to whether their tasks and duties are mainly similar to those of managers and supervisors or to those of other workers in the same area of work. This is because the status of 'working proprietor' is seen as related not to type of work performed but to 'status in employment' – corresponding to the 'self-employed' and 'employer' categories of the International Classification of Status in Employment (ICSE). However, one self-employed 'plumber' may have mainly managerial tasks but another may carry out the tasks of 'plumber' with very few managerial responsibilities, depending for example on the size of the firm. In the former case the job should be classified with managers and in the latter case with 'plumbers'.

In ISCO-88 both 'apprentices' and 'trainees' should be classified according to their actual tasks and duties as, if needed, these two groups may be separately identified through the 'status in employment' classification. ISCO-68 recommended that apprentices should be classified to the occupation for which they are being trained, but that trainees be classified according to their actual tasks and duties.

The problem of classifying jobs which have a broad range of tasks and duties should be handled by the application of *priority rules*, i.e. some tasks and duties are given priority in determining the occupational category to which a job should be classified, such as:

(a) in cases where the tasks and duties are associated with different stages of the process of producing and distributing goods and services, the tasks and duties related to the *production* stages should take priority over associated tasks and duties, such as those related to the sale and marketing of the same goods, their transportation or the management of the production process (unless either of these associated tasks and duties dominates). For example, the worker who bakes bread and pastries and then sells them should be classified as 'baker', not as 'sales assistant'; the worker who operates a particular type of machinery and also instructs new workers in how to operate the machine should be classified with the machine operators; the taxi driver who drives his/her own car and also keeps the accounts should be classified with motor-vehicle drivers; and

(b) in cases where the tasks and duties performed require skills usually obtained through different levels of training and experience, jobs should be classified in accordance with those tasks and duties which require the highest level of skill. For example: there are a number of jobs whose tasks and duties most of the time require a set of relatively easily obtained skills, but where the workers are also expected to have skills which require more training or experience which enables them to cope with unexpected and infrequent situations, for instance, to avoid accidents or injuries.

It is recognized that a certain amount of judgement and adjustment to national circumstances will be necessary in the choice and application of these priority rules.

Many users of the ISCO-68 found that its top aggregation level of nine groups meant that the differences within each group were too large for the groups to be useful for description and analysis. However, the next level of aggregation, with eighty-three groups, represented too much detail for many types of analysis, as well as for international reporting of occupational distributions, especially if the data are obtained through sample surveys. ISCO-88 therefore includes the 'sub-major' groups as a new level in the aggregation system – between the former major and minor groups, cf. Table 22.1.

COMPARISON WITH ISCO-68

In all areas of statistics it is important to achieve a balance between continuity of time series and needed adjustments and improvements in definitions, in methods of data collection and in classification systems. In developing ISCO-88, continuity was aimed for at the unit group level. The revision did, nevertheless, result in the splitting of a significant number of ISCO-68 unit groups. The numerical importance of many of these splits at the country level need not be important.

The unit group level is the most detailed level specified in the ISCO-88 structure. The previous versions of ISCO also specified a detailed set of occupational categories, although they were not discussed or approved by the ICLS. Those of the detailed ISCO-68 descriptions which are still relevant are made available to the users of ISCO-88 on diskette, upon request.

The emphasis on skill level and skill specialization as the main similarity criteria for the delineation of occupational groups in ISCO-88 is not such a dramatic change from ISCO-68 and related national classifications as it may seem. That skill was implicitly used in ISCO-68 can be seen through a closer analysis of its classification system. For example, the group 0/1, *Professional, technical and related workers*, contains occupations with tasks and duties which require, for the

most part, highly trained or skilled workers. Occupations of comparable skill requirements are otherwise only found in its major group
2, *Administrative and managerial workers*. Each of the other major
groups in ISCO-68 covers different broad areas of skill specialization.
For example, most of the occupations in major group 3, *Clerical and
related workers*, mainly require skills needed to deal with data and
information, while most of the occupations in major groups 4 and 5,
Sales workers and *Service workers* can be said mainly to require skills
needed in dealing with people. Similarly the distinctions between
different minor and unit groups within a major group can be seen as
distinctions between different skill specializations. Skill level is
explicitly discussed in the introduction to ISCO-68 in relation to
minor group 9-9, *Labourers not elsewhere classified*. The conclusion that
skill implicitly plays an important role in both ISCO-58 and ISCO-68
is also supported by the following quotation from the 'Introduction'
to ISCO-58:

Combinations (of occupations) may be based on materials worked on,
workplace, environment, the specialized equipment used (if any) and similar
relationships. The particular skills, knowledge and abilities of the workers
concerned have an intimate connection with such factors.

ISCO-88 consists of ten (nine) major groups, followed by 28 sub-
major groups, 116 (eighty-three) minor groups and 390 (286) unit
groups. (The numbers of ISCO-68 groups are given in parenthesis.)
When coding ISCO-68 groups to ISCO-88 we find that 55 per cent of
the ISCO-68 unit groups (157 out of 286) have been left unchanged or
have had their scope only slightly expanded or reduced. Fourteen of
the new unit groups have been created by combining two or three
ISCO-68 unit groups – using a total of thirty-one. The coding also
shows that ninety-six ISCO-68 unit groups were split – and that the
parts were coded to 174 different ISCO-88 unit groups. Twenty-four
of the split groups were 'not elsewhere classified' groups. A total of
thirty-two ISCO-88 unit groups contain no reference to any ISCO-68
unit groups or occupational categories. ILO, 1987, ILO, 1988 and ILO,
1990 should be consulted for further information about ISCO-88.

FOLLOW-UP WORK ON ISCO-88

Publications presenting ISCO-88 are available in English (1990),
French (1991) and Spanish (1991). In addition to presenting the main
principles and the treatment of special groups of jobs, they include
descriptions of all ISC O-88 groups and updated and revised versions

of the 'Expanded alphabetical list of titles' in ISCO-68 – with about 3,700 entries in the English volume, 2,800 in the French volume and 3,100 in the Spanish. The updating of these lists has used information obtained from national dictionaries of occupations in the three languages, as well as information obtained from experts in relevant areas. All entries in the updated lists have been coded to the most detailed groups of ISCO-88 and ISCO-68. The full text of the three publications, including the indexes, is available in machine-readable form, as are the descriptions of still relevant ISCO-68 occupational categories. The latter descriptions have been slightly edited but not updated.

A manual on the development and use of national occupational classifications and dictionaries will cover both client-oriented and statistical applications. Work on the manual has taken much longer than expected, but it is planned for publication in 1994.

The manual will discuss much more explicitly than has been done in the past the collection and processing of occupational responses to questions on both administrative forms and statistical questionnaires. The aim is to contribute to better and more uniform occupational statistics, both for those using ISCO-88 directly and for those using other occupational classifications for possible later linkage to ISCO-88 groups. This will improve the usefulness of occupational data both nationally and for international comparisons and communication. The need for well-designed and tested occupational questions is emphasized, as well as the fact that experience and experiments have shown that the best results are obtained when asking for both the occupational title of a job and for a brief description of the main tasks and duties. Guidance is given on how to train coders, control the coding process and ensure that coders receive feedback on their performance. The importance of a good index of occupational responses and the way such indexes should be created and used is explained. It is recommended that coding always should be carried out at the most detailed level supported by the information given by the respondent. Available evidence indicates that this strategy involves small marginal costs, in terms of coding errors and time used per response, compared to that of coding at a predetermined aggregation level. It is also recommended that the coding should distinguish clearly between responses which are incomplete and the 'not elsewhere classified' categories for particular occupations.

In discussing the mapping from national occupational classifications to ISCO-88, the recommended strategy is consistent with the coding strategy outlined above: mapping should be carried out at the lowest level of aggregation of each of the two classifications, i.e. the national occupational classification – which for many countries may be an only slightly modified version of ISCO-68 – and ISCO-88. Priority rules are specified for resolving problems of inconsistency between the two classifications.

The work programme and budget of the ILO Bureau of Statistics provide for the minimum amount of resources necessary for the ILO to maintain competence in the field of occupational classification. These limited resources will mainly be used to:

(a) provide technical advice on the development and use of national occupational classifications, whether or not they are based on ISCO-88. This technical advice may take the form of responding to simple requests for information or comments to draft plans or classifications, assisting in the preparation of plans to develop or revise national classifications or the backstopping of such projects;

(b) provide technical advice on the development of links between ISCO-88 and other occupational classifications, national and international;

(c) revise existing and develop new detailed occupational descriptions for priority areas;

(d) set up and run a small documentation centre and information service on national occupational classifications and their links to ISCO, and on activities relevant to the development of occupational classifications and their use.

So far work has been concentrated on activities (a) and (d).

It was originally expected that countries would want to consult the ILO on how to map their current occupational classifications into ISCO-88, in preparation for the requests for data according to this classification from the international community. This has not yet happened to the expected extent, probably because countries are waiting until they actually receive such requests. More countries than expected have initiated activities to develop or revise their national classifications according to the principles of ISCO-88 or by using ISCO-88 as a model. Australia should be mentioned first because it pioneered the approach used by ISCO-88 as well as provided much of the methodological basis both for its development and for guidelines on its implementation. Other OECD countries which now have ISCO-88 compatible classifications are New Zealand, the United Kingdom, Ireland and Italy, and we know that work is going on in Denmark, Iceland, Norway, Portugal and Spain, and is about to start in Sweden. Work to develop ISCO-88 based classifications has also started in many of the transition countries in Central and Eastern Europe and the former Soviet Union: Bulgaria, the Czech and Slovak Republics, Hungary, Poland, Romania, Slovenia, the Baltic states and Ukraine. Other countries or areas which already have ISCO-88 based occupational classifications include Barbados, Cyprus, Hong Kong, Papua New Guinea, Singapore, the United Republic of Tanzania and Trinidad & Tobago, while we have been informed that work has started in Fiji, India, Israel, the Philippines and Namibia. Initiative has been taken to develop a common ISCO-88 adaptation for the Pacific islands countries and a common statistical classification, ISCO-88(COM), has been developed for members of the European Community. This variant of ISCO-88 will also provide a framework for the EC work to revise and develop instruments to be used to facilitate labour mobility and the recognition of vocational and professional training within the Community. Some countries which recently have chosen to revise or update their national occupational classifications with little or no reference to ISCO-88 are: Canada, France, Germany, the Netherlands and Switzerland. The United States is carefully considering what role ISCO-88 should play in their forthcoming work to revise the U.S. SOC.

REFERENCES

ILO, 1987: *Revision of the International Standard Classification of Occupations*, Report IV to the Fourteenth International Conference of Labour Statisticians: Part I – *Background, principles and draft resolution*; Part II – *Draft definitions*, ILO, Geneva, 1987.

ILO, 1988: *Fourteenth International Conference of Labour Statisticians, Report of the Conference*, ILO, Geneva, 1988.

ILO, 1990: *The Revised International Standard Classification of Occupations (ISCO-88)*, ILO, Geneva, 1990.

Annex 8 (The ISCO-88 major groups) is to be found at the end of this volume.

23

Mapping a national classification of occupations into ISCO–88: outline of a strategy

E. HOFFMANN*

The purpose of this chapter is to outline a strategy for countries that wish to map a national occupational classification (NOC) into the revised International Standard Classification of Occupations (ISCO-88).

The focus of the chapter is on mapping the groups of a NOC into corresponding groups in ISCO-88. Other factors of importance for obtaining internationally comparable occupational information, such as data collection and coding strategies, will not be discussed here. Furthermore, the discussion is based on the assumption that the NOC is based on principles roughly consistent with those of ISCO-88; in particular, that the most detailed groups are defined in terms of type of work performed.

The chapter opens with a brief outline of why it may be useful and important to establish links between NOCs and ISCO-88. The next section outlines why and how mapping should always be carried out at the most detailed levels possible of the classifications. Then a short discussion follows of the procedure for establishing links at more aggregate levels and of the use of double coding. The last section outlines the role of the ILO in the establishment of links between NOCs and ISCO-88.

* This chapter was originally written as a paper for the ILO Seminar on Labour Statistics and Computerized Social Information System for Social Policy in Market Economies, Odessa, April 1993.

WHY MAP NATIONAL OCCUPATIONAL CLASSIFICATIONS INTO ISCO-88?

National occupational classifications should be mapped into ISCO-88 mainly because *national* users of occupational information want:

- to make comparisons between national circumstances and circumstances of other countries;
- to communicate occupational information with persons or institutions in other countries.

An additional consideration, but less important, is that users in *other countries* – including international organizations – also want to make comparisons and communicate occupational information internationally.

If only two countries are involved, the need for international comparable occupational information could be satisfied most effectively by directly linking their national classifications. However, as soon as more than two countries are involved, pairwise linking becomes impossible. Even if most comparisons are expected to be pairwise, it may be more efficient to use the indirect route of linking to a common reference classification in order to avoid having to establish many pairwise links. The obvious candidate for the role of a common reference classification is ISCO and, increasingly, its last version – ISCO-88.

It is important to remember when discussing international use of occupational information that this may involve both occupational statistics and information about the occupation of individuals, e.g. migrant workers. ISCO-88 is intended to facilitate international occupational communication for both client-oriented and statistical users, and it is an attempt to provide a basis for the different uses at the national level, while taking into account the special considerations which must follow from its international nature.

THE LINKS THAT MAY BE ESTABLISHED BETWEEN A NATIONAL OCCUPATIONAL CLASSIFICATION AND ISCO-88

Internationally comparable statistics on occupational groups are used mainly:

(a) to compare the *distribution* of the employed population or some other variable (such as wages, hours of work, accidents at work, income, consumption, reading habits) over occupational groups in two or more countries;

(b) to compare data on broadly or narrowly defined *individual sets of occupations* in two or more countries, for example, to compare the average wages of computer programmers in country *A* with those in country *B*, or the number of 'industrial designers' in the two countries;

(c) to merge data from different countries referring to comparable groups – in order, for example, to obtain enough observations to study the incidence of particular work-related accidents or diseases among workers believed to have similar exposure to particular working conditions or harmful substances.

Depending on the purpose of the study, 'occupation' may be regarded as the main variable, or it may serve as a background variable in a statistical analysis. Used as a background variable, it sometimes serves as a proxy for other variables, such as 'socio-economic groups' or 'working conditions', or it is used in the construction of other variables. Experience shows that at the international level many users of occupational statistics need data mainly at the higher level of aggregation – usually for type (a) descriptions. Among the exceptions are international studies of wages and earnings, work hazards and injuries and other conditions of work. Such studies often require that detailed occupational groups are defined, sometimes in cross-classification with the 'industry' and/or 'status in employment' variables.

The main *client-oriented* applications for a standard international occupational classification are in the international recruitment of workers and in the administration of short-term or long-term migration of workers between countries. An internationally developed and agreed upon set of descriptions for detailed occupational categories which can serve as a common 'language' for the countries and parties involved in such programmes may greatly increase the effectiveness of the communication necessary for their execution.

While the statistical use of type (a) above requires that the occupational classifications cover all jobs, the focus in other types of use – statistical or client-oriented – is on specific occupations or groups of occupations. Although the sum total of all users' interests in these types of use could conceivably also cover all occupations, in practice only some occupations are involved. The problem is to know which they are. Therefore the links have to be established for the whole range of occupations covered by the two classifications.

Because occupational information is needed at all levels of aggregation in international, as well as in national, applications, it follows that links between a NOC and ISCO–88 should also be established as far as possible at all levels of aggregation. In order to achieve this it is necessary, but not sufficient, to establish links at the most detailed level in the classifications. However, the links established at the detailed level will ease the establishment of links at more aggregate levels.

MAPPING AT THE MOST DETAILED LEVEL

Mapping one classification into another is equivalent to determining for each group in the first classification the most appropriate group in the other. This is in principle very similar to coding an occupational response on a questionnaire – an advantage being that in the case of mapping, one normally should have access not only to a title and very brief task information when assigning a code, but to a whole description of tasks and duties of jobs included in each occupational group in the NOC.

The first step when establishing links should always be to give to the most detailed groups of the NOC the code of the most detailed appropriate group in ISCO-88. Assuming that the most detailed level in the NOC is more detailed than the unit group level in ISCO-88, we will have the following cases:

(a) The NOC group belongs unambiguously to one of the ISCO-88 unit groups. This is of course the simplest situation and, if the NOC was developed on the basis of ISCO-68 or ISCO-88, this is likely to be the most usual case;

(b) The range of tasks and duties of the jobs belonging to the NOC group is partly outside those described for the most relevant ISCO-88 unit group, but falls within the same ISCO-88 minor group. In this case the group should be coded according to the numerical dominance priority rule outlined below, or, if this is not applicable, to the appropriate minor group;

(c) The range of tasks and duties of the jobs belonging to the NOC group is partly outside those described for the most relevant ISCO-88 unit group and they also fall partly outside the corresponding ISCO-88 minor group. In this case, the group should be coded to the ISCO-88 unit group determined by following the priority rules outlined below, invoked in the same order as they are described. If no unit group can be determined, then the same exercise should be carried out to determine the most appropriate ISCO-88 minor group, sub-major group or, as a last resort, major group.

The *numerical dominance* priority rule would say that in the case of a detailed NOC group not fitting into any ISCO-88 unit exactly, the group should be coded to the ISCO-88 unit group to which a large majority of the jobs, (e.g. around 80 per cent) in the national group belongs. If there is no such ISCO-88 unit group, then one should try to use the *skill level* priority rule.

The *skill level* priority rule would say that the national group should be coded to the ISCO-88 unit group that includes those tasks and duties of the national group corresponding to the highest ISCO-88 skill level. If no difference in skill level is involved in the different tasks and duties, then one should try to use the *production* priority rule.

The *production* priority rule would say that priority, when deciding to which ISCO-88 unit group to code, should be given to those tasks and duties directly related to the production of goods or services rather than to associated tasks and duties related to the sale and marketing of the same goods, their transportation or the management of the production process (unless these tasks and duties predominate among the workers in the NOC group). For example, when the tasks are baking bread and pastries and also selling them, the priority should be given to baking, not to selling; if the tasks are operating a particular type of machinery and also instructing new workers in how to operate the machine, then priority should be given to the machine operation; if the tasks are driving a taxi and also keeping the accounts, then priority should be given to driving.

The result from this coding exercise would be a list of detailed NOC occupational groups mostly given ISCO-88 unit group codes or the codes of even more detailed ISCO groups in areas where such groups may have been defined. This means that, when needed, the NOC groups can subsequently be aggregated to most of the relevant aggregate groups which have been defined in terms of ISCO-88 unit groups.

MAPPING AT THE AGGREGATE LEVELS

Unfortunately, data are seldom available for groups defined at the most detailed level in the NOC, because the census or survey returns have been coded at a higher level in the NOC. This makes it necessary to establish links directly between the aggregate NOC groups and the most detailed relevant aggregate ISCO-88 groups. The first step in this process is to look at the structure of the aggregate NOC groups for which data are available in terms of their component ISCO-88 unit groups, i.e. at the results of the exercise described in the previous paragraphs. Using the same priority rules as those outlined above, one may determine how one or the sum of several NOC aggregate groups can be used as a reasonably close approximation of an ISCO-88 unit group, minor group or sub-major group. In terms of closeness of approximation, this procedure obviously gives results which are much less satisfactory than those resulting from aggregating data using detailed national groups. This is one reason why it is recommended always to code to the most detailed level of the national classification, given the information in each census or survey response.

THE USE OF DOUBLE CODING

The most precise 'mapping' will be obtained by coding the original records simultaneously to both NOC and ISCO-88. This can be done by having a coding index, in machine-readable form, where each index entry has been given both the NOC and the ISCO-88 code. Coding will then be done by recording the number of the index entry, rather than the code(s) and letting the computer link the correct NOC code or ISCO-88 code, as needed, during the tabulation stage. This strategy is easier to implement when using a computer-assisted coding system (CAC) than when coding manually, but the most resource-demanding part is the work of assigning codes to the coding index, and that has to be done both for the CAC and the manual procedures.

In many cases coding to the NOC has already been completed by the time mapping to ISCO-88 is being considered. The procedure then used by some countries has been to code a random sample of responses from a population census or survey to both NOC and ISCO-88. The results from cross-tabulation between NOC and ISCO-88 has then been used to establish the distribution of ISCO-88 codes for each of the NOC codes, and this distribution has then been used to distribute the numbers for each NOC group, from a whole census or labour force survey, among the relevant ISCO-88 groups. However, the costs of this type of double coding may also be significant, especially if it has to be carried out frequently or for different types of populations in order to satisfy the assumptions required for the valid use of the conversions based on the results.

It should be noted that even though the results from double coding as described in the previous paragraph usually will be the best source of information for determining whether the numerical dominance priority rule can be applied, other sources and more unstructured general knowledge about the labour market and the population being coded may supplement or replace the results of double coding.

THE ROLE OF THE ILO

Mapping a NOC into ISCO-88 requires a good understanding of the national labour market and occupational structure, of the NOC itself and its principles, and of ISCO-88. Those who are responsible for the NOC and who have experience with its use are therefore best suited to establish the links between NOC and ISCO-88. However, because the exercise involves both classifications, it would be an advantage if those responsible for ISCO-88 could be given the opportunity to comment on a first draft of links between the two classifications, based on their knowledge of ISCO-88 and their experience with the difficulties of other countries and the way these have been resolved. Contacts should therefore be made with the ILO Bureau of Statistics before finalizing the links between the NOC and ISCO-88.

For work on NOCs which were originally developed on the basis of ISCO-68 – or to a lesser extent, ISCO-58 – the links established between ISCO-68 and ISCO-88 at the detailed level may prove useful. This material will be made available to countries both on paper and in machine-readable form.

24

Mapping the world of work: an international review of the use and gathering of occupational information

E. HOFFMANN*

An 'Occupational Classification and Dictionary' (OCD) may be loosely defined as a classification system for jobs and the persons who hold those jobs, with associated group definitions and descriptions. In this report the term 'NOCD' means an OCD which has been developed and is being used by a national (public) organization, normally the national statistical office or national employment service, which is seen as the responsibility of this organization and which carries its authority. (This does not necessarily mean that it is the national standard classification and that it is used by every user of such classifications.) The 'classification' element of an OCD consists of the specified groups, the definitions of the groups and their differences, as well as the rules and the coding index used to assign jobs and persons to the groups. The 'dictionary' element of an OCD consists of the group titles, the descriptive definitions and the non-defining parts of the group descriptions. These different elements may be more or less developed, and more or less coordinated between themselves and with the classification, e.g. descriptions may be formulated to be valid for groups which do not coincide completely with those defined by the classification structure.

National occupational classifications and dictionaries (NOCDs) have many similarities to geographic maps of a country, and this review will make use of these similarities, both in the organization of the presentation

* This chapter is based on a report originally prepared under Grant No.E-9-K-1-0013 from the US Department of Labor. The views expressed are those of the author and do not necessarily reflect those of the ILO, its Bureau of Statistics or the US Department of Labor. The author is also responsible for any errors or misunderstandings with respect to national practices. He is a member of the ILO Bureau of Statistics.

and to illustrate certain points. As with geographic maps, different users of the maps of the world of work (the OCDs) will ask for very different types of information (*content*) scaled to very different degrees of detail (*resolution*). Geographic maps range from small-scale outlines printed in a newspaper to indicate the location of the latest natural disaster, indicating only coast and borders and a few major cities, to large-scale location maps for a city's water and electricity supply systems. Maps of the world of work also range from consisting of a few broad occupational categories, used to organize information on the number of persons in a country who are doing different types of jobs, to detailed descriptions of tasks and duties of all the jobs in an enterprise, serving as basis for the fixing of remuneration and the organization of work. The *scope* (coverage) of both types of maps will also vary according to usage. Some basic topographical maps will be developed to cover the whole territory of the country and are intended to serve a wide variety of users, both as a source of information and as instruments for organizing in space other types of information. In the same way some OCDs will, as maps of the world of work, aim to cover all jobs in the economy and for many users provide a background variable, an instrument, for locating other information – about for example, income, working conditions, reading habits, divorce rates, training – in the world of work. Other maps, topographic or of the world of work, will be prepared only for those areas where the type of information they carry is relevant, and at a time when there is a specific need important enough for the user to be willing to cover the costs of data collection and map construction. Just as the common denominator of geographic maps is the spatial referencing of information, the common denominator OCDs is that they are focused on *the type of tasks and duties* that people do in their jobs. However, given this common denominator, the degree of resolution, the type and depth of thematic information and the coverage will vary between different maps of the world of work, corresponding to the needs of the different main users.

In this chapter reference will frequently be made to two different, but partly overlapping, distinctions. Both are relevant to any discussion of the development, use and maintenance of OCDs. One concerns the distinction between (a) *statistical* and (b) *client-oriented* usage of an OCD. The other refers to the distinction between (i) a *sorting function* and (ii) a *database function* (for occupation-related information). The latter distinction corresponds closely to the difference between the classification and the dictionary elements of an OCD. All statistical applications make use of the sorting function of the OCD, and they may also make use of the database function to determine where to sort particular jobs. Client-oriented users, concerned with making decisions affecting individuals and/or giving them advice, will be the primary users of the database function, but will also make use of the sorting function, i.e. to decide 'yes' or 'no' if this depends on whether the client has/had a job which belongs to a particular set of occupations; for example, to match job-seekers and vacancies and to provide input to statistics on operations of employment services.

To structure the presentation and discussion, this chapter will use the following 'model' of the work to develop, use and maintain or update an OCD (this does not imply that this is the way the work should or could be organized in practice).

(a) First, analyse how the OCDs are (to be) used and the users' require-ments' to arrive at conclusions concerning (i) who will benefit/suffer from the existence or not of an (up-to-date) OCD, and in what way and to what degree; (ii) the amount of resources which can be devoted to work on the OCD, both for the initial development and for follow-up work, as well as the division of labour between inter-ested and competent parties; (iii) the content of the information to be collected for the OCD; and (iv) the structure of the OCD.
(b) Collect the relevant information, using appropriate methods to ensure the required coverage, resolution, type and depth of information.
(c) Organize the collected information in ways which will facilitate the development of the OCD as a tool for sorting and as a database on occupations, as well as for easy maintenance and updating.
(d) Develop rules, guidelines and tools for using the OCD effectively.
(e) Develop and put in place procedures to ensure maintenance and updating of the OCD.
(f) Specify procedures for evaluation of the contents and structure of the OCD with a view to initiate revision if that is deemed necessary.

AN OVERVIEW OF NATIONAL OCCUPATIONAL CLASSIFICATIONS AND DICTIONARIES

Most countries have carried out some form of occupational mapping of their workforce, even if only at a very aggregate level and with instru-ments neither designed for nor adapted to their specific circumstances. Of the 126 countries, areas and territories for which information is avail-able at the ILO, 117 did use some type of occupational classification in the last pre-1990 population census.[1] Altogether, about 130 countries,

---

[1] See *Statistical Sources and Methods. Volume 5: Total and Economically Active Population. Employment and Unemployment (Population Censuses)*, International Labour Office, Geneva, 1990.

areas and territories have an NOCD, in this sense. In the majority of censuses the classification scheme used was that of the *International Standard Classification of Occupations* (ISCO) or a minor national adaptation of ISCO. Most of these countries used ISCO-68 as the basis for their coding of occupations, but some used an adaptation the first ISCO (ISCO-58). Some countries in Latin America used COTA, a regional adaptation of ISCO prepared by the Inter-American Statistical Institute for the 1960 and 1970 rounds of population censuses. For a significant number of countries the use of ISCO for coding was based on the recommendation by the United Nations that occupation be coded to the groups defined by the latest edition of ISCO, or consistent with these groups.[2] The widespread use of ISCO cannot in all cases be said to have been based on careful evaluation of whether this classification would be the most appropriate. However, the choice may very well have been cost effective, given the amount of resources available at the national level to develop the tools for obtaining occupational information.

The one common feature of the census classifications is that they cover the total employed population of the respective countries, and in this sense can be said to provide a base-map for their world of work. The degree of resolution ranged from five groups to 1,916. In most countries with some type of NOCD the resolution used in census coding is to a smaller number of, i.e. to broader, groups than those which exist at the most detailed level. Furthermore, the total number of different occupations separately defined at the most detailed level is below 2,500 in most NOCDs. Typically the maximum number of groups is between 800 and 1,200, and, judging by the number of jobs going into the different groups, the degree of resolution is very uneven between the different parts of the NOCD, partly reflecting different degrees of specialization between the jobs found in different parts of the economy.

Many of the census classifications have no further information about the type of work performed by the jobs classified to the different groups than that which is summarized in the titles of the groups, i.e. there is hardly any dictionary in the proper sense. In a number of NOCDs which have group descriptions, these contain only the basic information needed to distinguish groups from each other, i.e. short references to what is needed to carry out the tasks and duties of the jobs, such as subject matter knowledge required, materials worked with, products or services produced, or machines or equipment operated, as the case might be.

Based on the material available in the ILO we can estimate that in about fifty countries OCDs have been developed to serve client-oriented

---

[2] See United Nations, *Principles and Recommendations for Population and Housing Censuses,* Statistical Papers ST/ESA/STAT/SER, M67, New York.

users of OCDs, both for 'sorting' and for 'information about occupa-tions'. In many of the countries these OCDs are the same as, or close variants of, those used by the statistical authorities. However, reflecting the diversity of users' interests in some countries, OCDs which are quite different from those used for labour force statistics have been developed and are being used in client-oriented applications. They may differ from the statistical authorities' classifications in terms of the principles used for delineating groups, the degree of coverage and resolution, as well as in the type and depth of the information included in the descriptions. Many of these 'alternative' OCDs have some claim to be seen as a NOCD, at least for their area of concern. In some countries the decisions to develop separate OCDs for separate applications have been based on a deliberate choice, e.g. in France, while in others the development and use of different OCDs by different organizations seems to be mostly due to lack of communication or as a consequence of historical circum-stances. With the limited resources available for this type of work in most authorities, it has often been seen as less costly, and certainly quicker, for them to develop something adequate for their own use without having the trouble of co-ordinating with others. Classifications developed for coding statistical surveys have typically given higher priority to coverage and perceived data collection feasibility than those developed by, for example, vocational training authorities, and have been much less concerned with the resolution in certain areas or the type and depth of descriptions.

MECHANISMS FOR AND RESULTS FROM CONSULTATION WITH USERS OF NOCDs

Methods for communicating with users

In all the countries where an effort has been made to develop OCDs serving several different user requirements, the responsibility for this work has been given to (or taken by) an organization with a specific, strong user interest, e.g. the national statistical office or the employment services. However, tool-makers cannot know equally well all the appli-cations which are to be made of their tools, and most users will not know how to obtain the improvements they would like to see in these tools. Therefore formally organized bodies (steering groups, users' workshops, consultative committees), users' surveys and informal contacts have often been used to explore the requirements of other users. These channels of communication are useful and necessary also to mobilize resources and support from other organizations, to create necessary external pressure to honor commitments made to achieve progress, and to get guidance on proposals for both broad strategies and detailed content and solutions. The experience of different countries and of the ILO's own work strongly indicates that:

(a) users will generally express more useful and reflected opinions on the OCDs as reactions to a proposal or provocation, rather than spontaneously;

(b) concrete examples of the implications of alternative proposals will result in clearer advice from the users than general requests for advice on the current situation or on general principles; see, for example, the Australian survey of users' preferences for three alternative classification structures;

(c) while it may be fairly easy to identify both general and specific deficiencies in existing tools, it is in practice impossible to quantify the damage or loss to users, or their clients, of such deficiencies and therefore also impossible on this basis to specify the 'correct' amount of resources to invest in the development or improvement of the OCDs.

Main user requirements

In one or more of the countries surveyed the following areas have been identified as finding OCDs to be important tools:

- statistics
- job placements
- vocational guidance
- planning and design of vocational training and skill certification programmes
- immigration control
- monitoring occupational safety and health
- pay and human resource management systems

The user requirements of these areas are reviewed in the following sections.

Statistics   The statistical use of OCDs is to *sort and present* information according to the groups specified by the classification. The *degree of resolution* and the specific distinctions to be made will depend on the source and quality of the primary data, the needs of the main users of the particular set of statistics and the perceived costs to the statistical agency in terms of work-hours and errors to be corrected or adjusted for. *Information about the type of work* (tasks, working conditions, etc.) of the jobs to be classified to the different occupational groups is needed only to help the coding where the coding index is not adequate, for the updating and maintenance of this index and the classification, or to satisfy requests for regrouping of the basic categories according to criteria which are not used in the standard aggregation structure. As a consequence the descriptions in statistical classifications tend to be short and to focus on group differences.

The required coverage of the classification depends on the population to which the relevant statistics apply. The general statistical classifications are designed to cover all jobs in the economy, i.e. the whole employed population, but the classifications used for special statistical areas, such as various wage statistics in Sweden, will only cover those groups which are relevant in, for example, the manufacturing sector.

It is a common perception that statistics need mainly the aggregate parts of an OCD classification structure. This is only partly true, as a number of statistics-users want answers to questions like 'What is the number of dental assistants, plumbers, turners, farm labourers, secondary school science teachers or bus drivers in area A, and what are their average salaries?' However, in addition to such information about specific occupational groups, other users want to know the distribution of income, consumption, reading habits etc. over a limited number of broad groups defined with the help of the statistical variable 'occupation'. In the latter case 'occupation' serves as a background variable in the description or analysis. The logical and practical consequence of the need for statistics on detailed groups as well as for (shifting) aggregate groups is that coding should be carried out to the greatest detail supported by the information used as the basis for coding, namely in the statistical survey or the administrative records.

Job placements   The job placement agencies' use of the OCD is mainly for the sorting of job-seekers and vacancies, (i) to facilitate the matching process (which normally will involve also other characteristics of both the job and the job-seeker); (ii) to produce relevant statistics on job-seekers, registered unemployment, vacancies and placements; and (iii) to organize the work in the employment office. The sorting and matching process is used to reduce as much as possible the number of unsuitable jobs and candidates that the job-seeker and employer respectively will have to consider, while at the same time not eliminating possible opportunities or candidates. The first of these considerations would lead to very fine resolution in the sorting, while the other would indicate that sorting to broader and more general groups may be more appropriate, in particular for job-seekers who are looking for 'any job possible'. These considerations should lead to initial sorting (i.e. coding) to detailed groups combined with algorithms for matching which can take into account clusters of 'similar' occupational groups, where 'similar' is defined in terms of ease of transfer of skills between occupations. (The German system for vocational guidance as well as the French ROME system and the Swedish WAP 2000 system have developed a conceptual and visual basis for this. However, it is not certain that specific procedures have been implemented in actual matchings.)

A matching process relying heavily upon the use of correct occupational codes, as far as type of work is concerned, will in principle not need further information about the occupations than that which is needed for correct coding, i.e. it will use the same information as is needed for statistical coding (sorting). For this reason the employment officers often have as their main tool a summary version of the OCD used by their services, even though the communication process with both employers and job-seekers can be improved if the employment officers have *easy* access to information about the type of work (tasks and duties), skill requirements and typical working conditions of occupations, both to establish the particulars of the job/experience in question and to undertake vocational guidance where this is combined with placement. Present practices do reflect, however, the need to use both job- and person-specific information in the matching process and that many of the OCDs used are inadequately updated and maintained. The last point will be discussed further below.

It is worth noting in this context that the Dutch Central Bureau for Labour Exchange (CBA) has recently developed a system (FIT) for matching vacant jobs and job-seekers which focuses on the content (tasks and duties) of the jobs, rather than on occupations. A hierarchy of 120 clusters of around 2,000 tasks are specified in FIT, to be related to both the vacant jobs in question and the experience and training of the job-seeking individuals. In principle, this should provide for greater flexibility in the matching process than the use of occupational categories as the basis for sorting.

The coverage of the OCDs used for placement is very often curtailed because the employment services normally serve mostly the lower- and medium-skilled jobs in the labour market. Thus the French ROME has a very rudimentary coverage of occupations which require technical and higher education, and in the Swedish employment services these job categories are handled by special officers and routines.

Vocational guidance The term 'vocational guidance' is used here to cover all systematic efforts to inform and advise persons about job and career prospects, given the current situation, skills, interests, knowledge and mental and physical capacities of these persons. Guidance on choice of secondary and further education in the light of career opportunities, as well as choice of short vocational training courses, apprenticeships, rehabilitation training opportunities (if needed), and current job opportunities is also included. More types and depth of information is required from the OCDs for this type of use than for statistics or job placement. Information about tasks and duties, materials and machinery worked with, products and services produced, typical working conditions, mental and physical skill requirements, career opportunities and job prospects in the short and medium term, income range and 'typical personality profiles' suited for the jobs, is important, in addition to information about training opportunities and ways to gain relevant experience.

In principle, no particular sorting of the descriptions contained in the 'dictionary' part of the OCD or in separate guidance material would be better than others, if good indexes reflect the different types of information provided in the descriptions and there is a good system of cross-references between descriptions. Printed descriptions could well be sorted alphabetically by group title, and examples of alphabetically organized occupational dictionaries or guidance material can be found. However, in practice descriptions in general OCDs are almost invariably presented according to the classification structure, while printed guidance material is frequently sorted into broad 'activity areas' reflecting types of products or services produced. The number of different 'articles' in such material will tend to be much smaller than the number of occupational groups in the OCDs, especially as the coverage of the guidance material frequently is limited to those occupational groups which are deemed to require a significant amount of formal training beyond compulsory schooling, or to cover only those occupations for which training is well organized. Sometimes the clusters of occupations described in the guidance publications are formed on the basis of the type of training needed or typically followed to enter the occupations, or whether the occupations are commonly seen as steps in one career path. This means that the degree of resolution, judged by the number of different occupations identified in a cluster or by the number of persons working in the type of jobs covered by the group, will vary by several orders of magnitude. Numerically small occupations with well-developed training schemes or career paths will tend to be much better described than numerically larger and more 'open' occupations. This also reflects differences in the ease of collecting the relevant information.

Planning and design of vocational training programmes   Analysis of statistical information about the number of employed and unemployed persons in relevant occupational categories and of whether there is an increase or decrease in these groups, is used as background to decisions about the capacity of training programmes which are linked to the specific occupational categories (such as in Australia). The descriptions of occupations which can be found in certain of the OCDs are also consulted in the design of some training courses, but such courses are mostly developed through direct contacts between the respective training institutions and representative, sometimes tripartite, local, regional or national bodies. In the Netherlands this type of use seems to have influenced an OCD directly or to have led to the development of a special OCD, i.e. the OBIS system. In Germany there is a close relationship between many of the occupational descriptions, and the process for developing them, and the design and implementation of vocational training programmes. This is particularly so for those occupations (*Ausbildungsberufe*) for which there exists a legally based vocational training programme involving both employers and the schooling system. Another example may be the work on 'units of competence' of the National Vocational Qualification system under development in the United Kingdom by the National Council for Vocational Qualifications. This system is intended to influence both the extent and content of vocational training in that country.

Immigration control　For the production of relevant statistics, Australia has introduced relatively detailed occupational coding of all visa applications, as well as of passenger cards collected from overseas arrivals and departures. An NOCD code (i.e. ASCO code) is also given to all immigration applications and will provide part of the basis for assessing the skill level, an element in the points system used to determine whether permission to immigrate will be granted. Previously the Australian immigration authorities used a separate OCD which gave special emphasis to 'priority' occupations and lumped the rest into one or several groups. Systems similar to this are also used by immigration authorities in other countries, or by authorities charged with the administration or monitoring of citizens working abroad.

Monitoring occupational safety and health　The registration of occupation on death certificates and of type of work on reports of occupational accidents, injuries and illnesses has long represented an important example of classification to provide a basis for epidemiological studies on the work-related incidence of specific causes of deaths, accidents or illnesses, such as specific types of cancers (for example Sweden, Australia and the United Kingdom) or for general studies of social differences in mortality and morbidity.[3] For these types of studies there are also significant advantages to common international classifications, as they will represent a possibility of pooling data from several countries for small, possibly high risk, groups of the population. In cases where it has been possible to observe significant patterns of mortality or morbidity, warranting further investigations about possible causes, the occupational descriptions found in the OCDs will normally not give information which is detailed enough to identify possible risk factors. More accurate descriptions from this perspective, as well as possibilities for re-grouping detailed occupations according to known risk factors, are considered to be important ways of improving the OCDs currently used.

Pay and human resource management systems   Enterprise-specific and organization-specific systems for job classification and evaluation (JCE systems) are related to the OCDs reviewed in this chapter, but outside the scope of the review. However, there are some examples of overlapping between JCEs and OCDs. For example, both Sweden and Australia have systems of collective pay determination which have resulted in the use of industry-wide and country-wide wage and salary systems.

These collective agreement systems seem characterized by tailor-made distinctions between relevant groups. These groups are typically described mainly by their titles, which are well understood by the social partners who have negotiated the agreements and who together monitor their implementation at the workplace, where they are supplemented by agreed ranking-systems used for determination of the actual pay. These collective agreement systems are normally not linked to the NOCDs, but the Australian system for collective wage settlements is now being reformed and it is possible that the new system will make use of ASCO.[4]

Another example of overlap between JCEs and the NOCD has also been reported from Australia, where large corporations have used ASCO to analyse the staffing structures of enterprises with different JCE systems. Private management consultants have also used ASCO as a tool in their work. From Australia it has also been reported that as strong patterns of occupational segregation have been identified as one of the major structural impediments to equal pay and opportunity for women and men in the labour market, the Australian Affirmative Action Agency

---

[3] For studies of mortality, the cross-classification by industry of certain very detailed occupational groups will sometimes be needed to be able to isolate high-risk groups.

[4] A swedish project in the 1970s to develop an NOCD which could also be used in collective agreements had to be abandoned as the social partners could not reach consensus.

has recommended the use of ASCO in the compulsory reporting of progress in the implementation of affirmative action programmes. So far, consideration of the private sector's use of ASCO does not seem to have had any independent influence on its structure and content.

Summary statement about user requirements   Any review of users' demand concerning NOCDs will specify that information about 'occupations' is needed on a range of topics, the most important of which are:

- tasks and duties of the jobs
- materials and machinery worked with
- products and services produced
- typical, as well as limiting, working conditions and work situations
- mental and physical skill requirements
- career opportunities and job prospects
- range of income gained
- 'typical personality profiles' suited for the jobs
- training opportunities and ways to gain relevant experience

This information is both of interest in itself, in particular for vocational guidance and choice, and because it provides the basis for constructing relevant sorting tools (i.e. classifications) to be used to search for information of interest; to match job qualifications, experience and desires of persons to job openings, training and immigration opportunities; and to describe and analyse the situation and condition of occupationally defined groups of persons in terms of their present or past work experience.

Not many users seem concerned about the conceptual basis for the OCDs they use, and OCD-publications are generally rather vague in their presentation of this basis. However, the following description seems to cover the main practice and most users' requirements:

The primary units described and sorted by an OCD are the 'occupations'. An 'occupation' is defined as a set of 'jobs' with the same main tasks and duties, where a 'job' is a set of tasks and duties (designed to be) performed by one person. Persons are classified through their link with a job – past, present or future.

Different users tend to have different and sometimes conflicting views both about how finely the distinctions between different 'occupations' should be drawn, and about what should constitute 'similar occupations', i.e. what the main sorting tools should be. This issue is discussed further in the section below on the classification systems of the NOCDs. Most users do not have very precise ideas about the *form* which they would like for the occupational descriptions. In some countries researchers have developed interesting examples of formal typologies used to describe various aspects of the occupational groups. These can be found mainly in Australia, Canada, Germany, the Netherlands and the United States. These typologies have been developed mainly to satisfy needs of vocational guidance and rehabilitation, but have also been used for empirical studies of the functioning of the labour market and its impact on, for example income distribution, as well for studies of occupational differences in mortality and morbidity.

ORGANIZATION AND EXECUTION OF THE NOCD WORK

Dividing the NOCD work between different organizations

Some conclusions have emerged concerning the organization of NOCD work and the division of labour between the interested organizations, taking into account that it is difficult to find a country where there is one organization which sees this work as its core task (in contrast to geographic mapping which is the responsibility of a national mapping agency in most countries). Most countries seem to have a more or less formalized split of responsibilities between institutions or departments. The responsibility for the development of the main classification structure(s) has typically been 'given' (often by default) to the national statistical organization for which the sorting function is a major interest, while the responsibility for the informational content of the dictionary (i.e. the data-base function) rests with organizations with both a direct interest in the information as such and a network of collaborators and contacts through which the information can be collected. The main 'dictionary organization' will often be the national employment service, in particular if vocational guidance is seen as an important part of its duties. Problems of co-ordination do result from this split in responsibilities, in particular related to agreements on co-ordination of budgets and initiatives and on reasonable overlap of tasks, but one advantage is that each organization has an operational interest in the results of its own work. Another advantage is that the split in responsibilities may serve to ensure that some work will continue even if one of the partners fails to follow up its job for a period. The split may also provide some pressure for neglected work to start again.

It is also important to recognize that success in the work with the OCDs requires both top management support for the work and that the managerial and operational responsibility is given to strongly committed and competent persons who are willing and able to overcome institutional indifference as well as the technical challenges involved.

Collecting occupational information

A large number of different methods have been developed for collecting information for job descriptions and performing job analysis for individual organizations and enterprises.[5] However, there is very little documentation (outside the United States and Germany) about how information has actually been collected for NOCDs. The methods and results from enterprise-level job analysis work seem to have had only indirect influence, at best, on the information collected for the NOCDs. To a large extent this must be a consequence of the differences in the scale of the task of developing something which can describe up to a few thousand jobs in one organization on one hand and several million jobs in a country on the other. The lack of documentation is probably also related to the costs of performing 'satisfactory' job analysis. These costs may be acceptable when performed on a relatively small scale and with quite tangible benefits in terms of improved personnel management and improved control with wage and salary costs, but they are quite unacceptable on a national scale with much more diffuse benefits, even if satisfactory sampling and generalization procedures exist. French experts had planned to carry out 30,000 interviews over a four-year period for their major occupational dictionary, the *Répertoire française des emplois* (RFE), but they only managed to execute 10,000 over six years, using something like ninety work-years. The Australians used about forty work-years of staff resources over a three-year period for their *ASCO Working Draft*, which was published in 1983 and which has provided, with some updating, the basic information for the subsequent Australian work. No resource estimates have been reported from other countries, but in particular the work in Germany does clearly involve a large network of persons both in the public and the private sector, mostly consulted as specialists in a more or less systematic manner.

The most common approach to the development of occupational descriptions is exemplified by the Australian case. The Australians started from the descriptions found in the Canadian *Classification and Dictionary of Occupations* (CCDO), and carried out interviews with sector experts, management and work organization consultants, managers, supervisors and workers themselves to establish (a) whether the described occupations existed in Australia; (b) whether other occupations existed which were not described by the CCDO; (c) whether some of the 'specialisations' in the CCDO would be important enough in Australia to warrant their own descriptions; and (d) what modifications should be

[5] See, for example, S. Gael, ed., *The Job Analysis Handbook for Business, Industry and Government*, Vols. 1 and 2 (New York, Wiley, 1988).

made to the CCDO descriptions to reflect Australian circumstances and practices. On-site inspection of work operations were also used to some extent. As much as possible, the state and local employment offices were allocated descriptions for verification and updating on the basis of which occupations were thought to be particularly relevant in their geographic area. Standard formats and guidelines were used, but the range of work situations considered, the way informational inconsistencies were resolved or reflected and other aspects influencing the quality of the resulting descriptions depended inevitably upon the particular officers and their contacts. This process resulted in 2,208 individually described 'occupations' instead of the 6,700 described in the CCDO model.

The French data collection operation, on the other hand, did not start from an existing model or already existing descriptions. It was mainly based directly on studies of individual jobs, planned to span all different work situations. After initial studies to select firms, the activity (the 'unit') to be studied within the firm, and the particular job and worker, data were collected at the level of the firm, the unit and the worker to obtain both the context and the specifics of the work done. The worker interview was largely open, and carried out by well-educated persons who had been specially trained for the task. The resulting 10,000 job descriptions were consolidated into 810 'types of employment' (the term 'occupation' was deliberately avoided) or typical work situations, each covering a group of tasks offering common characteristics so that they can be performed by the same individual. In this consolidation process the following criteria were used:

- the position of the worker in the organization, his/her function and place in the technical process
- the way the worker operated in relation to people, to machines and to documents, using some reference to the typology used by the United States *Dictionary of Occupational Titles* (DOT)
- the degree of autonomy of the worker relative to the instructions received.

In the 23 volumes of 'type of employment' descriptions published as result of this exercise, mining occupations and jobs directly related to the production and distribution of energy are not covered. Neither are some of the professions, such as lawyers and medical doctors.

Updating the occupational information

In reviewing the work on different NOCDs one can easily get the impression that most of the organizations which have been able to develop a reasonably finished product tend to collapse from the effort after crossing the finishing line, at least as far the NOCD is concerned. The general picture is that no systematic effort and hardly any resources are spent on the updating and maintenance of the NOCDs for a good many years after they have been published. One reason for this seems to be that little care has been taken to distinguish between updating and maintenance, on the one side, and revision, on the other.[6] In principle maintenance and updates should be undertaken continuously, while the 'revision' of the NOCD, meaning a complete re-evaluation of its principles and structure, should only be considered once every fifteen to twenty years. One consequence of the lack of maintenance and update is that the quality of the OCD is slowly undermined, as it is getting out-of-date, with frustration and loss of confidence among users as one of the consequences.

The most notable exception to the lack of updating concerns the main instruments used for vocational guidance. These instruments are typically re-issued every two to three years with at least some updated information, in particular about training opportunities, but also with some new material about (groups of) occupations and about trends in employment opportunities. One reason why information about training opportunities may be easier to update than other types of occupational information is that the training courses are organized and revised by formal, permanent institutions, which are relatively stable (at least when run by the public sector) and with an interest in making their courses known to potential clients. The vocational guidance material distributed to school-leavers and job-seekers is one possible channel of free publicity for the training institutions.

The sources of occupational information used to update the vocational guidance material are typically the same type of industry specialists as those mentioned in the description of the Australian work above. In addition the training institutions themselves may also give information about what they see as trends in tasks and duties in relevant areas of work. One consequence of this is that the material may emphasize new technologies and methods rather than the typical ones. The new information on trends in tasks and skill requirements of occupations found in vocational guidance material will normally not, however, be used to update relevant parts of the NOCD. The main reason for this is probably that responsibility for the vocational guidance material is not located together with the responsibility for the NOCD.

---

[6] 'Maintenance' of course means the correction of mistakes and inaccuracies as they are discovered. 'Updating' means the renewal of descriptions as tasks and duties change, for example because of new types of machinery and work organization, and the addition of new occupations into the existing structure.

Statistical organizations normally make an effort to update the occupation coding indexes, but often only in connection with the preparations for the population censuses, which are carried out every five to ten years.

Organization of the information concerning each occupational group

Although some NOCDs will not have any information about the jobs other than that which can be understood from the group titles, most of them will have at least definitional statements which are mainly designed to make clear the dividing lines between different groups. They frequently consist of a short opening statement describing the general functions of the jobs classified to them. This may be followed by a more or less structured text enumerating main tasks and duties as well as tasks which may be of importance in certain jobs classified to the group but which are not necessarily considered as inherent for such jobs. Tasks which exclude jobs from a particular group may also be mentioned. Some OCDs will have lists of titles of occupations which are included in the respective groups and, in some cases, lists of related occupations which are classified to other groups. Supplementary occupational descriptions can in many countries by found 'outside' the OCDs. The German classification *Klassifizerung der Berufe* (KdB) has no occupational descriptions, descriptions found elsewhere have frequently been coded to KdB. The Swedish statistical classification NYK has only brief definitional statements, but Sweden used to have a dictionary which described in depth broader groups than those specified in the NYK. The French statistical classification PCS has established links to RFE, mentioned above, which has information about the type of firm and unit in which the jobs may be found; the limits to the type of employment and the occupation's relationship with others; tasks performed; level of responsibility and instructions received, implications of mistakes and relationships with other people; work environment; ways of access to the jobs and training required; further career opportunities. The graphic depiction of the last two types of information is one of the strong features of the French job-placement tool ROME.

Not many OCDs have followed DOT's example of using formal typologies (coding systems) for the description of aspects such as training and experience required, 'typical personality profiles' suited for the jobs, mental and physical skill requirements, working conditions, income range. Outside Canada and the United States the most interesting examples can be found in Australia, Germany and the Netherlands. The Australian ASCO Working Draft developed formalized occupational profiles expressed in coded form. The 'job content factors' (JFCs) covered a wide range of dimensions: formal preparation, including general education and post-school preparation; informal preparation, including on-the-job training and experience. In Holland the following categories were coded: special requirements; subject matter; equipment used; involvement in various mental activities, physical activities and social activities; environmental location and conditions; time constraints; rewards (pay); labour-market size; and industry code. Unfortunately, resources were not available to carry on this aspect of the Australian work after the ASCO Working Draft had been completed. In Germany and the Netherlands formalized typologies describing various aspects of occupations have been developed for vocational rehabilitation, for vocational guidance and for curriculum development. The typologies used seem to have been tailor-made for each system with little or no standardization, except where the same organization is responsible for several systems.

The classification systems of the NOCDs

Although in principle the entries in an OCD can be organized alphabetically by the titles of the described groups, most, but not all, have organized the material by a more or less hierarchical classification structure based on 'type of work performed' as described by the main tasks and duties. This structure is normally intended to be the main system for sorting (i.e. coding) jobs, persons holding those jobs and for searching for information about the jobs.

In most of the NOCDs developed before 1985, 'type of work performed' was seen as referring to some clearly and some more diffusely defined 'activity areas' such as 'health and social security', 'farming', 'transport' etc. which were considered to be related to the outcomes of the jobs' activities rather than those of the firms in which the jobs were performed. Thus these 'activity areas' were seen as clearly distinct from 'industry', the variable used to classify firms on the basis of their most important products. That many users, of occupational statistics in particular, found it difficult to understand the difference between 'activity area' and 'industry' was partly due to use of the same, or very similar, words to label the two types of groups, but also partly due to the strong correlation found in practice between the two variables. It was more serious, however, that although this way of organizing the information about different occupations was convenient for some users of that information, in particular for communication with employers and for organizing the work of collecting information about tasks and duties, it was virtually useless as a basis for description and analysis of labour markets and social structures and behaviour.

Giving priority to the description and analysis of social structures and behaviour, the French national statistical office (INSEE) developed in the early 1980s the socio-professional classification PCS, which give priority to social positions and perceptions for defining 'similar' occupations. The revisions of the Australian NOCD and of the ILO's ISCO gave priority to the needs of *labour market* description and analysis, resulting in a classification structure where broad distinctions are made on the basis of the *skill level* required to carry out the tasks and duties of the jobs, and the finer distinctions are based on *skill specializations* within the broad skill-level groups.

The conceptual basis for the new classification structure for ISCO was developed using the results of work carried out in Australia. Benefiting from these results, the ILO was able to develop a structure suited for a classification which serves both as a model for development and revision work in many countries and as a common denominator for the presentation of occupational statistics and other information from different countries. It also serves as an instrument for communicating occupational information between countries, e.g. in the international exchange of workers. In addition to having strong similarities to the Australian ASCO, the revised ISCO (ISCO-88) structure provides the basis for the work to develop a common occupational structure for the presentation of occupational statistics in the European Community (ISCO-88(COM)), as well as for work to develop new or revised NOCDs in a large number of countries or areas, e.g. United Kingdom, Ireland, Italy, the Netherlands, Denmark, Norway, Cyprus, Hong Kong, Singapore, Mauritius, Namibia, the United Republic of Tanzania, Barbados and Trinidad & Tobago, to mention some of the countries where the work has started or already been completed. ISCO-88 has also been used as the starting point for the development of occupational classifications in most of the transition countries in Eastern and Central Europe and the former Soviet Union, in particular for statistical use.

It is quite clear that classification structures based on either 'activity areas' or 'skill level and skill specialization' have no better claim to be the 'best' or 'better' than any of the other possible ones, even if many of the users who are monitoring labour-market trends or who are analysing its structure and development, have welcomed the use of a skill-based classification structure. The 'best' classification system can only be determined by the type of questions one wants to find answers to or the type of work one is trying to do. It is also clear that with modern computer technology, different classification schemes can be applied easily to the same basic (i.e. detailed) occupational groups, provided the right codes and keywords have been attached to or been integrated into the group descriptions. Strong differences between different users of a NOCD about the best classification structure for their respective work and clients, for example between the national statistical and employment services, should therefore not prevent them from co-operating on revising, updating and maintaining the basic descriptions of the NOCD and the development of tools for the effective use of the NOCD.

Tools, rules and guidelines for effective statistical use of OCDs

Many of the complaints voiced about statistics based on ISCO-68 and ISCO-based NOCDs were misguided in the sense that they were formulated as complaints about the structure and principles of ISCO when the problems which provoked them were really caused by inadequate updating and maintenance or improper use of the classifications, in particular when they were used for the coding of jobs and persons. Based on the experience of the ILO and the countries surveyed, and in particular the methodological work carried out in Australia, it is possible to formulate some 'golden rules' about occupation coding:

(1) The key to correct coding of jobs into occupations is the existence of a carefully constructed coding index reflecting the classification structure, both of which have been kept up to date.

(2) Coding should be based on relevant information about the job; normally this will be the occupational title and the job's main tasks and duties.

(3) Coding should be based on clear instructions about how and when the various elements in the occupational response should be used, and the coding index should be constructed to reflect these rules.

(4) Coding should always be to the most detailed level in the classification supported by the information available.

(5) 'Not elsewhere classified' categories are to be used only for the jobs specified as belonging to these groups. Inadequately described jobs, jobs which cut across defined groups, and jobs which for other reasons cannot be coded should be given special codes and referred as queries to supervisors and those responsible for the NOCD for resolution.

(6) Give coders feedback on queries and performance.

(7) Use systematically queries generated during the coding process to update the coding index and the classification.

Computer-assisted coding (CAC) systems have been developed for statistical use both in Australia and in the United Kingdom. They make it easier for the coder to follow the rules and guidelines necessary for high-quality, low-error coding than using the traditional short cuts, have led to occupational coding having error rates of up to 20 per cent. There is good reason to expect that such error rates are as common among employment officers as among statistical coders, even though the former may be expected to know the NOCD better (depending on their training and experience) and also to be able to get more information from job-seekers and employers. However, they also need tools such as those specified by the above 'golden rules'. Without tools such as (1) and (5) we must expect that an increasing number of vacancies and job-seekers will be coded to the 'not elsewhere classified' groups, with the result that 'occupation' increasingly becomes useless as a basis for matching or for statistical description.[7] It should be noted that CAC systems make the coding process more effective, but that proper coding procedures can also be followed without such systems. Some statistical organizations have also been using (partly) automated coding (AC) systems, which typically will code about 60–70 per cent of the responses in a census or survey. The remaining responses must be coded manually or interactively. The overall error rates seem to be about the same as for manual coding. Current developments seem to be leading to 'expert systems' which have features common to both CAC and AC systems.

Procedures for thorough evaluation of existing NOCDs

Little information has been made available to the ILO on how such evaluations are initiated, decided upon or executed. The report on the work in Australia makes it clear that strong signals had been received from various user communities, as well as from government-initiated inquiries, before the work to develop ASCO was started, and that consultations with users took place during the development process. The most interesting of these consultations is a users' requirement survey which asked the respondents to rank three different alternative models for classification structure, each presented in some detail. The work to develop a new Standard Occupational Classification (SOC) in the United Kingdom also started with a survey of the user community's perception of the existing instruments, but in a much less formalized way than that used by Australia. The extensive network in Germany, used to update the occupational information relevant for vocational guidance and planning, does not seem to have been much used to evaluate the classification structure. It seems clear that in many countries there is no formal evaluation of the existing NOCD before the responsible agencies decide that it needs to be revised. Such decisions seem to be based, in many cases, on a combination of pressure from dissatisfaction with the slowly

---

[7] This development has been described, for example, by experienced job placement officers in Sweden, who have developed informal strategies to cope with the problem.

deteriorating quality of a poorly updated and maintained NOCD and of the related statistics, and an inspiration-effect from developments in other countries and international organizations. Few persons take an active interest in the NOCDs, at least in most countries outside North America, and the persons who do therefore depend on inspiration and impulses from the international community. As the developer and guardian of ISCO, the ILO feels some responsibility both for communicating such inspirations and impulses and for emphasizing that the work at the national level should be based on national needs and priorities.

CONCLUDING REMARKS

It should be clear from what has been said that the main problems and shortcomings related to the development, use and maintenance of the NOCDs are related to the first and last of these activities. Concerning the use of the NOCDs it seems fair to say that well-developed and understood tools now exist, and the resources needed to bring them into use are not prohibitive, even considering the limited resources which normally are allocated to this area by the respective agencies. However, methods for proper development and updating of much of the occupational information which should form the basis and core content of the NOCDs seem to be much too expensive to be used in practice by most countries, with the exception of those countries, like Germany and the Netherlands, which give much importance to vocational education and related guidance. The work for vocational guidance and planning does not, however, extend to or feed into work on the classification in a systematic and continuous manner. As a result most countries have some good, detailed 'street maps' for individual enterprises or occupational areas, and some general 'small-scale maps' with limited information for the whole world of work. The latter are of variable and often doubtful quality. Given the limited resources normally made available for work with OCDs, the best prospect to improve on this situation is to learn how to improve the exploitation of the information contained in enterprise-level job descriptions and to generalize from them, as well as how to make more effective use of all the unstructured information about jobs which already exist. Unfortunately we cannot expect a technological breakthrough in the mapping of the world of work similar to that which remote sensing from satellites has brought to geographic mapping.

25

The revision of the Hungarian system of classifying occupations

J. FÓTI and G. LÁZÁR*

The first part of this chapter is based on a paper presented by the same authors during the ILO Workshop on the Role of National Occupational Classifiers of the Central and Eastern European Countries in the Economic Restructuring held in Geneva in December 1990. The original version has been only slightly modified, so this part reflects our views, opinions and plans at that time.

The second part gives a brief report about the work done for the development of the new Hungarian Classification of Occupations.

In the last part we discuss our further plans and potential problems concerning the 'transition period' (i.e. between the old classification and the new one).

SHORT HISTORICAL BACKGROUND AND EMERGING CHALLENGES

In Hungary, the Classification of Occupations that had been developed in 1975 (called FEOR) remained unchanged in its basic principles till 1992 – apart from the modifications and amendments executed in the meantime. Essentially, this system met the requirements of the centrally planned economy for almost two decades. With the recent developments, it became obvious that the system could not operate in its original form. The elaboration of a new classification based on an entirely new conception seemed to be imperative – in line with the transition to a market economy and with the need to get closer to the

* This chapter was originally written as a paper for the ILO Workshop on the Role of National Occupational Classifiers of the Central and Eastern European Countries in the Economic Restructuring, Geneva, December 1990.

statistical systems of the more developed countries.

The most important considerations for the revision of the classification system were as follows:

- the Hungarian system, its structure and principles were basically different from the international classification (ISCO), and as a whole it was different from the systems used by market-oriented countries;
- the system in its original form was inapplicable to the private sector and to the majority of the new economic organizations;
- extremely detailed activities caused great problems in a number of occupational groups, while some new occupations were difficult to classify;
- the strict separation of manual and non-manual work also caused difficulties for a flexible use of the system;
- as the system of wage categorization became outdated, the last two items of the eight categories fell into disuse.

In addition to the specific issues above, there were general methodological considerations as well. The requirements of the system at the time of its birth resulted in an eclectic mixture of sectors, qualifications and other aspects.

The following principles needed to be taken into consideration for the revision:

- First of all, the system of occupations must correspond to the international classification in accordance with ISCO's system – with allowance for Hungarian specialities as well. The experience of developed countries must be studied to provide assistance with practical adaptation.
- Another aspect that has to be taken into consideration is that the modernized system must be able to be linked to the old classification – to some extent. The need for comparability and for the preservation of continuous time series are essential requirements.
- The purpose of the classification system has to be clear: it has to serve primarily for the classification of labour, and it has to be applicable to population and establishment statistics as well. In addition, flexibility and the possibility of further development have to be assured (for example, to cope with new professions or new forms of organizations).
- The basis of the new classification – in contrast to the former one – should not be sectoral or organizational, but should be based rather on the contents of the professions or activities. On this basis, those categories and specifications which are not justified by practical

requirements should be omitted. The qualifications or skills of a worker should only be considered where they are necessary for the job.

On the basis of these considerations, the occupations could be aggregated into eight or nine main groups. The number of main groups might change – according to the requirements, and four, or maybe five, categories would be sufficient instead of the eight categories used before. It is necessary to proceed from the following considerations during the formulation of the main groups.

According to our judgement, ISCO's system can be followed in the case of non-manual workers. This implies that the modernized system will depart from the present one to some extent because the basis of the classification will consistently be the nature of the profession. Non-manual professions can be separated into three main groups.

The first main group would consist of top-level managers and executives. Separating company and institution leaders may appear to be a problem in forming this main group. Should we put central and local government administrators into separate groups, and in what form should the organizational structure appear here? The size of the organizational units (small, middle-sized, big companies, institutions) needs to be taken into consideration.

Highly qualified professionals would form the second main group. The nature of their professions would dominate the classification here, and that may concur with the sectoral scheme for some groups of activities (e.g. in the case of doctors, who carry out their activities mostly within health organizations). People who belong to other groups (e.g. engineers, technicians) may form groups that can be outlined by the content of their profession in different branches of material and non-material spheres. In short, the system has to allow for intersectoral aggregation as well.

Scientists, technicians or – corresponding to a market economy – representatives of business life and the banking system would be placed in this main group. An alternative classificatory system puts administrative experts and executives into this group also. Since a wide range of professions may evolve here, the question has been raised that it might be more practical to form a separate main group for them.

The third main group would contain middle-level technicians and people of the same sort. This way of forming a group seems to be simple and practical, because this group would contain technicians, assistants, etc., whose work is connected with those in the previous group. This main group may cross the border between manual and non-manual work, because it traces assistants up to the final stage.

For manual jobs – in our opinion – it seems necessary to depart from the ISCO system. In the Hungarian economy, the application of general criteria does not seem to be suitable, not even in the long run – considering the structural fundamentals and the coexistence of different economic forms. The specification which conforms to the characteristics of the profession seems to be temporarily more convenient for us. This would contain the following five main groups – manual workers in:

- manufacturing
- construction
- agriculture
- transport and communication
- commerce

If necessary, ISCO's system could be established by rearranging some of the major groups. Our proposal puts manual workers into five main groups – following the principles above.

Separating unskilled workers into another main group may appear to be a problem in the classification of manual occupations. We are inclined to think that it would be more appropriate to put them into different main groups, according to the nature of their profession. At least, it is reasonable to separate the group of agricultural and non-agricultural unskilled workers.

DEVELOPMENT OF A NEW CLASSIFICATION SYSTEM

According to the plans and outlined in the previous section (originally set out during the ILO workshop in December 1990), we started working on the new classification in 1991. The expert team consisted primarily of representatives of the CSO, the Ministry of Labour and the National Labour Centre (NLC), but in specific cases the advice of further experts was sought. So, in effect, the first proposal for the new, more up-to-date classification of occupations reflected the opinions and suggestions of a wide range of experts.

The first proposal was checked several times, for example with members of the Human Resources Department of the University of Economics. Useful advice was given also by ILO consultants concerning the direction of further development. We also had the opportunity – through bilateral consultation – of studying the systems and experiences of several countries, such as Austria, Germany, Australia and Canada.

The next important phase in the process of checking and amending the new system was the inter-agency discussion. In this context, we also had the opportunity to clarify several questions concerning the interpretation and application of the occupational classification system. The Information Committee of the National Council for Reconciliation of Interests also took the development of the new classification system onto its agenda. The results of all these consultations were taken into consideration during the finalization of the system.

Because of the relatively short time available the trials and testing of the new system were accomplished in parallel with the inter-ministerial consultations. Approximately seventy economic organizations of different types and sizes from a variety of industries were involved in the testing procedure. To gain useful experience we also recoded occupations using the new system within smaller parts of the 2 per cent sample of the population census for urban and village areas as well. The result of both approaches was that in the great majority of cases there were no difficulties at all in determining the new codes for occupations. In some cases we made the necessary modifications. After all these tests and amendments the system was modified in several parts and it became more detailed. During the development process we had several different alternatives. The last version – which integrated the requirements of the different users – was ready by the autumn of 1992.

The new Hungarian classification system, which took shape in this way, uses the main groups of ISCO-88 substantially unchanged. On the lower levels of aggregation it was possible and necessary to take into consideration the specific requirements of the Hungarian economy. In some cases the details also reflect the intention to allow for the continuation of our time series. These were the reasons for the final version's being a system, which is partly different from – in most cases more detailed than – ISCO-88. The difference is widest of course in the most detailed part, especially on the fourth level where the individual occupations are listed.

During the development process, as a result of a series of tests and discussions we had to depart in some cases from the plans outlined in the first section. The final results – compared to ISCO-88 – are displayed in Table 25.1. In the new Hungarian system – in accordance with the principles of ISCO-88 – the actual activity content is the starting point for defining and classifying occupations; nevertheless, important group-creating aspects are the level of skill, knowledge and education necessary to practise the various occupations as well. But the latter concepts can be interpreted only with the help of some measurable aspect. So it was unavoidable, as an auxiliary method, that we also had to examine the vocational qualification or educational level necessary or desirable for practising certain occupations in the new system.

Table 25.1: ISCO-88 and the new Hungarian classification (FEOR-93)

Aggregation levels	Number of items in	
	ISCO-88	FEOR-93
First level: major groups	10	10
Second level: sub-major groups	28	42
Third level: minor groups	116	133
Fourth level: unit groups	390	627

According to this, the Hungarian occupational classification uses qualifications – the same way as ISCO does – in the cases of main groups no. 2 to no. 9. But this is not considered as a rigid criterion, which could be handled independently of actual activity contents. So it can be stated only generally as a principle that occupations within main group 2 in most cases require qualifications equivalent to higher education (university or college). For main group 3 education to vocational secondary school level (medium-level professionals or technicians) is typical, but considering the formal educational qualification there are possible deviations in both directions, upwards and downwards too. In the main group no. 4 the general secondary school level (which does not provide a vocational qualification) and lower level vocational (non-manual) training is typical. In main groups nos. 5 to 8 are those occupations which need certain specific types of skills and vocational training. The necessary skill level in these groups can be different, to a great extent depending on the type of activity, from highly skilled to semi-skilled work. Main group 9 consists of those occupations which can be practised without any qualification or training, where the primary school educational level is sufficient.

To differentiate occupations the educational qualification is used as an auxiliary aspect, but another factor is the degree of freedom and independence in making decisions that is required in normal everyday practice in those specific occupations. The importance of this factor is vital, especially in those cases where the mechanical differentiation of occupations belonging to different main groups cannot be solved using only the former criteria. For example, in the case of technical occupations it is difficult to decide in many cases whether a specific occupation belongs to main group 2 or rather to main group 3. The existing formal qualification is not enough to make this decision. Professionals with a diploma of higher education may fill a job for which their degrees are not necessary, or they may fulfil tasks for which a medium-level qualification would be enough. In such cases the actual sphere of activity, the extent of responsibility for decisions can help to classify borderline jobs. In some exceptional cases it also can happen that somebody has not got a diploma or degree in higher education, yet because of their activities and great responsibilities belongs to main group 2.

In the case of manual occupations similar problems may occur between main groups 7 and 8, where also the possibility of making decisions and the extent of responsibility can help to determine the right classification.

The new Hungarian Standard Classification of Occupations (FEOR-93) and the proposal concerning its introduction got the official approval of the president of the Central Statistical Office on 1 November 1992. Taking into consideration that the new system is entirely different in its principles from the old one, it was decided not to introduce it on a particular date. So the year 1993 was considered to be a transitional year during which it is possible to switch over to the new system without bigger hitches. This time period can also be used to clarify and sort out the possible new questions raised by the use of the new system.

A separate publication was issued by the CSO after the approval of the new classification (the updated version of the Standard Classification of Occupations, FEOR-93, CSO, 1992 Budapest).

Chapter 1 of this publication gives methodological weight to the application of FEOR-93. It summarizes briefly the objectives of the new classification system, describes the structure of the nomenclature and gives an overview of the links with the international classification system. The other part of this methodological chapter describes the contents of the individual main groups and major groups and their classification principles. This part gives more details about the system and makes it possible to recognize what type of occupations belong to the different main groups and major groups. It also demonstrates the correct method of classifying occupations using the new system.

Chapter 2 contains the whole list of occupations. This shows clearly arranged the major groups, sub-major groups and minor groups and unit groups in increasing order of code-numbers, and contains all the 627 occupations of the 4-digit level.

Chapter 3 contains the list of occupations in alphabetical order.

To make the introduction of the new occupational classification system easier, *Chapter 4* compares and constrasts the former system and the new one on the 4-digit level. Because of the different structures and classification principles of the old and the new systems, a full one-to-one assignment is not possible, so the comparison can only be informative.

For a relatively large number of occupations in the new system there is no perfect equivalent in the old one, considering their activity contents.

FURTHER PLANS

For the full introduction of the new system it is of vital importance to take into consideration that the occupational classification must be made suitable not only for statistical data collections and data processing, but it has to be applicable for other very important objectives too (like personnel records, employment exchanges, career counselling, social insurance reporting etc.). To help these applications it will be necessary to publish an even more detailed list of occupations or jobs. According to our plans this will be accomplished on the fifth and sixth digits and in the future users will be able to use these as a reference.

For the 4-digit occupations this publication will also give a short description about the activity contents of the individual occupations which can also help in the classifying process and can be used in employment exchanges, for employment and training, counselling etc. This description will also contain the list of specific jobs belonging to the individual 4-digit occupations and will give information about the necessary skills, abilities and education for the specific occupations.

To compile such a publication needs a tremendous effort. (Maybe this was the reason why we never had such a publication for the old FEOR.) The suggestions of the ILO consultants can also help in the preparation of this publication, and close cooperation between the National Labour Centre and the CSO will be very useful too.

The NLC has been working on the compilation of an Occupational Handbook since 1989. First the descriptions were developed according to the former occupational classification. It was almost ready when the development of the new classification was begun, so it was not worth publishing it. Now the NLC team – with the help of many outside experts – is working on the new version which will be in accordance with FEOR-93. The Occupational Handbook which was planned to be ready for printing by the end of 1993 should contain for each individual occupation the following information:

- a short description of the activities
- the required education or qualification
- the physical burden
- the level of work
- working environment
- desired level of abilities
- factors of aptitude and interest

It can be seen that the full planned content of the Occupational Handbook would be too much for statistical purposes, but the short description of occupations required for the statistical publication can be made by extracting the necessary parts from the manuscript of the Handbook. This will be done by the NLC team with the coordination of the CSO.

The detailed description of each occupation and their activity contents will also contribute to the refinement of the classification itself, so this close cooperation between the Central Statistical Office and the Employment Services (i.e. the NLC) is very important and useful for both parties.

System of classification and description of occupations in the Soviet Union: structure, purpose and issues relating to improvements

S. MAKOVLEV and V. OUVAROV*

The main components of the system of classification and descriptions of occupations used in the Soviet Union were as follows:

- the All-Union Classifier: Occupations of Manual Workers, Posts of Non-Manual Workers and Wage-Rate Categories (OKPDTR);
- the Standard Wage-Rate and Skill Manual on the Jobs and Occupations of Manual Workers (ETKS);
- the Skill Manual on the Posts of Managers, Professionals and Non-Manual Workers (KS).

The OKPDTR was compiled on the basis of the ETKS and KS. Together, they formed a single set of inter-related documents describing the world of labour, work, the occupations of manual workers and the posts of non-manual workers.

However, by 1990 it was felt that they were in urgent need of improvement and further development. Quite apart from the need to remedy some obvious shortcomings, this was dictated by the aims and objectives of the country's radical economic reform and conversion to a regulated market economy.

The aim of this chapter is:

(a) to bring out the main features of the system of classification and descriptions of occupations that used to be in operation in the Soviet Union;

---

* This chapter was originally written as a paper for the ILO Workshop on the Role of National Occupational Classifiers of the Central and Eastern European Countries in the Economic Restructuring, Geneva, December 1990, but has been revised to take into account the passage of time.

(b) to present the structure, coding system, functions and main fields of application of the OKPDTR, ETKS and KS;
(c) to describe the work which was carried out with these documents at the enterprise level and at the All-Union level;
(d) to show the main ways in which they could be improved.

GENERAL OBSERVATIONS AND DEFINITIONS

The basic principles underlying the classification are the similarity of the nature of the tasks performed and the extent and content of the knowledge and skills needed to perform them.

On this basis, the entire workforce employed in the national economy was divided into two major groups: namely, manual workers and non-manual workers.

The first group comprised workers who were employed to perform primarily physical labour, in other words workers whose occupational activity chiefly involved physical effort. These were the workers who participated directly in the process of material asset formation and those employed in maintenance work, the carriage of goods, passenger transport, the provision of material services, etc. Their vocational training laid primary emphasis on the acquisition of proper skills needed for the performance of specific occupational functions. The second group comprised personnel engaged in primarily mental work, whose occupational activity chiefly involved intellectual, rather than physical, effort. In the process of their training, primary emphasis was given to in-depth theoretical knowledge and the skills needed for its application. Non-manual workers were subdivided into managers, professionals – characterized by a high-skill level (higher or intermediate specialized education) – and technical executives, employed in the primary processing of information, secretarial work and other support tasks.

In the OKPDTR, this initial classification was specified in terms of the occupations of manual workers and the posts of non-manual workers. The occupation of a manual worker was understood to refer to a type of occupational activity concerned with the performance of socially useful functions deriving from the social division of labour. An occupation presupposed a sum of knowledge and vocational skills acquired by a worker through a special system of education or by long-term practice.

The post of a non-manual worker referred to the service status of such personnel, which depended on the range of their duties, their official rights and the nature of their responsibility.

Accordingly, the subjects of classification were the occupations of manual workers and the posts of non-manual workers. Obviously, this distinction was to some extent conventional. Indeed, the introduction of new technology, the automation of production processes, the development of progressive forms of organization and labour incentives tended to modify the content of the tasks performed by manual and non-manual workers and blur the dividing line between them. In practice, however, the problems that arose in relating workers to one group or the other were fairly easy to deal with.

The version of OKPDTR discussed here took effect on 1 January 1987. It was a systematized compilation of 5,300 occupational titles for manual workers and 1,700 post titles for non-manual workers. The occupations of manual workers included in the OKPDTR were given in accordance with the ETKS, and the posts of non-manual workers (including managers, professionals and technical executives) in accordance with the KS and the Standard Nomenclature of Posts of Non-Manual Workers. The classification of the occupations of manual workers was based on the ETKS groups, arranged by type of industry and job, while that of the duties of non-manual workers proceeded from the nature and content of tasks performed, in accordance with the KS.

The Classifier and manuals amply covered the occupations of manual workers and the posts of non-manual workers. In this connection, it must be borne in mind that the characteristics given in the skill manuals described the basic and most common tasks associated with a particular occupation or post, according to the division of labour and cooperation established in each sector of the national economy. In effect, both the ETKS and the KS were manuals describing 'basic' tasks. In practice, the manuals served as a basis for enterprises to work out service instructions for non-manual workers, setting forth their direct duties, rights and degree of responsibility, and, as far as manual workers were concerned, as a basis for defining specifically the content and extent of tasks and the procedure for their performance, at every workplace. If necessary, occupations and posts could be derived from the 'basic' types. The Classifier and manuals covered only part of the existing posts of personnel working for economic and state administration bodies. They did not include military servicemen, the personnel of bodies in charge of internal affairs, collective farmers, members of the clergy or the occupations and duties of various other categories of personnel whose activities were subject to special provisions or regulations.

The OKPDTR did not directly give descriptions of the tasks associated with occupations or posts. These were given in the ETKS and KS. The latter were used for guidance in dealing with issues related to the division of labour between workers and ensuring standardization (including intersectoral standardization) in the specification of their duties and functions and skill requirements.

The OKPDTR, ETKS and KS were an integral part of the former Soviet Union's wage-rate system. Indeed, they were used to work out various components of the system such as wage-rate categories, wage-rate coefficients, wage scales, the salary scales of non-manual workers and a number of standard-setting instruments (for example, those specifying the procedure for determining various types of wage-related supplements or additional pay as an incentive to combine several occupations, multi-machine operation, etc.). The wage-rate system was designed to secure the principle of equal remuneration for work of equal value. It also served to regulate and differentiate the rates of pay of the various categories of personnel, thereby guaranteeing the provision of a minimum wage level to workers, depending on their skill level.

For these purposes, jobs were rated; in other words, a job category was determined (for manual workers) or jobs were related to a remuneration group (for non-manual workers) according to the complexity, nature and conditions of the work involved and the particular characteristics and significance of the type of economic activity and the worker's skill level. In relating tasks to a particular category an analytical method was used to assess task complexity on the basis of a number of factors, including the complexity of tools and work pieces, technological processes, the range of tasks performed (operations) and the workers' self-reliance in performing their tasks.

A worker's skill level was determined on the basis of the degree of complexity of the tasks he or she was able to perform. This was reflected in a level of proficiency in knowledge and vocational skills and measured by means of a wage-rate category. Each category was associated with a specific monthly, daily or hourly rate of pay.

Wage rates were set on a centralized basis according to the difficulty, intensity and conditions of work, taking account of the economic significance of the branch of activity concerned, in the form of fixed, standard values.

Each wage-rate category had a corresponding wage-rate coefficient, which reflected the relation between the rate of the given category and the rate of the first category, taken as the reference unit.

Wage scales reflected the sum total of skill-level categories and the corresponding wage-rate coefficients , which were used to establish a direct dependency link between a worker's remuneration and his skills. They were worked out for virtually every branch of the national economy. In most branches, the wage scales comprised six or eight categories. Accordingly, the first category was the starting skill level, while the sixth or eighth was the highest skill level.[1]

The application of the OKPDTR, ETKS and KS was mandatory in state enterprises (amalgamations and organizations), co-operatives and other social organizations throughout all branches of the national economy of the former Soviet Union. It is on the basis of these documents that enterprises established the titles of occupations and posts, rated jobs, related workers to skill categories, defined official duties and skill requirements and performed other operations. At the nation-wide and sectoral levels, these documents were in effect essential instruments in management and planning, the systematization of information on economic activity, statistical work and the analysis of labour resources. They were used to work out training and advanced training programmes for workers in all branches of the national economy.

PURPOSE OF THE CLASSIFIER

The OKPDTR was designed for the operation of an automated system of collecting and processing the data needed for the calculation, analysis, current and prospective planning of labour resources and the composition and distribution of skilled labour among the different categories of personnel (i.e. manual workers and service workers, including managers, professionals and technical executives), the calculation of wage funds, etc., at every level of management within the national economy. This classification made it possible to group occupations by type of economic activity and task, skill level, form and system of remuneration, conditions of work and degree of automation.

The Classifier was used in the statistical accounting of the occupational structure of the workforce employed in the former Soviet Union and changes in its structure occurring in response to the supply of new machinery and equipment to enterprises, the improvement of technological processes and the organization of labour in production facilities. Research was conducted separately on manual workers and non-manual workers.

Detailed information on the occupational structure of the workforce was gathered through full-scale surveys conducted once every five years

---

[1] The same category in different sectors did not necessarily imply that the work performed was of equal complexity. For this reason, one of the indicators used in establishing the skill level required for the performance of tasks of a particular degree of complexity was the time factor in the worker's training. Accordingly, the duration of vocational training reflected task differentiation by level of complexity in the inter-occupational cross-section, while wage-rate categories made it possible to reflect variations in the complexity of tasks within the same occupation.

in the main sectors of the national economy (including industry, construction, agriculture and transport). The primary purpose of these surveys was to determine the number of workers engaged in each occupation, by sex and skill level. On the basis of such survey data, conclusions could be drawn on the staffing of individual enterprises or sectors with skilled labour; on the appropriateness of the number of workers in a particular occupation in relation to installed plant; particular labour requirements could be identified; and forecasts could be made regarding the scale of training of additional skilled workers. The survey data were used to calculate a number of supplementary indicators pertaining to conditions and the organization of work and the degree of automation.

The statistical basis used in monitoring the utilization of the labour of non-manual workers within the national economy was a survey of the number of professionals with a higher or intermediate specialized education. This was conducted once every two years in all sectors of the national economy. The survey programme provided for the collection of data on the number of professionals by education (singling out those who had completed their studies within the past three years), sex and assignment of professionals to appropriate duties. The survey data made it possible to decide whether sectors or enterprises were saturated with particular professionals and whether they were distributed adequately, and to forecast the scale of training requirements for professionals in specific fields of specialization.

The OKPDTR, ETKS and KS served as source material for the compilation of the occupational dictionary (consisting of systematic and alphabetical dictionaries) used in coding replies to the questions on occupation[2] in census forms when the All-Union Population Censuses were conducted. The systematic occupational dictionary used in preparing the material for the 1989 census of the population of the former Soviet Union classified occupations into 260 groups, falling into 50 divisions.The grouping of occupations into groups and divisions was based either on an occupational-sectoral criterion (for example, the occupations of graphic artists, textile workers, builders, etc.), or on a functional criterion (for example, the occupations of planning and accounting personnel, the occupations of persons working on lifting and transport machinery, etc.). Occupations common to many sectors of the national economy were classified in a separate division.

---

[2] For the purposes of the census, 'occupation' was understood to refer to income-generating activity, i.e. a post, an occupation or work performed, but not to any specialization acquired as a result of education (this being a form of effectively performed work).

CODING SYSTEM

The OKPDTR was an integral part of the standard uniform system of technical and economic information classification and coding used in the automated management system of the national economy. It contained a systematic list of occupational titles of manual workers and post titles of non-manual workers, giving specific codes for each title.

The OKPDTR was divided into two parts, compiled on a uniform, methodical basis. Inside each part the titles of the classification subjects were arranged in alphabetical order. The first part, Classifier of the Occupations of Manual Workers, covered the occupations of manual workers in accordance with the Standard Wage-Rate and Skill Manual on the Jobs and Occupations of Manual Workers (ETKS). An excerpt from the first part is reproduced below:

Part I

Code	Control number	Occupational title	Range of categories	Manual number
19149	6	Turner	2-6	02
18809	9	Broad-profile lathe operator	2-8	02
Identification box		Box containing the title of the classification subject	Information box	

Part II, the classification of posts of non-manual workers, was compiled on the basis of the Skill Manual on the Posts of Managers, Professionals and Non-Manual Workers and other standard-setting instruments. The following excerpt is reproduced by way of example:

Part II

Code	Control number	Post title	Category code
22351	7	Labour organization and standard-setting engineer	2
Identification box		Box containing the title of the classification subject	Information box

Each entry in the classification comprised three boxes, namely:

- an identification box;
- a box containing the title of the subject of the classification;
- an information box.

The identification box was constructed by means of a serial, ordinal system of coding the subjects of the classification. The code of each title consists of five digits and a control number. The first digit of the codes in both parts of the OKPDTR serves to designate the worker's category (1 refers to the occupation of a manual worker and 2 to the post of a non-manual worker), while the other four digits are the ordinal numbers of the subjects of the classification (namely, the occupations of manual workers and the posts of non-manual workers). The control number is entered in the code in order to provide for the possibility of automatically detecting errors overlooked in transferring data from the original documents to the computer file. The structure of the coded designation of manual workers' occupations (posts of non-manual workers) can be represented schematically as follows:

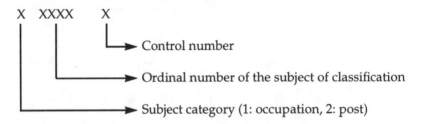

The box for the title of the classification subject gives the standard entry for the title of the specific occupation of a manual worker or post of a non-manual worker. This box also indicates the occupations of manual workers in the highest categories, which require a level of knowledge at least to the standard of intermediate specialized (technical) education.[3]

The information box provides for additional features characterizing each of the classification subjects, i.e. both occupations and posts.

The information box of the Classifier of occupations of manual workers gives the range of wage-rate categories for each occupation, together with the number of the issue of the Wage-Rate and Skill Manual on the Occupations of Manual Workers (ETKS). Additional symbols are also entered in this information box, characterizing the occupations of manual workers as follows:

---

[3] In 1990 the OKPDTR listed more than 400 such occupations.

- two digits: types of industry and tasks, in accordance with the Wage-Rate and Skill Manual on the Jobs and Occupations of Manual Workers (for example, the figure 01 is used to code workers' occupations that are common to all sectors of the national economy; the figure 02, foundry, welding and fitting-shop tasks; the figure 70, the tasks and occupations of workers engaged in livestock husbandry, etc.)
- one digit: wage-rate category (from 1 to 8)
- one digit: skill class (or group) (from 1 to 3)
- two digits: forms and systems of labour remuneration (for example, 10 stands for the application of a piece-rate form of remuneration; 20, for a time-rate form of remuneration, etc.)
- one digit: conditions of work (1: standard, 2: difficult and harmful, 3: very difficult and very harmful)
- one digit: degree of automation (1 indicates that the worker carries out his tasks on automats, automated systems, installations and apparatuses; 2, that the worker is assisted in his tasks by machinery and mechanisms, etc.)
- one digit: derivative occupations (1: senior, 2: assistant).

For example: OKPDTR coding of the occupation 'turner'.

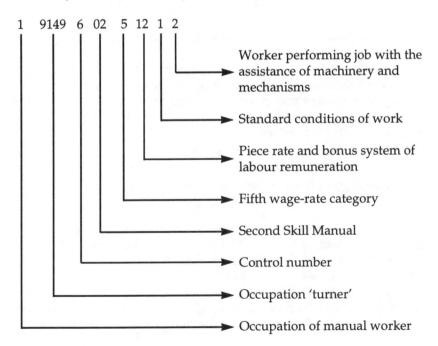

```
1    9149  6  02  5  12  1  2
```

Worker performing job with the assistance of machinery and mechanisms

Standard conditions of work

Piece rate and bonus system of labour remuneration

Fifth wage-rate category

Second Skill Manual

Control number

Occupation 'turner'

Occupation of manual worker

The information box in the Classifier of the posts of non-manual workers contains four digits characterizing posts as follows:

- one digit: category of posts (1: manager, 2: professional, etc.)
- two digits: derivative posts (01: deputy, 02: assistant, 03: chief, 04: senior, 05: shiftworker, etc.)
- one digit: skill category (1: first, 2: second, 3: third) for posts in respect of which skill categories are established for the purposes of remuneration.

For example: OKPDTR coding the post of 'chief engineer in labour organization and standard setting'.

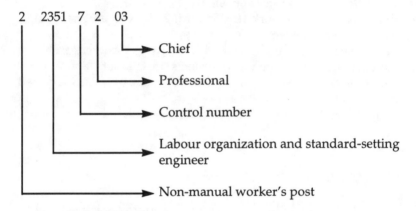

2   2351 7 2   03

→ Chief

→ Professional

→ Control number

→ Labour organization and standard-setting engineer

→ Non-manual worker's post

The layout and sequential arrangement of the information box reflect specifications determined on the basis of the Classifier. The information box can be expanded using the codes and titles of other All-Union Classifiers of technical and economic information, such as the codes of the All-Union Classifier of Economic Districts, the All-Union Classifier of Sectors of the National Economy of the USSR.

MANUALS DESCRIBING THE OCCUPATIONS OF MANUAL WORKERS AND THE POSTS OF NON-MANUAL WORKERS

In the Soviet Union there used to be separate manuals describing the occupations of manual workers and the posts of non-manual workers. These are still being used in most of the FSU countries.

The Standard Wage-Rate and Skill Manual on the Jobs and Occupations of Manual Workers (ETKS) was revised in the period 1982-86. It superseded the manuals introduced as from 1969 in respect of the production sectors, and from 1976 in respect of the non-production sectors, of the national economy. Before that, in the absence of a uniform manual, the sectoral wage-rate qualifications manuals established on a centralized basis were used instead.

The ETKS contains descriptions of the occupations of manual workers, grouped by industry and type of work. It consists of seventy-one separate issues (manuals) covering more than 200 types of industry, to which the specific occupations of manual workers are related. For example, Issue I covers 'occupations of manual workers common to all sectors of the national economy'; Issue II is concerned with eight types of industry, including 'foundry work', 'welding work' and 'fitting-shop and fitting-assembly work'; Issue VI, with two types of work, namely 'well drilling' and 'oil extraction'; etc. This grouping does not depend on the sector of the enterprises in which these industries or types of work are carried on.

As a general rule, the description of a particular occupation is given in only one of the sections. The description gives the characteristics of tasks and indicates the skills needed by a worker to perform such tasks. The characteristics take account of the requirements of scientific and techno-logical progress and the scientific organization of work in the application of progressive forms of labour organization and remuneration, in addition to the quality of production and the level of general education and specialized vocational training of workers. In principle, they are worked out in accordance with a wage scale comprising six categories, though a scale of eight categories is used for the performance of instru-ment work on general purpose equipment for making particularly delicate or complicated dies, stamps, instruments and equipment and for a number of other responsible tasks in various sectors.

Where the ETKS gives several categories (and, consequently, several wage-rate and skill characteristics) for a single occupation, a worker at a higher skill level must possess the knowledge, skills and ability to perform not only the tasks associated with the category assigned to him, but also those associated with the lower skill levels of the occupation in question. In some cases, workers in the higher categories are expected to be able to supervise workers in the lower categories of the same occupation.

ETKS wage-rate and qualification characteristics include examples of tasks associated with the worker's particular category. To the extent that such examples did not exhaustively cover all the tasks performed in each sector, the ministries, in agreement with the trade union, drew up and approved supplementary lists of examples of tasks for use in the enter-prises and organizations under their control, as were required for the purposes of standardization in rating tasks and relating workers to skill categories.

In terms of complexity, the tasks set out in supplementary lists had to match tasks described in the wage-rate and skill characteristics of occupations in the corresponding ETKS categories.

At the enterprise level, the ETKS served as a basis for:

* task rating
* the establishment of occupational titles
* the formulation of the specific content of the wage-rate and skill characteristics of workers' occupations
* the assignment of workers to skill categories
* the preparation of vocational training, retraining and advanced training curricula and programmes for workers.

In this connection, the requirement that had to be satisfied was the basic principle of labour-rating, namely, the category of a particular task was determined according to its complexity, and the category of the worker according to the category of the most characteristic tasks he performed.

The skill category of a worker, as established by the administration of an enterprise, was effective only in that particular enterprise. If a worker was transferred from one enterprise to another, his skill level was determined by the administration of the enterprise to which he was transferred, in accordance with his labour contract.

The re-rating of task and worker categories in an enterprise was permitted only in exceptional circumstances, e.g. in connection with a change in the characteristics of the production process, the introduction of new technology, the introduction of a new wage-rate and skill manual on the tasks and occupations of workers, etc.

The basic principle underlying the compilation of the Skill Manual on the Posts of Managers, Professionals and Non-Manual Workers (KS) is that of grouping by type of posts. The skill requirements of non-manual workers were determined by their official duties. And their official duties, in turn, determined their post title.

The posts themselves were classified according to the nature of the tasks performed. Non-manual workers were divided into three categories, namely, managers (managers of enterprises and their organizational subdivisions), professionals (engaged in the performance of technological, economic and other tasks), and technical executives (in charge of the preparation and formulation of documentation, accounting and auditing, industrial services). This approach stems from the fact that the functions of non-manual workers in enterprises and other institutions centre on management, decision-making and the preparation of the requisite information.

The characteristics of each type of post are broken down into three sections. The section 'official duties' lists the functions which may be fully or partly entrusted to the incumbent.

The section 'knowledge required' sets out the basic requirements that the worker must satisfy in terms of specialized knowledge, together with knowledge of legislative instruments, provisions, instructions, etc., and the methods and means that the worker must be able to apply in performing his official duties.

The section 'skill requirements' defines the level and content of the worker's specialized training, as required for the performance of the duties entrusted to him, together with requirements relating to his length of service.

The KS includes the skill characteristics of posts that are common to all sectors of the national economy. If necessary, individual enterprises could prescribe modifications to posts, such as deputy, assistant, head or chief, or categories of professionals under the same post title (for example, under the post 'economist' there may be established the following posts: economist, economist – second category, economist – first category). Such modifications and sub-classification are linked to the range of duties, the degree of responsibility and the level of remuneration.

The categories of professionals are determined by enterprise administrations on the basis of the evidence given by workers. The specific requirements for each skill category are laid down by the enterprise manager in consultation with the trade-union committee in the light of the characteristics of the organization of production, work and management, taking account of requirements relating to the level of training and length of service.

PROCEDURE FOR AMENDMENTS TO THE DESCRIPTIONS OF OCCUPATIONS OR POSTS AND THE CLASSIFIER

At enterprise level

By agreement with the trade-union committee, the management of an enterprise might extend the wage-rate and skill characteristics of workers' occupations. Extensions normally contained either descriptions of other types of tasks taken from the wage-rate and skill characteristics of workers' occupations as already given in the ETKS, or the characteristics of new tasks that had to be performed in the enterprise as a result of the introduction of new technology. At the enterprise, occupational characteristics were formulated taking account solely of the requirements of a specific work station and notified to the workers at least two months prior for their approval.

Wage-rate and skill characteristics of workers' occupations, formulated in an enterprise on the basis of 'basic' tasks given in the ETKS, were annexed to the collective labour contract and subject to annual approval. Information on the specifications of the characteristics of specific tasks in individual enterprises was not referred to the higher authorities.

Occupational titles had to be established in strict conformity with the ETKS. In particular, this restriction was dictated by the fact that, depending on their occupational titles or post titles and on the type of industry they were engaged in, manual and non-manual workers were in many cases entitled to specific privileges on retirement and in their receipt of pension benefits. Titles were attributed for work effectively performed, taking account of specific conditions in the industry concerned. Where a worker performed tasks associated with several occupations, his occupational title was established on the basis of the most characteristic tasks he performed.

The established procedure for supplements and changes to the ETKS and, consequently, to the OKPDTR, e.g. in connection with changes in occupational titles, the development of new occupations, the broadening of the range of categories, etc., used to be as follows:

(a) Enterprises under the control of the All-Union sectoral ministries submitted proposals to that effect to the competent ministries to which they were subordinate. The latter, after considering the proposals, drawing their general conclusions and reaching agreement with the trade-union bodies, submitted their own proposals to the State Committee on Labour and Social Affairs of the USSR (Goskomtrud USSR).
(b) Enterprises under the control of Republic authorities submitted their proposals, in agreement with the competent trade-union bodies, to Goskomtrud USSR through the competent Republic Committee on Labour. In this connection, it should be pointed out that since the Committees on Labour of the USSR lacked special services in charge of the consideration of such matters, these proposals were sent to Goskomtrud USSR without any amendments.

Pending approval by the State Committee of the USSR on Labour and Social Affairs, the rating tasks and the assignment of workers to skill categories in newly developed occupations were carried out by individual enterprises, in conformity with the titles and characteristics of similar occupations and tasks already covered by the ETKS, by notifying the ministry accordingly and providing it with the draft wage-rate and skill characteristics for the new occupations.

At the All-Union level

Orders for the development and formulation of skill manuals on 'basic' tasks in the occupations of manual workers and the posts of non-manual workers and the corresponding sections of the OKPDTR (and for amendments thereto in the intervals between re-editions) were given out by the State Committee of the USSR on Labour and Social Affairs, as appropriate, to the Central Office for Labour Norms (TsBNT) and the Scientific and Research Institute of Labour.

The functions of these organizations included the preparation of conclusions and proposals on supplements and amendments to the ETKS and KS, as required by the introduction in industry of new technology and new forms of production and labour organization. Experts from Goskomtrud USSR ministries, departments, scientific research organizations and enterprises also took part in such work.

On the basis of these proposals, the competent subdivisions of the Scientific Research Institute of Labour compiled a Collection of Amendments to the OKPDTR every two years.

The last issue of the Collection of Amendments to the OKPDTR was published in December 1988 and it covered supplements and amendments for 1987–88. In accordance with this Collection, five occupations were excluded from the section of the OKPDTR entitled 'Classification of occupations of manual workers', three new occupations were included and partial amendments and corrections were made to twenty-three occupations in the same section. In the section entitled 'Classification of the posts of non-manual workers', thirteen posts were excluded, 138 titles were included,[4] and partial amendments were made to sixteen posts.

All supplements and amendments to the ETKS and KS used to be approved by Goskomtrud FSU and by the former All-Union Central Council of Trade Unions, whereas those made to the OKPDTR, on the basis of recommendations by the State Committee of the USSR on Labour and Social Affairs, were approved by the State Committee of the USSR on Standards.

---

[4] The considerable number of new titles included was the result of the right granted to enterprises to work out characteristics in relation to the posts of non-manual workers in the light of the specific conditions prevailing in their branch of industry.

MAIN TRENDS IN THE IMPROVEMENT OF THE OKPDTR, ETKS AND KS

The necessity of expanding the Classifier and manuals stemmed from the need to ensure their fullest possible application in the process of economic reform which was under way in the USSR and, in particular, in the restructuring effected in respect of remuneration.

In working out (revising) the Classifier and description manuals on a centralized basis, it was realized that account should be taken of the need both to give enterprises more say in the rating of tasks and to limit the regulatory role of these instruments when they are used in specific work environments. It was considered desirable to work out – on the basis of the existing ETKS and KS – a uniform Skill Manual covering the entire workforce of the national economy.

The Classifier and the manuals on which it was based were planned to be effective instruments at every level of management in the national economy, especially in enterprises and organizations, and offer the possibility of prolonged use. They were intended to play a more important part in efforts to strike a better balance between the needs of increasing production on the one hand and their corresponding labour 'coverage', on the other; in job placement; in the development of vocational training and advanced training programmes and in placing emphasis on occupations for which there is a need in particular areas of economic activity.

The Classifier's structure was to be an effective means of analysing and forecasting the occupational and skill structure of the workforce and the degree of its development and modification resulting from technological modernization and the development of progressive forms of labour organization and remuneration.

The Classifier was to provide for the possibility of conducting wide-ranging international comparisons and using the ISCO-88 to that end. It was considered urgent that the classification in use in the USSR and the ISCO-88 should be adapted accordingly. This time-consuming task, once completed, would have made it possible not only to conduct a comparative analysis of the occupational structure of the workforce, but also to overcome many problems, including the practical difficulties confronting enterprises engaged in direct international relations and joint ventures in connection with the selection, assignment, education and remuneration of personnel.

The system was required to meet the needs of all of its potential users.

ILO-comparable annual employment and unemployment estimates: updated results and methodology (No. 3)

I. CHERNYSHEV and S. LAWRENCE*

I. THE ILO-COMPARABLE FRAMEWORK

The ILO-comparable framework was developed around the following four principles:

1. Consistency with ILO statistical standards as embodied in the ILO labour force framework, except where adjustments are negligible and can be disregarded;
2. Conformity with the Standardized Unemployment Rates published by the Organization for Economic Co-operation and Development (OECD) and consistency with other programmes of comparable estimates based on the ILO international standards;
3. Expression of estimates in terms of annual averages;
4. Estimates mainly based on regular household labour force surveys conducted at least once a year and capable of yielding consistent time series for the country.

II. THE ILO STATISTICAL STANDARDS (EXTRACTS)

Economically active population and the labour force framework

According to the ILO *Resolution concerning statistics of the economically active population, employment, unemployment and underemployment,* adopted by the Thirteenth International Conference of Labour Statisticians (October 1982), the economically active population

---

* This annex is an extract from the ILO *Bulletin of Labour Statistics*, No.4 (1990).

'comprises all persons of either sex who furnish the supply of labour for the production of economic goods and services as defined by the United Nations systems of national accounts and balances, during a specified time-reference period . . . Two useful measures of the economically active population are the usually active population measured in relation to a long reference period such as a year and the currently active population or equivalently the labour force measured in relation to a short reference period such as one week or one day . . . The labour force comprises all persons who fulfil the requirements for inclusion among the employed or the unemployed.'

This approach served as a basis for the development of a particular measurement framework denoted in the ILO international recommendations as the 'labour force framework'. Based on specific rules embedded in this framework, the population is divided into three basic categories: 'employed', 'unemployed' and 'not in the labour force'. The first rule of the labour force framework is that *a priori* persons be classified according to their activities during a short reference period, using the following priority rules:

Precedence is given to employment over unemployment; to unemployment over economic inactivity. Therefore, a person both working and seeking work is classified as employed, and a student attending school and also seeking work is classified as unemployed.

In addition, the following two rules should be applied within the labour force framework: the activity principle (a person's labour force status should be determined on the basis of what the person was actually doing during the reference period); and the reference period (preference should be given to a short reference period, i.e. one week or one day).

Employment

The ILO international definition of employment provides separate criteria for persons in paid employment and persons in self-employment in order to accommodate the idea that employment covers any work, be it for wage or salary, profit or family gain, including production for own consumption:

The 'employed' comprise all persons above a specific age who during a specified brief period, either one week or one day, were in the following categories:

(a) 'paid employment':
   (i) 'at work': persons who during the reference period performed some work for wage or salary, in cash or in kind;

(ii) 'with a job but not at work': persons who, having already worked in their present job, were temporarily not at work during the reference period and had a formal attachment to their job.

(b) 'self-employment':

(i) 'at work': persons who during the reference period performed some work for profit or family gain, in cash or in kind;

(ii) 'with an enterprise but not at work': persons with an enterprise, which may be a business enterprise, a farm or a service undertaking, who were temporarily not at work during the reference period for any specific reason.

For operational purposes, the notion 'some work' may be interpreted as work for *at least one hour*.

Unpaid family workers at work should be considered as in self-employment irrespective of the number of hours worked during the reference period. Apprentices who received pay in cash or in kind should be considered in paid employment and classified as 'at work' or 'not at work' on the same basis as other persons in paid employment.

Members of the armed forces should be included among persons in paid employment. They should include both the regular and temporary members.

Unemployment

The ILO international definition of unemployment is based on the following three criteria which should be satisfied simultaneously: 'without work', 'currently available for work' and 'seeking work'. Accordingly, the 'unemployed' comprise all persons above a specific age who during the reference period were:

(a) 'without work', i.e. were not in paid employment or self-employed;

(b) 'currently available for work', i.e. were available for paid employment or self-employment during the reference period, and

(c) 'seeking work', i.e. had taken specific steps in a specified reference period to seek paid employment or self-employment.

Notwithstanding the criterion of seeking work, persons without work and currently available for work who had made arrangements to take up paid employment or undertake a self-employed activity at a date subsequent to the reference period (future engagements) should be considered as unemployed.

Persons temporarily absent from their jobs with no formal job attachment (lay-offs) who were currently available for work and seeking work should be regarded as unemployed.

In this context, availability for work is interpreted as ability and readiness to work, provided the person is given a work opportunity. One purpose of the availability criterion is to exclude both persons who are seeking work to begin at a later date (a test of the current readiness to start work) and those who cannot start work for certain reasons. The validity of the 'current availability' criterion in terms of time should not be limited to the reference week or day but rather extended to one week or two weeks beyond the basic survey reference period.

The 'seeking work' criterion can be interpreted as activity or efforts undertaken during the specified reference period or prior to it in order to find a job. Such efforts may include:

(i)   ... registration at a public or private employment agency;
(ii)   being on call at a personnel office or any other professional register;
(iii) placing or answering advertisements;
(iv)   writing letters of application;
(v)   seeking assistance from friends or relatives;
(vi)   awaiting a reply from an employer, etc.

The job search period is not limited to the specified reference period (one week or one day) but may be longer – one month or the past four weeks including the survey reference period.

III. COUNTRY NOTES AND ADJUSTMENT PROCEDURES

For each country below, the information presented indicates:

Source: The source of the employment and unemployment statistics used most widely in the national context, which is the basis for obtaining data for the comparable estimates, as well as the type of national data published;

Population covered: The age coverage and type of population included by selected source;

National data: The type of data published by the country: as of a point-in-time or averages;

Differences: Differences between the national employment and unemployment concepts and definitions used and the ILO international standards where 'total employment' refers to the civilian labour force employed plus career and conscript members of the armed forces and the 'total labour force' represents 'total employment' plus 'unemployment';

Adjustments: The specific adjustments made to harmonize the national figures with the international standards, and/or the cases where no adjustments were considered necessary due to the insignificance of the numbers;

Averaging: The method used to compute the annual average data where national data refer to point-in-time estimates.

To facilitate the quick reference utility of this presentation, the following usages have been adopted:

Excluded: means excluded from the national concepts and definitions; should be included according to the ILO international standards and is referred to under 'Adjustments' made within the ILO-comparable framework;

Included: means included in the national concepts and definitions; should be excluded according to the ILO international standards and is referred to under 'Adjustments' made within the ILO-comparable framework.

• *Bulgaria*[1]

Source: Compulsory regular labour statistics reporting system, special surveys and population censuses. This covers all establishments, enterprises and organizations in the State and cooperative sectors engaged in material and non-material production.

Population covered: All persons aged 16 years and over plus those 15 year-olds engaged in socialized production and foreigners working in the country under special intergovernmental agreements. Armed forces are excluded.

National data: Annual averages.

Differences:

  Employment:
  Excluded:
  (a) Armed forces.
  (b) Others, i.e. persons employed in individual subsidiary farming, persons engaged in religious organizations, individual services, catering activities, private craftsmen, priests of all religions, other self-employed.

  Unemployment:
  In 1989 the Labour Force Survey concepts and definitions were under consideration.

Adjustments: For reasons of confidentiality, (a) cannot be included at present, (b) have been included with no adjustments.

Averaging: National data are annual averages.

---

[1] Estimates up to 1989.

• *Czechoslovakia*[2]

Source: Statistical employment reports, compulsory for all State and cooperative enterprises, farms and organizations, all types of educational establishments, special surveys and population censuses.

Population covered: All persons aged 15 years and over who are engaged in the national economy. Persons performing their military service are excluded.

National data: At 31 December of each year.

Differences:
   Employment:
   Excluded:
   (a) Armed forces.
   (b) Persons on maternity leave, with a formal job attachment.
   (c) Persons temporarily engaged in housework, with a formal job attachment.
   (d) Paid apprentices and trainees.
   Unemployment:
   In 1989 the Labour Force Survey concepts and definitions were under consideration.

Adjustments: (a) (including civilian employees and students in military academies), (b), (c) and (d) are included.

Averaging: Method ILO–2 (see below).

• *Hungary*[3]

Source: The Compulsory Annual Survey conducted within the uniform labour statistics data collection system; monthly and quarterly statistical labour reports prepared by sectoral departments of the Central Statistical Office; special surveys conducted by the Social Insurance Service and National Association for Small-Scale Industries and Retail Traders; Population Censuses and Microcensuses.

Population covered: The working-age population covers men 15–59 years, women 15–54 years, 14 year-olds engaged in socialized production and employees beyond working age (re-employed retired people).

National data: End of the year.

Differences:
   Employment:

___

[2] Estimates up to 1989.   [3] Estimates up to 1989.

Excluded:

(a) Mothers receiving child-care allowance, even though they maintain a formal job attachment.

(b) Unpaid family workers, temporary and seasonal workers in agriculture, working less than three months in the year.

(c) Rentiers (pensioners).

Unemployment:

In 1989 the Labour Force Survey concepts and definitions were under consideration.

Adjustments: (a) have been included. Among the unpaid family workers employed in agriculture, (b), those who correspond to the criterion 'active wage earner' (in both the socialized and private sectors) are included in the comparable data. The number of persons not meeting this criterion and those under (c) are not significant. Employment data by branch of economic activity in division 3 include divisions 2 and 4 and division 8 includes division 9.

Averaging: Method ILO-2 (see below).

• *Poland*[4]

Source: Compulsory monthly reports from industrial, construction, transport, communications, internal and foreign trade units, quarterly and annual reports on all sectors of the national economy (material and non-material production), Population Census and Microcensus for the rural population involved in private agriculture.

Population covered: All persons aged 18 years and over as well as persons aged 14 to 17 who are engaged in the national economy.

National data: Annual averages.

Differences:

  Employment:

  Excluded:

(a) Armed forces.

(b) Paid apprentices and trainees.

(c) Mothers on child-care leave, maintaining a formal job attachment.

(d) Persons living on income from rents.

  Unemployment:

In 1989 the Labour Force Survey concepts and definitions were under consideration.

---

[4] Estimates up to 1989.

Adjustments: For reasons of confidentiality, data on (a) could not be included, (b) and (c) have been included. The number of (d) is insignificant and does not influence the national employment figure.

Averaging: National data are annual averages.

• *USSR*[5]

Source: Compulsory Statistical Labour Reports from all State enterprises, cooperatives, organizations and institutions, secondary and higher educational establishments,   special sample surveys and population censuses.

Population covered: All persons aged 16 years and over plus 15-year-olds. Those who are engaged in the national economy. The Armed Forces are excluded.

National data: Annual averages.

Differences:
   Employment:
   Excluded:
   (a) Armed forces.
   (b) Mothers receiving child-care allowance who have a strong job attachment.
   (c) Family members of wage earners and salaried employees engaged in individual subsidiary farming.
   Unemployment:
   The concepts, definitions and data collection methods were under consideration.

Adjustments: (a) have been included from 1987; for earlier years only civilian employment is available. (b) and (c) are included.

Averaging: National data are annual averages.

ILO-2: METHOD FOR CALCULATING AVERAGE ESTIMATES FOR ANNUAL EMPLOYMENT FROM STATE CURRENT REPORTING SYSTEM, ETC.

Let us use X_t to indicate annual employment estimates obtained from State current reporting system and/or other occasional observations in year t, X_{t+1} for annual employment estimates obtained from the same source in year $t+1$ and $\overline{X}$ for the annual average of the two consecutive years.   The annual average for year $\overline{X}_t$ is thus:

$$\overline{X}_t = \frac{X_t + X_{t+1}}{2}$$

---

[5] Estimates up to 1989.

Table A1.1 ILO-comparable estimates of labour force, employment and unemployment by sex (annual averages in thousands)

Country sex year	Working-age population	Labour force			Employment		Unemployment	
		Total	Civilian	Participation rate (%)	Total	Civilian	Total	Unemployment rate (%)
Bulgaria								
Total								
1981	6 807	.	.	.	.	4 418	.	.
1982	6 831	.	.	.	.	4 452	.	.
1983	6 849	.	.	.	.	4 466	.	.
1984	6 875	.	.	.	.	4 460	.	.
1985	6 892	.	.	.	.	4 460	.	.
1986	6 908	.	.	.	.	4 473	.	.
1987	6 935	.	.	.	.	4 487	.	.
1988	6 957	.	.	.	.	4 468	.	.
1989	6 892	.	.	.	.	4 365	.	.
Canada								
Total								
1981	18 443	11 974	11 899	64.9	11 076	11 001	898	7.5
1982	18 684	12 002	11 926	64.2	10 694	10 618	1 308	10.9
1983	18 881	12 185	12 109	64.5	10 750	10 675	1 434	11.8
1984	19 071	12 391	12 316	65.0	11 007	10 932	1 384	11.2
1985	19 267	12 609	12 532	65.4	11 298	11 221	1 311	10.4
1986	19 474	12 823	12 746	65.8	11 608	11 531	1 215	9.5
1987	19 721	13 090	13 011	66.4	11 940	11 861	1 150	8.8
1988	19 968	13 353	13 275	66.9	12 323	12 245	1 031	7.7
1989	20 220	13 582	13 503	67.2	12 565	12 486	1 018	7.5
1990	20 509	13 760	13 681	67.1	12 572	12 572	1 109	8.1
1991	20 824	13 835	13 757	66.4	12 418	12 340	1 417	10.2

Country sex year	Working-age population	Labour force			Employment		Unemployment	
		Total	Civilian	Participation rate (%)	Total	Civilian	Total	Unemployment rate (%)
Males								
1981	9 063	7 120	7 051	78.6	6 625	6 556	494	6.9
1982	9 172	7 078	7 009	77.2	6 305	6 236	773	10.9
1983	9 258	7 121	7 052	76.9	6 272	6 203	849	11.9
1984	9 342	7 169	7 100	76.7	6 377	6 308	792	11.0
1985	9 427	7 236	7 167	76.8	6 497	6 428	739	10.2
1986	9 521	7 313	7 244	76.8	6 636	6 567	677	9.3
1987	9 643	7 403	7 332	76.8	6 780	6 709	623	8.4
1988	9 762	7 492	7 422	76.7	6 946	6 876	546	7.2
1989	9 884	7 595	7 525	76.8	7 047	6 977	548	7.2
1990	10 028	7 631	7 561	76.1	7 018	6 948	613	8.0
1991	10 186	7 638	7 569	75.0	6 820	6 751	817	10.7
Females								
1981	9 380	4 855	4 849	51.8	4 451	4 445	403	8.3
1982	9 511	4 922	4 916	51.8	4 388	4 382	534	10.8
1983	9 622	5 063	5 057	52.6	4 478	4 472	585	11.6
1984	9 730	5 223	5 216	53.7	4 631	4 624	592	11.3
1985	9 838	5 372	5 365	54.6	4 801	4 794	572	10.6
1986	9 952	5 509	5 502	55.4	4 971	4 964	539	9.8
1987	10 078	5 687	5 679	56.4	5 160	5 152	527	9.3
1988	10 205	5 861	5 853	57.4	5 376	5 368	485	8.3
1989	10 334	5 986	5 978	57.9	5 516	5 508	470	7.9
1990	10 481	6 128	6 119	58.5	5 633	5 624	496	8.1
1991	10 638	6 197	6 188	58.3	5 598	5 589	599	9.7

Czechoslovakia

Total

Year								
1981	11 593	.	.	.	8 181	7 815	.	.
1982	11 623	.	.	.	8 184	7 822	.	.
1983	11 649	.	.	.	8 200	7 837	.	.
1984	11 681	.	.	.	8 251	7 887	.	.
1985	11 718	.	.	.	8 317	7 953	.	.
1986	11 761	.	.	.	8 379	8 011	.	.
1987	11 823	.	.	.	8 409	8 039	.	.
1988	11 902	.	.	.	8 449	8 078	.	.
1989	12 000	.	.	.	8 431	8 075	.	.

Males

Year								
1981	5 553	.	.	.	4 395	4 074	.	.
1982	5 568	.	.	.	4 387	4 069	.	.
1983	5 581	.	.	.	4 388	4 068	.	.
1984	5 596	.	.	.	4 408	4 087	.	.
1985	5 615	.	.	.	4 426	4 105	.	.
1986	5 637	.	.	.	4 450	4 125	.	.
1987	5 668	.	.	.	4 448	4 122	.	.
1988	5 708	.	.	.	4 464	4 137	.	.
1989	5 757	.	.	.	4 440	4 132	.	.

Females

Year								
1981	6 040	.	.	.	3 786	3 741	.	.
1982	6 055	.	.	.	3 797	3 753	.	.
1983	6 068	.	.	.	3 812	3 769	.	.
1984	6 085	.	.	.	3 843	3 800	.	.
1985	6 103	.	.	.	3 891	3 848	.	.
1986	6 124	.	.	.	3 929	3 886	.	.
1987	6 155	.	.	.	3 961	3 917	.	.
1988	6 194	.	.	.	3 985	3 941	.	.
1989	6 243	.	.	.	3 991	3 943	.	.

Country sex year	Working-age population	Labour force			Employment		Unemployment	
		Total	Civilian	Participation rate (%)	Total	Civilian	Total	Unemployment rate (%)
Hong Kong								
Total								
1985	4 059	2 632	2 623	64.8	2 552	2 543	80	3.0
1986	4 154	2 705	2 697	65.1	2 632	2 624	73	2.7
1987	4 213	2 734	2 727	64.9	2 689	2 681	46	1.7
1988	4 281	2 770	2 762	64.7	2 733	2 725	37	1.3
1989	4 326	2 759	2 752	63.8	2 730	2 723	29	1.1
1990	4 353	2 754	2 747	63.3	2 719	2 712	35	1.3
1991	4 418	2 804	2 797	63.5	2 755	2 749	49	1.7
Males								
1985	2 088	1 677	1 669	80.3	1 621	1 613	56	3.3
1986	2 137	1 720	1 712	80.5	1 671	1 663	49	2.9
1987	2 159	1 734	1 727	80.3	1 705	1 698	29	1.7
1988	2 197	1 761	1 754	80.2	1 738	1 730	24	1.3
1989	2 208	1 757	1 750	79.6	1 739	1 732	19	1.1
1990	2 217	1 754	1 747	79.1	1 732	1 725	22	1.3
1991	2 230	1 759	1 752	78.9	1 726	1 719	33	1.9
Females								
1985	1 971	955	954	48.4	931	930	24	2.5
1986	2 017	986	985	48.9	961	961	24	2.5
1987	2 054	1 000	1 000	48.7	983	983	17	1.7
1988	2 084	1 009	1 008	48.4	995	995	14	1.3
1989	2 118	1 002	1 002	47.3	992	992	10	1.0
1990	2 136	1 000	1 000	46.8	987	987	13	1.3
1991	2 189	1 046	1 046	47.8	1 030	1 030	16	1.5

Hungary

Total

Year								
1981	6 681	.	.	.	5 690	.	.	.
1982	6 635	.	.	.	5 662	.	.	.
1983	6 614	.	.	.	5 631	.	.	.
1984	6 602	.	.	.	5 603	.	.	.
1985	6 582	.	.	.	5 585	.	.	.
1986	6 559	.	.	.	5 585	.	.	.
1987	6 538	.	.	.	5 569	.	.	.
1988	6 501	.	.	.	5 527	.	.	.
1989	6 459	.	.	.	5 489	.	.	.

Males

Year								
1981	3 459	.	.	.	3 001	.	.	.
1982	3 438	.	.	.	2 986	.	.	.
1983	3 428	.	.	.	2 956	.	.	.
1984	3 420	.	.	.	2 926	.	.	.
1985	3 409	.	.	.	2 899	.	.	.
1986	3 402	.	.	.	2 892	.	.	.
1987	3 394	.	.	.	2 888	.	.	.
1988	3 370	.	.	.	2 855	.	.	.
1989	3 341	.	.	.	2 821	.	.	.

Females

Year								
1981	3 222	.	.	.	2 688	.	.	.
1982	3 197	.	.	.	2 676	.	.	.
1983	3 186	.	.	.	2 675	.	.	.
1984	3 182	.	.	.	2 678	.	.	.
1985	3 173	.	.	.	2 686	.	.	.
1986	3 157	.	.	.	2 693	.	.	.
1987	3 144	.	.	.	2 680	.	.	.
1988	3 131	.	.	.	2 672	.	.	.
1989	3 118	.	.	.	2 667	.	.	.

Country sex year	Working-age population Total	Labour force Total	Labour force Civilian	Labour force Participation rate (%)	Employment Total	Employment Civilian	Unemployment Total	Unemployment rate (%)
Philippines								
Total								
1986	34 331	21 405	·	62.3	18 889	·	2 516	11.8
1987	34 546	22 660	·	65.6	20 166	·	2 494	11.0
1988	35 564	23 497	·	66.1	21 266	·	2 231	9.5
1989	36 608	24 157	·	66.0	21 935	·	2 222	9.2
1990	37 681	24 269	·	64.4	22 224	·	2 045	8.4
1991	38 693	25 686	·	66.4	22 956	·	2 730	10.6
Males								
1986	17 006	13 623	·	80.1	12 022	·	1 601	11.8
1987	17 170	14 309	·	83.3	12 846	·	1 463	10.2
1988	17 626	14 818	·	84.1	13 545	·	1 273	8.6
1989	18 095	15 161	·	83.8	13 935	·	1 226	8.1
1990	18 693	15 306	·	81.9	14 169	·	1 137	7.4
1991	19 132	16 056	·	83.9	14 565	·	1 491	9.3
Females								
1986	17 325	7 782	·	44.9	6 867	·	915	11.8
1987	17 376	8 351	·	48.1	7 320	·	1 031	12.3
1988	17 938	8 679	·	48.4	7 721	·	958	11.0
1989	18 513	8 996	·	48.6	8 000	·	996	11.1
1990	18 989	8 963	·	47.2	8 055	·	908	10.1
1991	19 560	9 630	·	49.2	8 391	·	1 239	12.9

Poland					
Total					
1981	...	...	18 006	...	...
1982			18 209		
1983			18 375		
1984			18 384		
1985			18 531		
1986			18 595		
1987			18 596		
1988			18 474		
1989			18 438		
Males					
1981			9 769		
1982			9 555		
1983			9 587		
1984			9 565		
1985			9 560		
1986			9 737		
1987			9 716		
1988			9 806		
1989			9 828		
Females					
1981			8 737		
1982			8 653		
1983			8 787		
1984			8 819		
1985			8 972		
1986			8 858		
1987			8 783		
1988			8 669		
1989			8 611		

Country sex year	Working-age population	Labour force			Employment		Unemployment	
		Total	Civilian	Participation rate (%)	Total	Civilian	Total	Unemployment rate (%)
United States								
Total								
1981	172 272	110 812	108 670	64.3	102 539	100 397	8 273	7.5
1982	174 451	112 384	110 204	64.4	101 705	99 526	10 678	9.5
1983	176 415	113 750	111 550	64.5	103 033	100 834	10 717	9.4
1984	178 602	115 763	113 544	64.8	107 224	105 005	8 539	7.4
1985	180 440	117 695	115 461	65.2	109 384	107 150	8 312	7.1
1986	182 831	120 079	117 834	65.7	111 841	109 597	8 237	6.9
1987	185 010	122 122	119 865	66.0	114 697	112 440	7 425	6.1
1988	186 837	123 893	121 669	66.3	117 192	114 968	6 701	5.4
1989	188 600	126 077	123 869	66.8	119 550	117 342	6 528	5.2
1990	190 217	126 955	124 788	66.7	120 081	117 914	6 874	5.4
1991	191 883	127 421	125 303	66.4	118 995	116 877	8 426	6.6
Males								
1981	82 476	63 939	61 974	77.5	59 361	57 397	4 577	7.2
1982	83 514	64 440	62 450	77.2	58 261	56 271	6 179	9.6
1983	84 536	65 051	63 047	77.0	58 791	56 787	6 260	9.6
1984	85 625	65 855	63 835	76.9	61 111	59 091	4 744	7.2
1985	86 499	66 441	64 411	76.8	61 920	59 891	4 521	6.8
1986	87 828	67 452	65 422	76.8	62 922	60 892	4 530	6.7
1987	88 935	68 243	66 207	76.7	64 143	62 107	4 101	6.0
1988	89 860	68 930	66 927	76.7	65 276	63 273	3 655	5.3
1989	90 744	69 821	67 840	76.9	66 296	64 315	3 525	5.0
1990	91 590	70 173	68 234	76.6	66 374	64 435	3 799	5.4
1991	92 443	70 302	68 410	76.0	65 485	63 593	4 817	6.9

Females								
1981	89 796	46 873	46 696	52.2	43 178	43 000	3 696	7.9
1982	90 937	47 944	47 755	52.7	43 445	43 256	4 499	9.4
1983	91 879	48 699	48 503	53.0	44 242	44 047	4 457	9.2
1984	92 977	49 908	49 709	53.7	46 114	45 915	3 794	7.6
1985	93 941	51 255	51 050	54.6	47 464	47 259	3 791	7.4
1986	95 003	52 627	52 413	55.4	48 920	48 706	3 707	7.0
1987	96 074	53 879	53 658	56.1	50 555	50 334	3 324	6.2
1988	96 977	54 963	54 742	56.7	51 917	51 696	3 046	5.5
1989	97 857	56 256	56 030	57.5	53 253	53 027	3 003	5.3
1990	98 627	56 782	56 554	57.6	53 707	53 479	3 075	5.4
1991	99 440	57 119	56 893	57.4	53 510	53 284	3 609	6.3
USSR								
Total								
1987	...	.	.	.	143 287	138 287	.	.
1988	...	.	.	.	142 798	138 798	.	.
1989	159 369	.	.	.	143 077	139 077	.	.
Males								
1987	...	.	.	.	73 076	68 076	.	.
1988	...	.	.	.	72 827	68 827	.	.
1989	82 051	.	.	.	72 969	68 969	.	.
Females								
1987	...	.	.	.	70 211	70 211	.	.
1988	...	.	.	.	69 971	69 971	.	.
1989	77 318	.	.	.	70 108	70 108	.	.

.   Not applicable.   ...   Not available.

Decimal figures are separated by a period.

Methodological description of the Labour Force Survey in the Russian Federation

1. TITLE OF THE SURVEY

    Population Sample Survey of Employment (PSSE).

2. ORGANIZATION RESPONSIBLE FOR THE SURVEY

    The State Committee on Statistics of the Russian Federation (GOSKOMSTAT of Russia).

3. COVERAGE OF THE SURVEY

    (a) *Geographical*: The whole country.
    (b) *Persons covered*: All permanent residents aged 15–72 years, including those temporarily absent.

    Excluded are:
    (1) persons on long-term missions (six months and longer);
    (2) students living in hostels and schoolchildren living in boarding schools;
    (3) inmates of penal and mental institutions;
    (4) military personnel (conscripts and career) living in barracks;
    (5) foreign citizens.

4. PERIODICITY OF THE SURVEY

    Currently the survey is annual.

5. REFERENCE PERIOD

    The calendar week.

6. TOPICS COVERED

The survey provides information on the following topics: employment (main and secondary), unemployment, hours of work, duration of unemployment, reasons for not being employed, discouraged workers, occasional workers, industry, occupation, status in employment and level of education.

Information on the informal sector is provided to the extent that survey respondents report on their activities. As regards underemployment, the only data available are statistics on persons working part-time for economic and other relevant reasons.

7. CONCEPTS AND DEFINITIONS

(a) *Employment*: Employed persons are:
  (1) all persons who, during the reference week, did any work at all as paid employees, in their own business, profession, or on their own farm, or who worked at least one hour or more as unpaid family workers in an enterprise operated by a member of a family; and
  (2) all those who were not working but who had jobs or businesses from which they were temporarily absent because of illness, bad weather, vacation, advance qualification training, labour-management disputes, or personal reasons, whether they were paid for the time off or were seeking other jobs.

Included in the totals are:
  (1) full- and part-time workers seeking other work during the reference period;
  (2) full- and part-time students working full- or part-time;
  (3) persons who performed some work during the reference week while being either retired and receiving a pension; or registered as jobseekers at an employment office or receiving unemployment benefits;
  (4) paid and unpaid family workers (irrespective of the number of hours worked);
  (5) private domestic servants;
  (6) members of producers' cooperatives;
  (7) members of the armed forces (conscripts and career).

Each employed person is counted only once. Those who held more than one job are counted in the job which they consider to be the major one.

Excluded are persons whose only activity consisted of work around the house (painting, repairing, or own housework); volunteer work for religious, charitable and similar organizations and unpaid apprentices and trainees. Those are considered as not economically active.

(b) *Unemployment*: Unemployed persons are all civilians who had no employment during the reference week, were available for work, except for temporary illness, and had taken specific steps to find employment.
    Note: Temporarily not working paid/unpaid family workers are considered to be unemployed or not economically active depending on whether or not they were seeking work during the reference week.

Included in the unemployed are full- and part-time students seeking full- or part-time employment, provided they are currently available for work (if they are seeking work for some future date, such as for the summer months, they are considered inactive).

The 'specific steps to find employment' include any of the following steps: registration at a state or commercial/private employment office; writing letters of application; seeking assistance from friends or relatives; placing or answering advertisements; waiting at a designated labour pick-up point, etc.

(c) *Hours of work*: They relate to the actual number of hours worked during the reference week (including overtime but excluding meal breaks, paid or unpaid days off and approved time away from work). For persons working in more than one job, the figures relate to the number of hours worked in all jobs during the week.

8. CLASSIFICATIONS USED

Both employed and unemployed persons are classified by industry, occupation, and level of education. The unemployed are classified by the industry, occupation and status of their previous job.

(a) *Industry*: The classification used is the former All-Union Classification of Economic Sectors (OKONH). For the purpose of international comparisons, the results are converted into ISIC Rev. 3.

(b) *Occupation*: The classification system used is the former All-Union Classification of Wage-Earner Occupations and Salaried-Employee Posts and Tariff Rates. (Conversion into ISCO-88 is not possible.) Work is under way to develop a new Russian Occupational Classification.

(c) *Status in employment*: Five major groups of the International Classification of Status in Employment are used. The Russian Classification of the Status in Employment is being developed.

(d) *Level of education*: Six groups of level of education are used. There is no link with the International Standard Classification of Education (ISCED-1976).

9. SAMPLE DESIGN

(a) *The sample frame*: The PSSE sample is built up on the basis of the decennial Population Census (conducted in 1989) and compiled from the lists of census enumeration districts.

(b) *The sample*: The sampling procedure is based on the search for an optimal variant of the sample according to the following eight variables: number of population, gender, age, family size, source of means of subsistence, education (first level), nationality, 'household belongs to'. The full sample is based on a stratified two-stage random sampling design with a sampling fraction of 0.6 per cent of the population aged 15–72 years. At the first stage the census enumeration districts are selected. At the second stage ultimate sampling units (households and persons) are selected. Substitution of ultimate sampling units is made only if nobody lives at the selected address. The sample is stratified by household size and by the census indicator 'household belongs to'. An update of the sample will be made for the next round of the survey.

(c) *Rotation*: It is expected that the rotation size for the next round of the survey will be about 20 per cent.

10. DOCUMENTATION

The results of PSSE were published in December 1993.

Questionnaire used in a sample survey of the population on employment (Labour Force Survey) in the Russian Federation

Those covered are all persons aged 15-72 years, excluding foreign citizens

Respondent's Card No. _____

Portfolio No. _____ Census schedule No.[1] _____

Address: Autonomous Republic, Territory (Krai), Region _____
District _____ Rural Council _____
Settlement (town, township, village) _____
Boulevard (prospect), street, square, lane_____
House No. _____ Apartment No. _____
Telephone No. _____

Name: _____

Gender: M F (to encircle) Age _____

A. Source of information (to encircle)
1. Respondent
2. Respondent's family member
3. Other person

---

[1] If the questionnaire is filled out for persons living at the same address but who are not listed among those selected for the survey, the Census Schedule No. should be marked with '*'.

B. Reasons for non-response (to encircle)
   1. Respondent's refusal
   2. Respondent's long illness
   3. Respondent's absence, mission, vacation
   4. Other reasons (specify) _____

C. Information about further co-operation[2]
   1. Agree   2. Do not agree

Interviewer

Name _____

Enumeration district No. _____

Date _____

Approved by the
State Committee on
Statistics of the
Russian Federation

on 02. 06.92, No. 38

To be filled out for all persons aged 15-72 years, excluding foreign citizens

1	2	3	4	5	6
Territory	Locality (town-1, village-2)	Enumeration district	Respondent	Portfolio	Census schedule
Code					

---

[2] To be completed at the end of the interview.

QUESTIONNAIRE: POPULATION SAMPLE SURVEY OF EMPLOYMENT
All questions should cover the reference week
from ___ to _____ 199_

The information collected during this interview is **confidential** and will only be used in summarized totals for the purpose of statistical analysis of employment and unemployment.

1. Did you work for pay or profit during the reference week?

No.	Question	Code	Skip
1	Did you work for pay or profit during the reference week? You must include all paid work even if it is for a few hours and if you are self-employed or work for individualpersons.		
	Yes	1 —> 5	
	No	2 —> 2	
2.	Even though you were not working, did you have a job or business that you were temporarily away from last week? (Because of illness, vacation, education, production stoppage or any other reason)		
	Yes	3 —> 5	
	No	4 —> 3	
3.	Did you perform any unpaid work on the farm or in the business of some member of yourfamily?		
	Yes	5 —> 5	
	No	6 —> 4	
4.	Even though you did not perform any unpaid work, were you engaged in agricultural production, flower growing, fishing, hunting, collecting mushrooms or berries for profit? (in order to sell; already sold)		
	Yes	7 —> 5	
	No	8 —> 26	

EMPLOYED

5. Are you (READ OUT):

    - student or full-time schoolchild ....   9 —> 6
    - pensioner ....   10 —> 6
    - military serviceman ....   11 —> 22
    - priest or related category ....   12 —> 41
    - none ....   13 —> 6

6. The following questions cover only that activity
    which you consider to be your **main employment**.

    Last week, were you employed by:
    - state enterprise or state organization .   14 —> 10
    - producers' cooperative ....   15 —> 7
    - collective farm ....   16 —> 7
    - association ....   17 —> 7
    - leased enterprise ....   18 —> 10
    - private collective enterprise ....   19 —> 7
    - private individual or family enterprise.   20 —> 8
    - farm ....   21 —> 8
    - stock-holding enterprise ....   22 —> 10
    - consumer-union enterprise ....   23 —> 10
    - public organization or its enterprise ..   24 —> 10
    - individual person ....   25 —> 10
    - were you self-employed? ....   26 —> 9
    - other (specify) _____ ......   27 —> 7

7. Did you work as an employee?

    Yes ....   28 —> 10
    No ....   29 —> 14

8. Were you (READ OUT):

    - employee ....   30 —> 10
    - self-employed worker/employer..........   31 —> 9
    - unpaid family worker ....   32 —> 14

9. In your job or business did you have
    employees?

    Yes ....   33 —> 14
    No ....   34 —> 14

10. Was your work (READ OUT):

  - permanent ....   35 —> 12
  - temporary ....   36 —> 11
  - casual ....   37 —> 11

11. Why did you have a temporary job?

  - unable to find a permanent job ....   38 —> 12
  - unwilling to accept a permanent job ....   39 —> 12
  - other reasons (specify) _____ ....   40 —> 12

12. According to your contract, were you employed:

  - full-time ....   41 —> 14
  - part-time ....   42 —> 13

13. Why did you have part-time work?

  - unable to find full-time work ....   43 —> 14
  - unwilling to take full-time work ....   44 —> 14
  - transferred by administration ....   45 —> 14
  - other reasons (specify) _____ .....   46 —> 14

14. Could you please give the complete name of your employer:

  _____

  (If it is not possible to define from the above
  name the branch of industry this enterprise
  belongs to, clarify the main type of activity
  of the enterprise or own business)

  _____   —[3]> 15

15. What was your occupation or post or what was the nature
     of your work?
  _____ 67 —[3]> 16

16. How many hours do you **usually** work per week in your
     main employment or own business?

  _____ hours ....   68 —[3]> 17

---

[3] To be filled out by statistical organization.

17. How many hours did you **actually** work in your main
     employment (own business) during the reference week
     including overtime, paid or not, but excluding meal
     breaks?

     _____ hours ....   69 —⁴> 18
     0 (zero) hours ....   70 —> 19-2

18. Please specify whether in your main employment
     (business) you worked last week (READ OUT):

     - more hours than usual ....   71 —> 20
     - fewer hours than usual ....   72 —> 19-1
     - the same number of hours as usual ......   73 —> 20

19-1. Why did you work less than usual that week?

19-2. Why did you not work **at all** during the reference week?

     Specify the main reason:
     - own illness or injury, looking after
          a sick person ....   74 —> 20
     - annual leave or days off, compensatory
          leave or compensation for overtime
          work, or for work on red-letter
          days/days off ....   75 —> 20
     - statutory pregnancy leave, maternity or
          child-care leave ....   76 —> 20
     - education, attending a training course
          away from own workplace, education
          leave ....   77 —> 20
     - paid or unpaid leave by the initiative
          of the administration ....   78 —> 20
     - transferred to another daily time-table
          of work by the initiative of the
          administration ....   79 —> 20
     - special conditions of work or activity .   80 —> 20
     - strike ....   81 —> 20
     - began new employment during the
          reference week ....   82 —> 20
     - resigned ....   83 —> 20
     - other reasons..........................   84 —> 20

⁴ To be filled out by statistical organization.

20.   During the reference week, did you have any other paid
      or unpaid job or business in addition to the one you
      have just told me about? (Including work without pay
      on a farm or in an enterprise operated by a member of
      your family)

      Yes ....   85 —-> 21
      No ....   86 —-> 22

21.   Approximately how many hours did you work in your
      secondary (extra or side-line) job(s)?
      _____ hours ....   87 —*> 22

22.   Were you looking for a different or additional
      work during the reference week?

      Yes: different work ....   88 —-> 23
           additional work ....   89 —-> 24
      No ....   90 —-> 41

23.   Why were you looking for work?

      - Forthcoming release ....   91 —-> 24
      - End of the term of employment ....   92 —-> 24
      - Not satisfied with the wage/salary of
        present work ....   93 —-> 24
      - Work not according to the occupation
        acquired ....   94 —-> 24
      - Other personal reasons ..   95 —-> 24

24.   Were you looking for (READ OUT):

      - permanent work ....   96 —-> 25
      - fixed term ....   97 —-> 25
      - casual work ....   98 —-> 25
      - no preference ....   99 —-> 25

25.   Were you looking for (READ OUT):

      - full-time work ....   100 —-> 41
      - part-time work ....   101 —-> 41
      - no preference ....   102 —-> 41

PERSONS WITHOUT WORK

26. Are you (READ OUT):

      - student/full-time schoolchild...........   103 —> 27
      - old-age pensioner, occupational
           pensioner ....   104 —> 27
      - pensioner by disability ....   105 —> 27
      - called up for military service ....   106 —> 41
      - running a home ....   107 —> 27
      - not employed ....   108 —> 27

27. Last week, were you looking for paid work or
      did you try to organize your own business?

      Looked for work ....   109 —> 28
      Took steps to organize own business ......   110 —> 33
      Neither ....   111 —> 32

28. In what way were you looking for work (READ OUT):

      Registered at employment office:
      - state ....   112 —> 29
      - commercial (private) ....   113 —> 29
      Through the press and/or advertisement ...   114 —> 29
      Private contacts ....   115 —> 29
      Direct contacts with managements and/or
           employer ....   116 —> 29
      Other methods ....   117 —> 29

29. If you had been offered work during the reference week,
      could you have started work immediately?

      Yes ....   118 —> 30
      No ....   119 —> 41

30. Would you like to have (READ OUT):

      - permanent work ....   120 —> 31
      - fixed term ....   121 —> 31
      - casual work ....   122 —> 31
      - no preference ....   123 —> 31

31. Would you like to have (READ OUT):

    - full-time work ....   124 ——> 33
    - part-time work ....   125 ——> 33
    - no preference ....   126 ——> 33

32. Why were you not looking for work?

    - Got a new job, will begin to work next
      week ....   127 ——> 33
    - Found a new job, waiting for
      notification ....   128 ——> 33
    - Registered at employment office as
      "looking for work" ....   129 ——> 33
    - Attending training course organized by
      an employment office ....   130 ——> 33
    - Waiting for invitation from the last
      place of work ....   131 ——> 33
    - Was ill during the reference week ......   132 ——> 33
    - Believed no jobs were available ....   133 ——> 41
    - No need to work ....   134 ——> 41
    - Other reason ....   135 ——> 41

33. How many months have you been looking for work
    or tried to organize your own business?

    - Less than one month ....   136 ——> 34
    - From 1 to 3 months ....   137 ——> 34
    - From 3 to 6 months ....   138 ——> 34
    - From 6 to 9 months ....   139 ——> 34
    - From 9 to 12 months ....   140 ——> 34
    - More than 12 months ....   141 ——> 34
    - Have not been looking for work, it was
      proposed to me ....   142 ——> 34

34. Are you registered as unemployed?

    Yes ....   143 ——> 35
    No ....   144 ——> 36

35. Do you receive unemployment benefits?

    Yes ....   145 ——> 36
    No ....   146 ——> 36

36.   Have you ever worked before for pay
          or had a profitable business?

Yes ....   147 —> 37
No ....   148 —> 38

37.   Have you worked for pay or had a profitable business
          during the last 12 months?

Yes ....   149 —> 38
No ....   150 —> 38

38.   Which of the following corresponds to your reason for
          not being employed?

Released because of redundancy ....   151 —> 40
Released at your own request ....   152 —> 40
Put off from career service in the Armed
    Forces because of their reduction ....   153 —> 40
Released for other reasons ....   154 —> 40
Closure/liquidation of own business ......   155 —> 40
Dissolution (liquidation/closure) of
    cooperative, collective farm, association,
    or private collective enterprise ....   156 —> 40
No job after completion/cessation of study   157 —> 39
No job after conscript service in the Armed
    Forces...................................   158 —> 39
No job after imprisonment ....   159 —> 39
Other reason ....   160 —> 39

39.   Do you have any occupation or profession
          and what is your occupation, profession?

Yes:_____   161 —5> 41
No ....   162 —> 41

40.   In your last job what was your occupation,
          post or what was the nature of your work?

_____   163 —5> 41

---

5 To be filled out by statistical organization.

GENERAL QUESTIONS

41.   What type of education do you have?

- Higher	164 —> 42
- Not completed higher	165 —> 42
- Specialised secondary	166 —> 42
- General secondary	167 —> 42
- Not completed secondary	168 —> 42
- Primary, no primary	169 —> 42

42.   What is your marital status?

Married	170 —> 43
Single	171 —> 43
Widowed..................................	172 —> 43
Divorced	173 —> 43

43.   Do you agree to participate in the same
interview next year?

Yes	174 the end
No	175 the end

THANK YOU FOR YOUR UNDERSTANDING AND CO-OPERATION!

44.   Tick off the gender of the respondent

- male	176
- female	177

45.   Age of the respondent[6] .... | 178 _____

---

[6] To be filled out by the interviewer from the respondent's card.

Conceptual and technical outline of the Hungarian Labour Force Survey

SAMPLE AND ROTATION SCHEME

In 1991 the old USHS sample (USHS stands for Unified System of Household Surveys) was used. It was based on the 1980 census and had been introduced in 1983. The USHS sample design required a two-stage stratified probability sample. Stratification was determined mainly by geographic units and the size of settlements. The sampling frame for the 1990s was to be based on the 1990 census, and a new sample was to be selected from this frame. Though the basic principles of the sample design were to be maintained, some essential improvements in stratification were envisaged.

In this note two aspects of the Hungarian Labour Force Survey will be considered:

– how the standard estimator of the old USHS sample is to be modified to meet the requirements of the LFS, and
– how a feasible rotation scheme may be devised.

We note that the rotation method described below would probably be used only from the second year of the new sample, i.e. in 1993 for the first time. In spite of this it seemed useful to present it here, as it would not be affected by the changes in sample design.

In the following we mean by 'sample' the old sample in 1991 as well as the new sample from 1992 – unless the opposite is stated explicitly. The sample contains about 30,000 households and is split by random method into three subsamples denoted by S1, S2 and S3. Households in S1, S2 and S3 are to be interviewed during the second week of the month according to the following schedule shown in Figure A4.1:

(a) The alternative use of the subsamples S1, S2 and S3

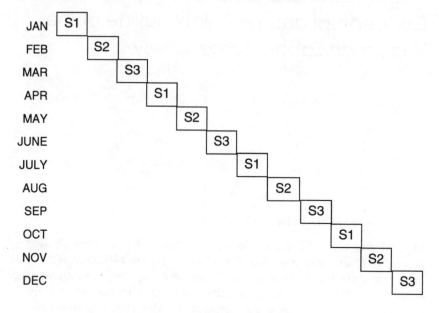

(b) The changes in subsample S1 in four consecutive quarters

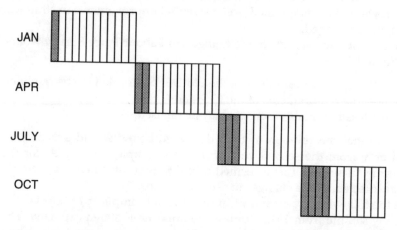

Changing segments are indicated by hatched rectangles. Segments of the subsamples S2 and S3 are changed by the same pattern as those of S1.

Fig. A4.1   Rotation scheme for the Hungarian Labour Force Survey

Subsample	Months of Interview
S1	January, April, July, October
S2	February, May, August, November
S3	March, June, September, December

For the purposes of rotation of the *new* sample each subsample is to be split into twelve equal segments randomly. In each month one segment of the *current* subsample (i.e. that used at that time) is to be replaced by a new one, and the outgoing segment is never to be used again. (Recall that no rotation was planned for 1992.)

Remarks: (i) This method implies that every sample household remains in the sample for at least one year, and from the second year every new sample household remains in the sample for three years. (ii) The sample is also used as a rolling sample, i.e. data will be estimated not only for calendar quarters, but also for non-calendar quarters that may be defined as periods consisting of three arbitrary consecutive months, e.g. February, March, April. Under the rotation method described above the overlap of subsamples for any two consecutive *calendar* quarters will amount to $11/12 = 92$ per cent of the 30,000 households.

We shall also consider an alternative rotation scheme such that one-eighth of each subsample is changed on each occasion; this would imply that new entrants remained in the sample for *two* years.

ESTIMATION METHODS

The standard estimator available for the old USHS sample is of the following form:

$$(*) \qquad Y = \sum_j W_j Y_j$$

where

Y_j is the value of characteristic observed

W_j is sample weight

     } for sample unit j,

and summation is taken over some subclass of the sample. A sample subclass may correspond to a geographic area or to some demographic group defined by sex and age. Sample units belonging to the same stratum of the sample have the same weight W_j.

(*) serves the purpose of estimating *totals*. *Means* or *ratios* are estimated from the USHS sample in the form Y/X where X has similar representation as Y above. We note that a very good method is available for calculating the sampling error of USHS estimates: this method was originally developed for the purpose of the World Fertility Survey in 1977. Unfortunately, this method will probably no longer be suitable for USHS estimates – in particular, for labour force estimates – if the modifications outlined below are carried out.

In what follows we refer to the estimator (*) by the term *simple direct estimate*. For the purpose of the Labour Force Survey some more complex estimators will be needed. Let us introduce the following notations:

N population count
E the number of employed
U the number of unemployed
L labour force, $L = E + U$
R unemployment ratio, $R = U/L$
P labour force participation rate, $P = L/N$

All these quantities will refer to estimates, mainly to simple direct estimates for some subclass or group of the population. In the following considerations the notion of simple direct estimates will be used, though they will never occur in practice in pure form, as they will be, just as in CPS, adjusted

– for non-response, and
– for deviations from updated population counts N based on the last census.

Let us consider now a non-calendar quarter (see the preceding paragraph), e.g. that consisting of February, March and April. (We note here that non-calendar quarters also include the 'normal' quarters as special cases.) For $i = 1, 2, 3$ let N_i, E_i, U_i, etc. denote the monthly sample direct estimates for February, March and April, respectively. We define now the following quarterly estimates:

(**) $E = (E_1 + E_2 + E_3)/3$
$U = (U_1 + U_2 + U_3)/3,$
$L = E + U$
$R = U/L$
$P = L/N$

We note that – as a consequence of adjustments – N in the last equation is consistent with the updated census counts, and is therefore not affected by sampling error in the majority of cases.

It is worth stressing here that the sample variance of E (or U) is one-third of the averaged variances of E_1, E_2, and E_3 (or U_1, U_2 and U_3, respectively):

$$\text{Var}(E) = \text{Var}((E_1 + E_2 + E_3)/3) = 1/3^2 \left(\text{Var}(E_1) + \text{Var}(E_2) + (\text{Var}(F_3))\right)$$

This means in terms of standard errors that the quarterly estimate E based on the 30,000 households of the whole sample is on the average $\sqrt{3}$ times as precise as any of the monthly estimates E_1, E_2 and E_3 which are based on subsamples consisting of about 10,000 households. (The same holds for U_1, U_2, U_3 and U.)

The estimators marked by (**) are obviously feasible for the Hungarian Labour Force Survey in 1991, and there is probably no better alternative in the specific situation. To complete the methodology for 1991 two more issues should be considered, namely:

– measuring changes in the labour force over time, and
– computing sampling error for the estimates.

The use of the estimation method described above implies that changes over time can best be measured by comparing the estimates of consecutive *calendar* quarters; in this case we have a panel survey which is optimal for observing such changes. On the other hand, it is very likely that the method used hitherto to estimate USHS sampling errors would no longer be feasible if raking ratio adjustments were used; in that case the application of some version of balanced half-sample replications might be recommended. The details of this application will be elaborated later.

Our preliminary design concludes with an extension of the estimators (**); this relates to the new sample at the period when rotation is used, i.e. after 1992. Consider two consecutive calendar quarters denoted by $t - 1$ and t, respectively. For t we need the following concept notations:

E, U, L, R and P are quarterly estimates defined by (**);

E_0, U_0, L_0, R_0 and P_0 are quarterly estimates calculated from the overlap of the samples belonging to t–1 and t, thus they are closely related to E, U, L, etc. (Recall that the size of overlap amounts to 92 per cent);

E^*, U^*, L^*, R^* and P^* are the *final* composite estimates of the indicators in consideration.

We shall denote the values of these estimates pertaining to the previous quarter t–1 by an additional prime: $E', U', \ldots, E'_0, U'_0, \ldots, E^{*\prime}, U^{*\prime}, \ldots$, etc. In particular, we assume that in the quarter t $E^{*\prime}, U^{*\prime}$ and $L^{*\prime}$ are known. Our composite estimator is the following:

(***)
$$E^* = aE + (1-a)\,(E^{*\prime} + E_0 - E'_0)$$
$$U^* = aU + (1-a)\,(U^{*\prime} + U_0 - U'_0)$$
$$L^* = E^* + U^*$$
$$R^* = U^*/L^*$$
$$P^* = L^*/N$$
$$a = 0.6$$

It is easy to see that this estimator is based on the same principle as the CPS estimator; in the absence of rotation it reduces to (**). On the other hand, if the sample is rotated, (***) is superior to (**), as it reflects through the terms $E_0 - E'_0$ and $U_0 - U'_0$ the changes over time better than the latter. This composite estimator may also be used with rotation schemes other than that described at the beginning of this Annex.

Labour force sample survey for Czechoslovakia

Questionnaire A: Household Questionnaire

Interviewer No.	District No.
Date of interview	Flat No.
Reference week	Household No.
	(in the flat)

Instruction for interviewer: establish who is head of household (HOH) and list all other household members (including those temporarily absent, but not those whose absence is prolonged) sharing common accommodation, in terms of their relationship to head of household and socio-demographic data; if 10 or more persons, continue on another form of Questionnaire A, renumbering person nos. as 11, 12, etc. Ring respective codes to mark the answers.

Person No.   1 2 3 4 5 6 7 8 9 10

1. Relationship to HOH:
   - person at the HOH   1 1 1 1 1 1 1 1 1 1
   - spouse of HOH   2 2 2 2 2 2 2 2 2 2
   - son, daughter   3 3 3 3 3 3 3 3 3 3
   - son-in-law, daughter-in-law   4 4 4 4 4 4 4 4 4 4
   - grandson, granddaughter   5 5 5 5 5 5 5 5 5 5
   - parents, father-in-law, mother-in-law   6 6 6 6 6 6 6 6 6 6
   - brothers & sisters of head of household   7 7 7 7 7 7 7 7 7 7
   - others   8 8 8 8 8 8 8 8 8 8

2. Sex:
   - male   1 1 1 1 1 1 1 1 1 1
   - female   2 2 2 2 2 2 2 2 2 2

3. Citizenship:
   - CSFR   1 1 1 1 1 1 1 1 1 1
   - others   2 2 2 2 2 2 2 2 2 2

4. Nationality:
   - Czech   1 1 1 1 1 1 1 1 1 1
   - Slovak   2 2 2 2 2 2 2 2 2 2
   - Moravian   3 3 3 3 3 3 3 3 3 3
   - German   4 4 4 4 4 4 4 4 4 4
   - Polish   5 5 5 5 5 5 5 5 5 5
   - Russian, Ukrainian 6 6 6 6 6 6 6 6 6 6
   - Hungarian   7 7 7 7 7 7 7 7 7 7
   - Gipsy   8 8 8 8 8 8 8 8 8 8
   - others   9 9 9 9 9 9 9 9 9 9

5. Day,   - - - - - - - - - -
   month   - - - - - - - - - -
   and year of birth: - - - - - - - - - -

6. Age: - - - - - - - - - -

7. Marital status:
   - single   1 1 1 1 1 1 1 1 1 1
   - married   2 2 2 2 2 2 2 2 2 2
   - divorced   3 3 3 3 3 3 3 3 3 3
   - widow, widower 4 4 4 4 4 4 4 4 4 4
Person No.   1 2 3 4 5 6 7 8 9 10

8. Economic activity:
   - working (excluding items below) 1 1 1 1 1 1 1 1 1 1
   - apprentice   2 2 2 2 2 2 2 2 2 2
   - student of secondary school   3 3 3 3 3 3 3 3 3 3
   - undergraduate   4 4 4 4 4 4 4 4 4 4
   - woman on maternity leave   5 5 5 5 5 5 5 5 5 5
   - woman taking care of family   6 6 6 6 6 6 6 6 6 6
   - retired   7 7 7 7 7 7 7 7 7 7
   - unemployed   8 8 8 8 8 8 8 8 8 8
   - child under 15   9 9 9 9 9 9 9 9 9 9
   - others   10 10 10 10 10 10 10 10 10 10

Instructions for interviewer:
After filling in all socio-demographic data (questions 1-8) for all house-
hold members go to interviewing person No. 1 according to
Questionnaire B, and successively all other persons in the household,
over 15.
After completing the interview of the last person over 15 according to
Questionnaire B, go on interviewing with question No. 9 of the
Questionnaire A.

	Code		Skip to
9. Does your household have a telephone installed?			
– Yes	1	->	10
– No	2	->	End
10. Will you permit your household's next interview to be done by telephone?			
– Yes	1	->	11
– No	2	->	End
11. What is your telephone number?	——	->	End

End: Thank you for the interview.

Signature of the
interviewer

Questionnaire B: Questionnaire for household members over 15

Household member to whom   District No.
this questionnaire relates   Flat No.

Respondent household member   Household No.
providing information   (in the flat)

Interviewer No.

Date of interview   Reference week

Question No.	Code	Skip to

1. Did you do any paid work last week
   for a wage, salary or other remuneration
   or for profit?

	Code	Skip to
– Yes	1	-> 4
– No	2	-> 2

2. Even though you were not working, did
   you have a job or employment that you
   were away from?

	Code	Skip to
– Yes	1	-> 3
– No	2	-> 36

3. Give the main reason why you were
   away from work last week

	Code	Skip to
– sick or injured	1	
– leave/holiday	2	
– maternity leave or additional maternity leave	3	
– study leave/attending a training course	4	
– laid off work for technical and organizational reasons	5	4
– strike or lock-out	6	
– conscription for military service/ training	7	
– bad weather	8	
– other family or personal reasons	9	

Date of interview   Reference week

Question No.	Code	Skip to

4. Was the work/jobs you were in
   (or away from) last week

	Code	Skip to
– your permanent main job or employment	1	-> 8
– your permanent main as well as second job	2	
– second (additional) job	3	-> 5
– temporary, casual or seasonal job	4	

5. Have you any other main job in
   addition to this job?
   – Yes   1   ->   8
   – No   2   ->   6

6. Did you do this type of job because
   – you were not able to find a permanent   1
       job or
   – this type of job suits you and you are
       not looking for a permanent job or   2   ->   7
   – you have another reason?   3

7. How long have you been working
   (without interruption) in your last
   temporary job?
   – less than one month   1
   – 1 month but less than 3 months   2
   – 3 months but less than 6 months   3   }   ->   9
   – 6 months but less than 12 months   4
   – more than 1 year   5

8. How long have you been working in
   your present main job (your present
   work) with the same employer or as
   a self-employed person?
   – less than 6 months   1
   – more than 6 months but less than
       12 months   2
   – more than 12 months but less than
       3 years   3
   – more than 3 years but less than   ->   9
       5 years   4
   – more than 5 years but less than
       10 years   5
   – more than 10 years but less than
       20 years   6
   – over 20 years   7

9. What is produced, what services rendered
   or what operations performed at the
   working place (plant, operational unit)
   where you are doing your main (or

sole) job? (State the kind of activities
processing, distribution, services
etc., produce manufactured there,
material processed, etc.)

....   ---   ->   10

....

10. Give the name of the district and the
county where you work.

....   ---   ->   11

11. What kind of work do you do (at
present)?
(a) give the name of your profession,
occupation or employment

....

(b) describe exactly what work you are
doing at the place where you work

....   ---   ->   12

....

12. Do you work in your main or the only
job as
– an employee   1
– cooperative member   2
– self-employed without employees   3   ->   13
– self-employed with employees   4
– as a helping household member?   5

13. Do you work in your main or only
job
– full-time (i.e. full working hours) or   1   ->   15
– part-time or   2   ->   14
– were you absent from work more
than 4 weeks due to illness, maternity
leave, etc.?   3   ->   23

14. Give the reason why you work
part-time (the main reason).

– cannot find suitable full-time work	1		
– at the initiative of the employer (work shortage)	2		
– for health reasons (invalidity)	3		
– child care	4	->	15
– school or specialized course attendance	5		
– I also have another job (second job)	6		
– the part-time job suits me	7		
– other reasons	8		

15. How many hours do you usually work in your main or the only job? Give the number of hours or average hours per week. --- -> 16

16. How many hours did you work in your main or the only job or at your place of work last week?
    – number of worked hours   ---   ->   17
    – I did not work last week   0   ->   19

17. Was the number of hours worked last week in your main job
    – lower than the working hours agreed with you   1   ->   18
    – the same as the working hours agreed   2   ->   19
    – higher than the working hours agreed   3
    – or is it up to you to decide on your working hours?   4   ->   23

18. Give the main reason why you did not work the full working hours last week.
    – confirmed illness or injury   1
    – leave/holiday   2
    – study leave/attending a training course away from own workplace   3
    – laid off work for technical or organizational reasons   4   ->   19
    – strike or lock-out   5
    – bad weather   6
    – other reasons   7

19. How often do you work overtime?
    – every week   1 ⎫
    – usually in two or three weeks
      per month   2 ⎬ ->   20
    – rarely, in one week per month at
      most   3 ⎭
    – I never work overtime   4   ->   23

20. How many hours did you work
    overtime last week (paid or unpaid)
    in your main job?   --- ->   21

21. You usually work a different
    number of overtime hours than you did
    last week. Give their usual number in
    the past 4 weeks   --- ->   22

22. Give the main reason why you do
    work overtime:
    – at the manager's (management's
      order)   1 ⎫
    – I do not need to work overtime,
      but I want to earn more   2 ⎪
    – I want to fulfil my duties which
      I cannot cope with in normal   3 ⎬ ->   23
      working hours
    – the character of my job necessitates
      overtime work   4 ⎪
    – for other organizational or technical
      reasons   5 ⎪
    – for other personal reasons   6 ⎭

23. Besides your main job do you also
    do another job or paid work?
    – Yes   1   ->   24
    – No   2   ->   31

24. Give the main reason why you have
    an additional job besides your main
    job.

– I am not able to work full-time
in my main job   1
– I am interested in extra earnings   2   ⎫
– my second job is my hobby   3   ⎬   ->   25
– other reasons   4   ⎭

25. Do you work in your second job as
– an employee working for a wage,
salary or other remuneration   1   ⎫
– cooperative member   2   ⎪
– self-employed on your own   3   ⎬   ->   26
– self-employed with employees   4   ⎪
– as a helping household member?   5   ⎭

26. What is produced, what services are
rendered or what operations performed
at the working place (plant, operational
unit) where you are doing your second
job? (State the kind of activities –
processing, distribution, services, etc.,
produce manufactured there, material
processed, etc.)

....   ---   ->   27

....

27. Give the name of the district and the
county where do you do your second
job.

....   ---   ->   28

28. What kind of work do you do as a
second job?
(a) give the name of profession or
employment

....

(b) describe exactly what work
you perform

....

....   ---   ->   29

29. How many hours do you usually work
per week in your second job,
or at other paid work?
 – less than 5 hours   1
 – more than 5 and less than 10 hours   2
 – more than 10 and less than 15 hours   3 } ->   30
 – more than 15 and less than 20 hours   4
 – more than 20 hours   5

30. Do you work in your second job or
other paid work
 – regularly as a permanent job or only   1   ->   31
 – casually or seasonally?

31. Are you seeking another or second job,
although you already have one?
 – Yes   1   ->   32
 – No   2   ->   33

32. Why are you seeking another or
second job? Give the reason for it
(only one).
 – uncertainty or the fear that you might
   lose your present job   1
 – a substantial change in the character
   of your present work   2
 – higher earnings   3
 – better self-assertion (better use of   4 } ->   33
   your qualification)
 – better aspects of the job (for example
   commuting unnecessary, better work
   environment, etc.)   5
 – other reasons   6

33. What was your gross wage (i.e. before
the tax is paid) in your main job, or
your part of profit used as the
entrepreneur's reward last month in
Cks (without family allowances and
the state compensating allowance and
bonuses)?
   ....   ---   ->   34

34. What was your gross monthly average

share of bonuses and rewards for the
last month?

....   ---   ->   35

35. If you have worked besides your main
job in another paid job, give the
total income from these jobs in the
past month (if the second job was an
entrepreneurial activity, state how much
of the profit was used as the so-called
entrepreneur's reward).

....   ---   ->   55

36. Have you ever had a permanent paid job?
- Yes   1   ->   37
- No   2   ->   43

37. How long ago did you leave your
last job?
- less than 1 month ago or 1 month ago   1
- more than 1 month – 3 months ago   2
- more than 3 months – 6 months ago   3   ->   38
- more than 6 months – 1 year ago   4
- more than 1 year – 2 years ago   5
- more than 2 years – 5 years ago   6
- more than 5 years   7   ->   43

38. Why did you leave your last job?
- I have wound up my business activities   1
- the employer has wound up his
  business   2
- I have been dismissed as redundant   3
- I have been dismissed for other
  reasons   4
- my temporary job has ended   5   ->   39
- I have left the job myself from
  personal or family reasons   6
- I have left the job for health
  reasons   7
- I have started my studies   8
- because of being conscripted to army
  service or a substitute service   9
- I have been retired   10
- for other reasons   11

39. What was produced, what services
    were rendered or what operations were
    performed at the place of work (plant,
    operational unit) where you did your
    last job? (State the kind of activities –
    processing, distribution, services, etc.,
    produce manufactured, material
    processed, etc.)

    ....
    ....   ---   ->   40

40. Give the name of the district and the
    county where you worked in your
    last (past) job.

    ....   ---   ->   41

41. What kind of work did you perform in
    your last job?
    (a) give the name of profession or
        employment

    ....
    (b) describe exactly what you did
    ....   ---   ->   42

42. Did you work full-time or part-time?
    – full-time   1 ⎱   ->   43
    – part-time   2 ⎰

43. Were you seeking a paid job (in the
    last 4 weeks)?
    – Yes   1   ->   44
    – No   2   ->   54

44. Indicate in what way you were
    seeking a job (in the last 4 weeks)?
    – through the Labour Office   1
    – newspaper ad. etc. (paid by yourself)   2
    – I follow newspaper ads.   3
    – with the help of my friends   4   ->   45
    – I visit various enterprises   5
    – through private employment agencies   6
    – I use some other means   7

45. What were you doing before you
started to look for a job?
    - I worked full-time for a wage, salary
      or other kind of remuneration   1
    - I was a cooperative member   2
    - I was self-employed on my own   3
    - I was self-employed with employees   4
    - I did casual jobs   5
    - I worked as a helping family member   6   ->   46
    - I was training for my future profession
      at school or at a training institution   7
    - I was a housewife   8
    - I was working in another job   9
    - I was retired   10

46. Are you seeking a job (do you want to
work) as
    - an employee for a wage, salary or
      another kind of remuneration   1
    - cooperative member   2
    - entrepreneur   3   ->   47
    - I am seeking any job   4
    - I have not yet decided   5

47. Are you seeking a job (do you want
to work)
    - full time or   1   ->   48
    - part time or   2   ->   49
    - no preference?   3   ->   50

48. If you are not able to find a full-time
job, would you accept a part-time job?
    - Yes   1
    - No   2   ->   50
    - I don't know   3

49. If you cannot find a part-time job,
will you accept a full-time job?
    - Yes   1
    - No   2   ->   50
    - I don't know   3

50. Are you willing to attend a
    requalification course?
    – Yes   1 ⎤
    – No   2 ⎬ ->   51
    – I do not know   3 ⎦

51. How long have you been seeking a job?
    – less than one month   1
    – more than 1 month, less than 3 months   2
    – more than 3 but less than 6 months   3 ⎬ ->   52
    – more than 6 but less than 12 months   4
    – more than 1 year but less than 2 years   5
    – more than 2 years   6

52. If you find a job, would you be able
    to start within 14 days?
    – Yes   1   ->   55
    – No   2   ->   53

53. Why would you not be able to
    start your job within 14 days?
    – I must finish school or training   1 ⎤
    – I must finish my requalification   2 ⎪
    – for personal or family reasons   3 ⎬ ->   55
    – for illness or disability   4 ⎪
    – for some other reasons   5 ⎦

54. Why are you not seeking any job
    (give the main reason)?
    – I am a pensioner (old-age pensioner,
      invalidity pensioner)   1
    – I am being trained in a training
      institution   2
    – I am attending a secondary school   3
    – I study at a university   4
    – I am attending a requalification course   5
    – I look after my family   6 ⎬ ->   55
    – for health reasons   7
    – I don't believe I would find a job,
      although I should like to work   8
    – I don't want/don't need to work   9
    – I have already found a job, the start
      has been fixed for later   10
    – for other reasons   11

55. Are you registered at the Labour Office
    as a job-seeker?
    – Yes   1   ->   56
    – No   2   ->   58

56. Do you get income support before
    taking up a job   1 ⎫
    or the requalification allowance   2 ⎬ ->   57
    or other social benefit during   ⎪
    unemployment   3 ⎭
    or none?   4   ->   58

57. What was your income support before
    taking up a job or the requalification
    allowance or other social benefit during
    unemployment for the last month?
    ....   ---   ->   58

58. What is your education (highest level only)?
    – primary   1   ->   60
    – completed apprenticeship   2 ⎫
    – vocational training   3 ⎪
    – completed apprenticeship with   4 ⎬ ->   59
       school-leaving examination   ⎪
    – completed secondary technical   5 ⎭
    – completed secondary general   6   ->   60
    – university   7   ->   59
    – never had any full-time education 8   ->   60

59. Name the subject you are studying
    (including apprenticeship or
    training).
    ....   ---   ->   60

60. Do you have any disabilities which
    limit the kind of work that you can do?
    – no   1 ⎫
    – yes, some disability   2 ⎬ ->   END
    – yes, severe disability   3 ⎭

END = skip to surveying next person over 15.

Signature of the interviewer: ....

Hungarian Labour Force Survey questionnaire

CENTRAL STATISTICAL OFFICE
Unified System of Household Surveys
Labour Force Survey
Social-demographic Data
1992-1994

County:
Region:
District:
Dwelling No:
Sample No:
Year ...... Month .... Failure

1.
2.
...............................county   3.
...............................town   4.
...............................street   5.
...............................street number 6.

Family No.	Household members	Person No.	Year of birth	Economic Act. Q.			CODE OF CHANGE					
				1992	1993	1994	1.	2.	3.	4.	5.	6.
				(Persons between 15-74)			interview					
			01									
			02									
			03									
			04									
			05									
			06									
			07									
			08									
			09									
			10									

1. Serial number of the person

2. Serial number of family

3. Sex: male (1)   female (2)

4. Year of birth

5. Marital status:
    unmarried (1) – married (2) – widowed (3) – divorced (4)

6. Family standing:
    husband (1) – wife (2) – cohabitant (3) – single
    parent (4) – child (5) – grandparent (6) –
    other relative (7) – non relative (8) – single (9)

7. Highest educational attainment: less than 8 classes
    in elementary school (1) – elementary school
    finished (2) – apprentice school (3) – vocational
    school (4) – grammar school (5) – other secondary
    school (6) – college (7) – university (8)

8. Type of highest educational qualification
    Does . . . have any other one which has the same level?

9. Manual qualification

10. Is . . . a regular student?
    Yes (1)   No (2)

11. Does he/she receive maternity allowance?
    Yes (1)   No (2)

12. Does he/she receive pension?
    Yes (1) . No (2)

13. Native language:
    Hungarian (10   other (2)

14. Knowledge of languages:

CENTRAL STATISTICAL OFFICE
Unified System of Household Surveys
Labour Force Survey
Economic Activity Questionnaire
1992

County:
Region:
District:
Dwelling No:
Sample No:
Household No:
Date: Year: Month:
Person No in the HOH:

....
town

---

1. Did . . . do at least one hour work for pay
   or profit *last week*?

   EXCLUDE HOUSEHOLD WORK AND WORK AROUND
   THE HOUSE!

   – Yes (1)
   – No (2) ——> GO TO 4.   28

2. How many hours did . . . work *last week*?

   ACTUAL HOURS. INCLUDE OVERTIME.
   EXCLUDE TIME OFF!

   – in main work either as employee, self-employed,
   – unpaid family member or casual worker   29-30
   – in other work as employee or casual worker   31-32
   – in other work as self-employed or unpaid
   – family member   33-34

   ALTOGETHER   35-37

   IF 35-37 = 36 OR MORE GO TO 17
   ON MAIN WORK.

3. Does . . . *usually* work 36 hours or more a week
   in all work?

– Yes (1) What is the reason . . . worked less
than 36 hours *last week*?

MARK PRIMARY REASON.

– illness (01)
– vacation (02)
– holiday (03)
– labour dispute (04)
– bad weather (05)
– new job started during week (06)
– job terminated during week (07)
– number of hours worked varies (08)
– work slack (09)
– other (specify in notes) (10) ....

– No (2) What is the reason . . . *usually* works less
than 36 hours a week?

MARK PRIMARY REASON.

– full time work not available (1)
– work slack (2)
– doesn't want full-time work (3)
– full-time work week under 36 hours (4)
– illness (5)
– other (specify in notes) (6) ....

GO TO 17 ON MAIN WORK.

4. Does . . . have a gainful work from which he/she
was temporarily absent *last week*?

DO NOT COUNT CHILD-CARE LEAVE
AS EMPLOYMENT.

– Yes (1)
– New job is to begin within 30 days (2) ——> GO TO 12.
– No (3) ——> GO TO 6.

5. Why did not . . . work *last week*?

MARK PRIMARY REASON.

– illness (1)
– maternity leave (2)
– vacation (3)
– labour dispute (4)
– bad weather (5)
– number of hours worked varies (6)
– temporary lay off (7)
– other (8) (specify in notes) ....

☐

GO TO 17.

6. Was . . . looking for work *in the last 4 weeks*?

– Yes (1)
– No (2) ——> GO TO 12.

☐

7. What was . . . doing in the *last 4 weeks* to find work?

MARK FIRST THAT APPLIES.

– checked with public employment agency (1)
– checked with private employment agency (2)
– checked with employer directly (3)
– placed or answered ads (4)
– checked with friends and relatives (5)
– other (6) (specify in notes)   ....
– nothing (7)   ——> GO TO 12.

☐

8. Why was . . . looking for work?

– lost job (1)
– quit job (2)
– his or her business went bankrupt or gave it up (3)
– left school (4)
– wanted temporary work (5)
– change in home or family responsibilities (6)
– left military service (7)
– wanted to work while in school (8)
– other (9) (specify in notes) ....

☐

9.   How many weeks has . . . been looking for work?   ☐☐

10. Has . . . been looking for full-time or part-time work?

     – full-time (1)
     – part-time (2)
     – any (3)   ☐

11. Could . . . have taken a job *last week* if one had
     been offered?

     – Yes (1)
     – No (2)

     Why not?

     – new job starting in 30 days (1)
     – training course for adults learning a new
       profession at Central Labour Office (2)
     – illness last week (3)
     – going to school (4)
     – other (5) (specify in notes) ....   ☐

12. When did . . . last work in a job or business on a
     regular basis?

     DO NOT COUNT HOLIDAY WORK.

     – within last 12 months (1)
       which month (01-02)
     – 1-2 years ago (2)
     – 2-3 years ago (3)
     – 3-4 years ago (4)
     – 4-5 years ago (5)
     – more than 5 years ago (6)
     – worked only as unpaid family member (7)
     – never had regular work (8)   ☐

13. Why did . . . leave this work?

    – lay off (01)
    – quit because of
      – family reasons (02)
      – health problems (03)
      – school (04)
      – work arrangements (05)
      – other (06)
    – gave up his or her business (07)
    – his or her business went bankrupt (08)
    – child-care leave (09)
    – seasonal work terminated (10)
    – temporary work terminated (11)
    – retired (12)
    – worked only as unpaid family member (13)
    – never had regular work (14)
    – other (15) (specify in notes) .... ☐☐

    IF 6 = 2 OR
       7 = 6 OR 7   GO TO 14.
    OTHERWISE GO TO 17 ON THIS
    WORK.

14. Does . . . want a regular work either full or
    part time?

    – Yes (1)
    – No (2)   ––> GO TO 16.   ☐
    – Does not know (3)

15. What is the reason . . . is not looking for work?

    – believes no work is available in line of work or
      area (01)
    – couldn't find any work (there are too many
      unemployed) (02)
    – lacks necessary schooling, training, skills or
      experience (03)
    – too young or too old (04)
    – waiting to be called back (05)

– ill or physically or mentally disabled (06)
– can't arrange child care (07)
– family responsibilities (08)
– in school or other training (09)
– other (10) (specify in notes) ....
– doesn't know (11)

16.   Does . . . intend to look for work of any kind in
       the next 12 months?

       – Yes (1)
       – No (2)
       – Doesn't know (3)

       GO TO 17 ON LAST WORK.

17.   DESCRIPTION OF WORK

a)   Employer ....
       (name, industry, location)

b)   Occupation, work duties ....

c)   Status in employment ....

d)   How many hours does . . . usually work
       (or worked) a week in this job?

       – number of hours
       – doesn't know, because
         – number of hours worked varies (1)
         – this isn't his/her regular job (2)

e)   Never had regular work (1)

18.   Is . . . registered at the public employment
       agency as unemployed?

       – Yes (1)
       – No (2)

19. Does . . . receive unemployment benefit?

    – Yes (1)
    – No (2)   ☐

Conceptual outline of the planned Romanian Labour Force Survey

PERIODICITY

The survey is to be conducted on an annual basis. The collection of data is to be carried out during a 4–5 week period in March-April, when seasonal influences are at their lowest, and no legal or religious holidays occur.

REFERENCE PERIOD

The reference period is the full calendar week (from Monday to Sunday) preceding the interview week.

COVERAGE

Geographical: the whole country.

POPULATION: all persons living in ordinary households. A part of the institutional population is also covered, specifically those who maintain family ties with the household during their temporary absence:
   – members of the armed forces living in barracks or camps;
   – children and students living in boarding schools;
   – sick persons in hospitals, sanatoria, clinics and the like;
   – workers living in dormitories;
   – detainees in prisons or reformatory institutions;
   – aged persons living in asylums.

MAIN CONCEPTS AND DEFINITIONS

Employment

All persons aged 14 years and over who, during the reference week, worked for pay or profit are counted as 'employed'. Thus, the following population categories are included:

(1) persons *at work*, who had a job and during the reference week worked as employees, unpaid family workers, self-employed workers, employers;
(2) temporarily absent persons, who during the reference period were *not at work* but had a job to which they kept a formal attachment (reasons for absence: vacation, sickness, maternity, educational, training or unpaid leave, temporary disability, strike or lock-out, temporary work stoppages due to bad weather, slack work, raw material shortages, technical or energy breakdowns;
(3) persons temporarily laid off without pay (partial unemployment);
(4) full- and part-time workers seeking other work;
(5) persons who during the reference week worked for pay or profit, although being under compulsory schooling, or retired and receiving a pension, or registered as jobseekers at an employment office, whether or not receiving unemployment benefits;
(6) pupils and students working full-time or part-time;
(7) unpaid family workers, including those who were temporarily absent during the reference week;
(8) paid apprentices and trainees who worked full-time or part-time;
(9) paid domestic staff;
(10) members of the armed forces.

Unemployment

All persons aged 14 years and over, that during the reference week met all of the following requirements:

(1) did not work and had no job;
(2) were available to start work within 15 days;
(3) were actively seeking work, that is had taken specific steps during the last four weeks to seek paid employment or self-employment.

There are also included:

(a) persons without a job and currently available for work who made arrangements to start a new job on a date subsequent to the reference week;
(b) pupils and students actively looking for work.

Underemployment

All persons who during the reference week were employed but worked for involuntary reasons less hours than the normal hours expected for that activity, and were seeking additional work are counted as 'under-employed'.

Hours of work

Information is required on both:

(1) hours usually worked during the reference week at the main job;
(2) hours actually worked at the main job.

CLASSIFICATION USED

Employed and unemployed persons that have work experience are to be classified by:

– industry
– occupation
– status in employment
– educational attainment.

All data is to be classified by sex, and most of the characteristics are to be classified by age groups as well.

SAMPLE SIZE AND DESIGN

The 1992 Population and Housing Census will provide the sampling frame. A two-stage area sampling will combine systematic sampling with cluster sampling.

The probable size of the sample will be around 40,000 households.

The rotating sample is completely changed after 3 years, and there is a permanent overlap of two-thirds of it from one year to the next.

RESULTS AND PUBLICATION

Some 80 tables will break down the main population categories first by activity status and then by one or more cross-criteria:

– sex
– age groups
– occupation
– industry

– educational attainment
– marital status
– reasons (for unemployment, non-activity, part-time employment, etc.).

Tables containing activity and unemployment rate, data on duration of unemployment, on the methods used for work-seeking, on households, and on annual social and professional labour force mobility are also to be produced.

QUESTIONNAIRE DESIGN

The questionnaire is conceived as a combination of:

- a cover form, meant to be filled in over the three consecutive years, that is the period of time during which a household is kept in the sample; it should mainly contain:
  – identification data (address, area number, etc.);
  – data on the living quarters;
  – data on the household composition (relationship to the reference person);
  – demographic data (age, sex, nationality, marital status);
- an individual questionnaire with questions referring to the economic activity. Only persons aged 14 years and over are to be asked this set of questions, which are grouped into five modules;
  – general questions, principally probing questions, acting as a filter towards one of the following modules;
  – questions addressed to the employed persons;
  – questions addressed to unemployed and non-active persons;
  – questions regarding educational and vocational attainment;
  – questions regarding social and occupational mobility, addressed only to those that were not in the survey in the previous year.

Questions are direct and use standardized terminology for consistency. Most of them are closed, multiple choice, and pre-coded.

The content of the questionnaire is subject to several consecutive revisions, especially after the two pretests that are to be conducted on smaller subsamples.

DATA COLLECTION

Data are to be collected by interviewing all the members of the household aged 14 years and over, preferably, but proxy response is to be admitted. The method to be used is that of the personal visit paid by specially trained interviewers hired part-time – teachers and college students will be particularly encouraged to apply.

Recruitment of interviewers will be performed on the basis of certificates that attest to their high-school graduation. A month before starting the field operations they are to attend a 2-3 day training course. A reference manual will also be at their disposal.

Annex 8

The ISCO-major groups

1. LEGISLATORS, SENIOR OFFICIALS AND MANAGERS

This major group covers occupations whose main tasks consist of planning, formulating and deciding on policies, laws, rules and regulations of national, state, regional or local governments or legislative assemblies, or of planning, formulating, organizing, co-ordinating, controlling and directing policies and operations of enterprises and organisations. The core content of this group is the same as that of major group 2, *Administrative and managerial workers*, in ISCO-68, but occupations with similar tasks classified under other ISCO-68 major groups have been added. This major group has been divided into three sub-major groups, eight minor groups and twenty-five unit groups – reflecting differences in tasks associated with different areas of authority and different types of enterprises and organizations.

Sub-major and minor groups

11   Legislators and senior officials
    111   Legislators
    112   Senior government officials
    113   Traditional chiefs and heads of villages
    114   Senior officials of special-interest organizations

12   Corporate managers[1]
    121   Directors and chief executives

---

[1] This sub-major group is intended to include persons who – as directors, chief executives or specialized managers – manage enterprises requiring a total of three or more managers.

     122   Production and operations department managers
     123   Other department managers

13   General managers[2]
     131   General managers

2. PROFESSIONALS

This major group covers occupations whose main tasks require a high level of professional knowledge and experience in engineering, natural sciences, social sciences, humanities and related fields. The main tasks consist of engaging in the practical application of scientific and artistic concepts and theories, increasing the existing stock of knowledge by means of research and creativeness, and teaching about the foregoing in a systematic manner. All occupations classified under this major group were classified under major group 0/1, *Professional, technical and related workers*, of ISCO-68. This major group has been divided into four sub-major groups, eighteen minor groups and fifty-five unit groups – reflecting differences in tasks associated with different fields of knowledge and specialization.

Sub-major and minor groups

21   Physical, mathematical and engineering science professionals
     211   Physicists, chemists and related professionals
     212   Mathematicians, statisticians and related professionals
     213   Computing professionals
     214   Architects, engineers and related professionals

22   Life science and health professionals
     221   Life science professionals
     222   Health professionals (except nursing)
     223   Nursing and midwifery professionals

23   Teaching professionals
     231   College, university and higher education teaching professionals
     232   Secondary education teaching professionals
     233   Primary and pre-primary education teaching professionals
     234   Special education teaching professionals
     235   Other teaching professionals

---

[2] This sub-major group is intended to include persons who manage enterprises on their own behalf, or on behalf of the proprietor, with the assistance of no more than one other manager and/or some non-managerial help.

24   Other professionals
    241   Business professionals
    242   Legal professionals
    243   Archivists, librarians and related information profes-
            sionals
    244   Social science and related professionals
    245   Writers and creative or performing artists
    246   Religious professionals

3. TECHNICIANS AND ASSOCIATE PROFESSIONALS

This major group covers occupations whose main tasks require the experience and knowledge of principles and practices necessary to assume operational responsibility and to give technical support to *Professionals* in engineering, natural sciences, social sciences, humanities and related fields. The core content of this major group consists of occupations which were classified under major group 0/1, *Professional, technical and related workers* , in ISCO-68. Occupations with skill requirements at a similar level, which were classified under other ISCO-68 major groups, especially major groups 3, *Clerical and related workers* , and 4, *Sales workers,* are also classified under this major group. This major group has been divided into four sub-major groups, twenty-one minor groups and seventy-four unit groups – reflecting differences in tasks associated with different fields of knowledge and different areas of specialization.

Sub-major and minor groups

31   Physical and engineering science associate professionals
    311   Physical and engineering science technicians
    312   Computer associate professionals
    313   Optical and electronic equipment operators
    314   Ship and aircraft controllers and technicians
    315   Safety and quality inspectors

32   Life science and health associate professionals
    321   Life science technicians and related associate profes-
            sionals
    322   Modern health associate professionals (except nursing)
    323   Nursing and midwifery associate professionals
    324   Traditional medicine practitioners and faith healers

33   Teaching associate professionals
    331   Primary education teaching associate professionals

	332	Pre-primary education teaching associate professionals
	333	Special education teaching associate professionals
	334	Other teaching associate professionals

34	Other associate professionals	
	341	Finance and sales associate professionals
	342	Business services agents and trade brokers
	343	Administrative associate professionals
	344	Government associate professionals
	345	Police inspectors and detectives
	346	Social work associate professionals
	347	Artistic, entertainment and sports associate professionals
	348	Religious associate professionals

4. CLERKS

This major group covers occupations whose main tasks require the knowledge and experience necessary to record, organize, store and retrieve information, compute numerical, financial and statistical data, and perform a number of client-oriented clerical duties, especially in connection with money-handling operations, travel arrangements, business information and appointments. The core content of this group consists of occupations that were classified under major group 3 *Clerical and related workers*, in ISCO-68. This major group has been divided into two sub-major groups, seven minor groups and twenty-two unit groups – reflecting differences in tasks associated with different areas of specialization.

Sub-major and minor groups

41	Office clerks	
	411	Secretaries and keyboard-operating clerks
	412	Numerical clerks
	413	Material-recording and transport clerks
	414	Library, mail and related clerks
	419	Other office clerks

42	Customer services clerks	
	421	Cashiers, tellers and related clerks
	422	Client information clerks

5. SERVICE WORKERS AND SHOP AND MARKET SALES WORKERS

This major group covers occupations whose main tasks require the knowledge and experience necessary to provide protective services, personal services related to travel, housekeeping, catering and personal care, or to sell and demonstrate goods for wholesale or retail shops and similar establishments. The core content of this group consists of occupations that were classified under major group 4, *Sales workers* , or 5, *Service workers,* in ISCO-68. This major group has been divided into two sub-major groups, nine minor groups and twenty-three unit groups – reflecting differences in tasks associated with different areas of specialization.

Sub-major and minor groups

51		Personal and protective services workers
	511	Travel attendants and related workers
	512	Housekeeping and restaurant services workers
	513	Personal care and related workers
	514	Other personal services workers
	515	Astrologers, fortune-tellers and related workers
	516	Protective services workers
52		Models, salespersons and demonstrators
	521	Fashion and other models
	522	Shop salespersons and demonstrators
	523	Stall and market salespersons

6. SKILLED AGRICULTURAL AND FISHERY WORKERS

This major group covers occupations whose tasks require the knowledge and experience necessary to grow and harvest crops, breed, feed or hunt animals, gather wild fruit and plants, catch or breed fish, or cultivate or gather other forms of aquatic life. The core content of this group consists of occupations that were classified under major group 6, *Agricultural, animal husbandry and forestry workers, fishermen and hunters,* in ISCO-68. This major group has been divided into two sub-major groups, six minor groups and sixteen unit groups – reflecting differences in tasks associated with different areas of specialization, and differences in market orientation.

Sub-major and minor groups

61   Market-oriented skilled agricultural and fishery workers
    611   Market gardeners and crop growers
    612   Market-oriented animal producers and related workers
    613   Market-oriented crop and animal producers
    614   Forestry and related workers
    615   Fishery workers, hunters and trappers

62   Subsistence agricultural and fishery workers
    621   Subsistence agricultural and fishery workers

7. CRAFT AND RELATED TRADES WORKERS

This major group covers occupations whose tasks require the knowledge and experience necessary to extract and treat raw materials, manufacture and repair goods, and construct, maintain and repair roads, structures and machinery. The main tasks of these occupations require experience with and understanding of the work situation, the materials worked with and the requirements of the structures, machinery and other items produced. The core content of this group consists of occupations that were classified under major group 7/8/9, *Production and related workers, transport equipment operators and labourers*, in ISCO-68. This major group has been divided into four sub-major groups, sixteen minor groups and sixty-seven unit groups – reflecting differences in tasks associated with different areas of specialization.

Sub-major and minor groups

71   Extraction and building trades workers
    711   Miners, shotfirers, stone cutters and carvers
    712   Building frame and related trades workers
    713   Building finishers and related trades workers
    714   Painters, building structure cleaners and related trades workers

72   Metal, machinery and related trades workers
    721   Metal moulders, welders, sheet-metal workers, structural-metal preparers, and related trades workers
    722   Blacksmiths, tool-makers and related trades workers
    723   Machinery mechanics and fitters
    724   Electrical and electronic equipment mechanics and fitters

73	Precision, handicraft, printing and related trades workers
	731 Precision workers in metal and related materials
	732 Potters, glass-makers and related trades workers
	733 Handicraft workers in wood, textile, leather and related materials
	734 Printing and related trades workers

73 Precision, handicraft, printing and related trades workers
   731 Precision workers in metal and related materials
   732 Potters, glass-makers and related trades workers
   733 Handicraft workers in wood, textile, leather and related materials
   734 Printing and related trades workers

74 Other craft and related trades workers
   741 Food processing and related trades workers
   742 Wood treaters, cabinet-makers and related trades workers
   743 Textile, garment and related trades workers
   744 Pelt, leather and shoemaking trades workers

8. PLANT AND MACHINE OPERATORS AND ASSEMBLERS

This major group covers occupations whose main tasks require the knowledge and experience necessary to operate vehicles and other mobile equipment, to tend, control and monitor the operation of industrial plant and machinery, on the spot or by remote control, or to assemble products from component parts according to strict rules and procedures. The tasks of these occupations require mainly experience with and understanding of the machinery worked with. The core content of this group consists of occupations that were classified under major group 7/8/9, *Production and related workers, transport equipment operators and labourers*, in ISCO-68. This major group has been divided into three sub-major groups, twenty minor groups and sixty-eight unit groups – reflecting differences in tasks associated with different areas of specialization.

Sub-major and minor groups

81 Stationary plant and related operators
   811 Mining and mineral-processing-plant operators
   812 Metal-processing-plant operators
   813 Glass, ceramics and related plant operators
   814 Wood-processing- and papermaking-plant operators
   815 Chemical-processing-plant operators
   816 Power-production and related plant operators
   817 Automated-assembly-line and industrial-robot operators

82	Machine operators and assemblers
	821 Metal- and mineral-products machine operators
	822 Chemical-products machine operators
	823 Rubber- and plastic-products machine operators
	824 Wood-products machine operators
	825 Printing-, binding- and paper-products machine operators
	826 Textile-, fur- and leather-products machine operators
	827 Food and related products machine operators
	828 Assemblers
	829 Other machine operators and assemblers

83　　　Drivers and mobile plant operators
　　　831　Locomotive engine drivers and related workers
　　　832　Motor vehicle drivers
　　　833　Agricultural and other mobile plant operators
　　　834　Ships' deck crews and related workers

9. ELEMENTARY OCCUPATIONS

This major group covers occupations which require the knowledge and experience necessary to perform mostly simple and routine tasks, involving the use of simple hand-held tools and in some cases certain physical effort, and, with few exceptions, only limited personal initiative or judgement. The core content of this group consists of occupations that were classified under minor group 9-9, *Labourers not elsewhere classified,* in ISCO-68. Occupations with skill requirements at a similar level classified under other ISCO-68 minor and major groups, especially major groups 5, *Service workers,* and 6, *Agricultural, animal husbandry and forestry workers, fishermen and hunters,* are also classified under this major group. This major group has been divided into three sub-major groups, ten minor groups and twenty-six unit groups – reflecting differences in tasks associated with different areas of work.

Sub-major and minor groups

91　　　Sales and services elementary occupations
　　　911　Street vendors and related workers
　　　912　Shoe cleaning and other street services elementary occupations
　　　913　Domestic and related helpers, cleaners and launderers
　　　914　Building caretakers, window and related cleaners

915   Messengers, porters, doorkeepers and related workers
916   Garbage collectors and related labourers

92   Agricultural, fishery and related labourers
921   Agricultural, fishery and related labourers

93   Labourers in mining, construction, manufacturing and transport
931   Mining and construction labourers
932   Manufacturing labourers
933   Transport labourers and freight handlers

0. ARMED FORCES

This major group covers the same occupations as those covered in the group *Members of the armed forces* in ISCO-68, which was defined as follows:

> Members of the armed forces are those personnel who are serving in the armed forces, including women's auxiliary services, whether on a voluntary or involuntary basis, and who are not free to accept civilian employment. Included are regular members of the army, navy, air force and other military services, as well as temporary members enrolled for full-time training or other service for a period of three months or more. Excluded are persons in civilian employment, such as administrative staff of government establishments concerned with defence questions; police (other than military police); custom inspectors and members of other armed civilian services; members of military reserves not currently on full-time active service; and persons who have been temporarily withdrawn from civilian life for a short period of military training.

Sub-major and minor groups

01   Armed forces
011   Armed forces